Financing Higher Education

D0165668

Higher education is a key element in national economic performance. A modern economy needs a high-quality university system, and needs to make it accessible to everyone who can benefit. But mass higher education is expensive and competes for public funds with pensions and health care – to say nothing of nursery education and schools. This is the dilemma that many countries offering free or subsidised higher education face today.

Financing Higher Education focuses on the UK debate, examining the head-on collision between the economic imperatives of student loans with regulated market forces and the political imperative of 'free' higher education. The first part of the book contains selected writing by the authors from the late 1980s about two key elements in the puzzle: the proper design of student loans (writing which was picked up and promptly implemented in other countries), and the role of regulated market forces, an area which remains a political minefield in most countries. The book traces those twin elements through the 1990s and into the twenty-first century, culminating in important – and perhaps path-breaking – legislation in 2004.

The authors have been active in the UK debate on higher education since the late 1980s and, individually and jointly, have advised governments and others at home and abroad. *Financing Higher Education* offers lessons both about policy design and about the politics of reform, which are of particular relevance to countries that have not yet addressed the issue.

Nicholas Barr is Professor of Public Economics at the London School of Economics, and the author of *The Economics of the Welfare State* and numerous other books and articles. He has been a Visiting Scholar at the IMF, and worked for the World Bank on reforming welfare states in post-communist countries.
Iain Crawford obtained a BSc (Econ.) from the London School of Economics, where he was subsequently Head of Public Relations. He has a long history of political campaigning, and was a Parliamentary candidate in 1987.

Financing Higher Education

Answers from the UK

Nicholas Barr and Iain Crawford

Routledge
Taylor & Francis Group

LONDON AND NEW YORK

First published 2005
by Routledge
2 Park Square, Milton Park, Abingdon, Oxon OX14 4RN

Simultaneously published in the USA and Canada
by Routledge
270 Madison Ave, New York, NY 10016

Routledge is an imprint of the Taylor & Francis Group

© 2005 Nicholas Barr and Iain Crawford

Typeset in Baskerville by
Florence Production Ltd, Stoodleigh, Devon
Printed and bound in Great Britain by
The Cromwell Press, Trowbridge, Wiltshire

British Library Cataloguing in Publication Data
A catalogue record for this book is available from the British Library

Library of Congress Cataloging in Publication Data
A catalog record for this book has been requested

ISBN 0–415–34620–7 (hbk)
ISBN 0–415–34857–9 (pbk)

Iain Crawford

Iain Crawford died in March 2004 after a long illness. In 1988 he and Nick Barr, while holding down their respective 'day jobs', embarked upon a sustained campaign for an income-contingent student loan system for the UK. Their message, often not well understood, was for a long time unpopular with the stakeholders, reluctant to reform. The process took its many interesting twists and turns, and for years it seemed that it was easier to deliver the Barr-Crawford message abroad than at home.

The campaign, like their friendship, was provocative and enduringly positive, the sum being greater than its parts. There was a solid foundation. Dubbed at times 'fanatics' by some, it is an enormous tribute to them both that the 2004 Higher Education Bill, which contains a good deal of their model, was given a Second Reading by the House of Commons in January this year.

It was just that Iain lived to see it, and for those of us who knew him personally, it serves as a mark of his political ability, his lateral thinking and downright determination.

Louise Crawford
Ardnamurchan
June 2004

Contents

Foreword

Professor Lord Desai

This is the book that launched a revolution, one that is yet to finish its course, but I have no doubt that it will come to fruition. Like Lincoln Steffens I have seen the future and know it works. Indeed I had my first glimpse of the future in 1988 when Nicholas Barr, as a younger colleague at the LSE, sent me the first draft of his paper on loan-funded higher education. It was the summer holiday, in France, which for a university academic meant spending the time reading, writing and catching up with academic work not done in term-time. The proposal was quite innovative and I was immediately engaged by it. Nick Barr was exploring whether one could charge for higher education by giving income-contingent loans to the students in higher education, who (if full time and not 'mature') were then receiving it free. As a member of the Labour Party – and indeed Chair of one of its constituency parties – I was perfectly entitled to wear blinkers and argue that free higher education for all was the core of our beliefs, or of the British welfare state, or of socialism. Some of my House of Commons colleagues did just that when the Higher Education Bill was finally introduced early in 2004. But I knew then, as I know now, that we do not have universal free higher education at all. Only those who went on to higher education immediately after A levels were likely to receive full funding from their Local Education Authorities. The rest – part-time or mature students, or those in further education – were likely to be charged a fee. I did not cavil at the Barr idea because I knew that higher education, far from being a necessity, is a career choice. It benefits the receiver in terms of higher income over the life cycle of employment. Thus, while higher education may benefit society by various externalities, it is also a gift to those selected to receive higher education. Are the recipients deserving? This is where the debate gets muddied.

As of now the middle classes (A and B, and a few C1 in occupational categories) are overrepresented in higher education, and thus prima facie the gift of free higher education is a regressive transfer. The working-class students (C2, D and E) do not get their proportionate share. Originally this had nothing to do with fees charged, because if they qualified to go in at 18 years there was no fee; and there was until 1998 a maintenance grant on a means-tested basis. So the low incidence of working-class students had nothing to do with the expenses incurred. The reason for the low incidence was that few working-class students 'stayed on' in school beyond 16 years, i.e. beyond O levels or GCSEs. This could be partly due to the quality of schooling, especially the low expectations teachers had of those students, or because of higher value placed on earning an income immediately. The former requires a better schooling system; the latter is a matter of cost-benefit calculus. If there is an unhealthy myopia among working classes, it can be ameliorated by better information and counselling. Some pupils who do not go on to A levels or higher education may, of course, choose to go back in later years as mature students. Thus the inequity of the lower representation of working-class students can be dealt with by measures independent of the mode of financing higher education.

Alas, politics is never that simple, and the fact that higher education provision is financed almost exclusively from public funds – much like health care – makes politics central to the issue. Economists have known for a long time that the sectional interests of the entrenched receivers of public subsidies are often dressed up as the national interest. Thus during the Corn Law agitation, landlords argued how vital agriculture was to England's military strength and public welfare. They also accused manufacturers of exploiting their workers, hoping thereby to split the alliance of industrial workers and industrialists against the Corn Laws. Karl Marx, no slouch at denouncing exploitation, still took the view that the Corn Laws needed to be abolished because cheap grain was good for the economy as well as for the buyers of grain. But between Ricardo's discovery (simultaneously with Malthus and Barton) of the theory of rent in 1814 and the abolition of the Corn Laws in 1846, there is a gap of 32 years. What is more the Anti Corn Law League was a formidable political machine which put up candidates for Parliament and carried out a vigorous campaign for voter registration.

No such popular campaign has taken place for higher education financed by income-contingent loans. Indeed the campaign has been entirely for regressive subsidies masquerading as one for access of working-class students to higher education. The English middle classes have an ability to defend their subsidies on the grounds that if abolished poorer people will suffer. Universality becomes a battle cry in the full knowledge that despite universality the particular benefit will be a middle class capture. Indeed the Conservative Party which has its antennae close to the heartbeats of middle-class England (Scotland is a separate case and Wales is beginning to be different after devolution), took this into account when it expanded access to higher education in the Great Education Reform Bill (GERBIL). Instead of charging the better-off for money to fund greater access, it kept the higher education grant pretty much the same and allowed the unit of resource to shrink. This cowardice cost the universities dear, and for ten years after 1989 the steady impoverishment of universities was the untold horror story of English social life.

The story remained untold because English higher education is crippled by the existence of Oxbridge; and the public image of universities on TV and in the print media is of dreamy spires with clean-cut lawns, lazy summer punts and fellows running around in gowns and mortar boards. The great English public thinks all universities are places of privilege and prosperity. This has deprived the universities of any public sympathy in their fight for more money, and given politicians a stick to beat universities with. This is the cry for access, i.e. access to Oxbridge colleges for students from comprehensive schools, especially those from working-class background. This issue is separate from that of funding but mixing the two up has benefited the opponents of the Barr-Crawford proposals. The result has been a sorry mangled debate on the Higher Education Bill in the Commons with the simplicity of the original proposals messed up by many restrictions and concessions.

But even so I believe that the Barr-Crawford proposals will win support in the end in their full simplicity. The other part of the duo, Iain Crawford, was politically savvy and knew the electoral pressures that drive such debates. He was not himself from a privileged background and had made his way to LSE as a mature student. He knew the Scottish angle and could translate his proposals to suit other systems, as they did in Hungary. Barr and Crawford are acutely aware of equity issues as they are on the ground, rather than as mythologised by middle-class pressure groups to terrify MPs. If you have income-contingent loans you are borrowing against your future income to pay for the education which guarantees you that higher future income. Thus while parental incomes of potential entrants to higher education are unequal, their future incomes after higher education are much less unequal. Thus *ex post* equity is a better way of judging the proposals than equity *ex ante*. This is where the beauty of the proposal lies, because given the uncertainty it is better to rely on *ex post* outcomes. Of course the payments have to be upfront. The loan proposal says that the government pays up front and then collects the money from the beneficiaries as a fraction of their subsequent earnings. Those MPs who have put constraints on the proposals have kept the present inequities even as they claim to speak for the less well-off.

The intellectual journey is set out very clearly in this collection of articles. What is harder to convey is the sheer thrill of being part of a revolution in the mode of thinking about the finance of higher education. This was partly because Nicholas Barr is a superb pedagogue but also because Iain Crawford could tell great stories and make even the most technical economic argument lively. I feel lucky to have been there right from the beginning, and hope to be still here when the revolution is complete.

Meghnad Desai
May 2004

Preface

In November 1987, the Secretary of State for Education, Kenneth Baker (now Lord Baker of Dorking) published a White Paper (UK Department for Education and Science 1987) foreshadowing the 1988 Education Reform Act which, in effect, nationalised Britain's universities. On 27 January 2004, the House of Commons, after bitter dispute and by a majority of only five, gave a Second Reading to a Higher Education Bill which restored a measure of autonomy and competition. The Bill received Royal Assent in July 2004.

In policy terms, therefore, this is a story with a happy ending. But it is clearly also a long one. Iain and I first met by chance in late 1987. He was finishing an undergraduate degree at the London School of Economics (LSE), which he had started as a mature student, but from which he had taken time out to fight a Parliamentary seat in the 1987 General Election. At the time, he had just accepted a part-time job with a specific remit to consider the School's position in connection with some of the White Paper's proposals. I had recently published the first edition of *The Economics of the Welfare State* (1987), which applied the then fairly new economics of information to the welfare state, considering in particular where markets were likely to work well (e.g. food) and where badly (health care, school education). The book included a short section on student loans (Chapter 2, this volume).

We both attended a meeting at LSE in March 1988 to discuss how academics might head off the worst features of the Education Reform Bill. Iain's view was blunt: 'Don't start from here.' Instead, he argued, we should set the scene for the next time the issue became salient. In short order, he engineered a slot for me to appear on the 'Today' programme on BBC Radio 4, with more to follow, and encouraged me to write an article for *The Times Higher Education Supplement* about my current research on student poverty.

The mix worked instantly, so that we were able to do together what neither of us could have done alone. To some extent, my main contributions were the analytics and the writing, Iain's the political nous and understanding of the media, but that oversimplifies the nature of the joint creative process, which was driven by a shared passion to widen access and an increasing fascination with the broader topic of higher education finance. That passion emerged in very different ways from two very different people. I remember at an early stage making the academic's comment that 'it's nice to get the argument right'. Iain, the politician, commented darkly, 'it's nice to win!'.

The process involved endless discussion. Writing together would often see Iain pacing up and down the room talking; I would sit at the keyboard, assembling words whose correlation with what Iain was saying could be total, partial or zero; periodically he would peer over my shoulder to approve or to suggest revisions. Over time, there was some crossover in our skills, though we continued to rely on each other when the chips were down.

The process was also enormous fun. Much of this book was originally written for academic journals, government inquiries or Parliamentary Select Committees (we were always prepared to talk to politicians of any political party who wanted to talk to us), so that the language tends to be formal, but I hope that some of the fun emerges even there, and perhaps more obviously in some of the newspaper articles interspersed among the chapters.

Apart from the first and last chapters, which are new, the rest of the book is a selection of our published work. Articles are left almost entirely as they were written. The inevitable price – some repetition – is deliberate. The book is not only a about the state of play today, but an account of the 16-year campaign as it really was, and a sobering reminder of how many times an idea has to be pressed before it is translated from journal article into legislation.

This volume is aimed at a broad readership. Though much of the writing is about the UK debate, the book is written to bring out the more general lessons for other countries, and is thus acutely relevant to policymakers in the OECD, and in post-communist and middle-income developing countries, including officials in Ministries of Finance and Education, and in international organisations such as the International Monetary Fund, the World Bank and the United Nations. In the academic world, it should be of interest to economists and colleagues in departments of social policy and public policy. It should be of interest also in related areas such as political economy, as illustrating the difficulties of implementing change and pointing to some of the tools necessary to bring it about. Readers who are short of time should read Chapters 1 and 16, after which any of the remaining chapters can be read as free-standing.

Our ideas were clear from an early stage. They would not, however, have come to fruition without generous help from many friends and colleagues – none of whom should be blamed for the result. Our starting point was to advocate student loans with income-contingent repayments, i.e. repayments calculated as $x\%$ of the borrower's subsequent earnings, rather than a fixed sum of $£x$ per month, like a mortgage or bank overdraft. The history of the idea is set out more fully in Chapter 6: it was first proposed by Milton Friedman (1955; see also Friedman 1962, pp. 103–5) and, in a UK context, by Peacock and Wiseman (1962) and Prest (1962) in evidence to the Robbins Report (UK Committee on Higher Education 1963) and by Glennerster, Merrett and Wilson (1968). The 1960s debate is summarised by Blaug (1970, pp. 293–307), and Robbins' conversion to this type of loan in Robbins (1980).

More immediately, many people helped me with *The Economics of the Welfare State* which was the intellectual foundation of our work. Early in our higher education campaign, the persistent advocacy of education vouchers by John Barnes, then in LSE's Department of Government, gave me the impetus to think things through and to realise that the analytical basis of my hostility to vouchers for school education did not follow through into higher education: students are better informed than school children and hence better able to make choices; and it is possible to construct voucher schemes with a strong redistributive gradient.

Mervyn King (then a colleague in the Economics Department at the School, now Governor of the Bank of England) suggested in a conversation in July 1988 that piggy-backing student loans on National Insurance contributions, as well as having administrative advantages, also made clear the idea that student loans are a form of redistribution to oneself over the life cycle, analogous to pensions, thus providing an idea with great resonance, which did a great deal to build early support for income-contingency.

Many others gave enthusiastic help in the early days and hence had a major impact on the writing in Part 1. Meghnad (now Lord) Desai took time from his summer holiday, as did Gail Wilson, to comment on early drafts. Mark Blaug patiently tutored me in the economics of education. Alan Peacock gave generous support, both through supportive comments, and in a practical way by encouraging the David Hume Institute to co-publish two early pieces of writing. Tony Atkinson and Nicholas Stern, successive Chairs of LSE's Suntory-Toyota International Centre for Economics and Related Disciplines, gave consistent support including research funding for an early study of student poverty (Barr and Low 1988), for a conference on 'The Future Funding and Management of British Higher Education' at the LSE in September 1988 and for co-publishing some of our work with the David Hume Institute. I am grateful also to Gervas Huxley and Maureen Woodhall.

The chapters in Part 2, particularly the quantitative estimates of the effectiveness of different loan regimes, draw on joint work with Jane Falkingham using LIFEMOD, a microsimulation model she had helped to develop. Some of those chapters, and even more those in Part 3, owe a great deal to Colin Ward, till 2003 Chief Executive of the UK Student Loans Company, the publicly-owned loans administration, who shared our commitment to student loans as part of a strategy to promote access and contributed in important ways on factual matters, policy thinking and technical design. From 1999–2001 we advised the Hungarian government on the design and implementation of an income-contingent student loan scheme in collaboration with Colin Ward and his colleague Hugh Macadie, from whom we learned a huge amount about the practicalities of loans administration, which fed into our evidence to the UK Education Select Committee (Chapters 15–17).

Government and Parliament – notwithstanding that for most of the period we were guerillas fighting government policy – also deserve thanks. Early loan proposals were sent to Robert Jackson, then Minister for Higher Education. We come from different political backgrounds, and disagreed strongly over some aspects of the proposals; but the disagreement was always constructive and helped to improve the scheme. The House of Commons Education Select Committee also played an increasing role under the chairmanship of Margaret Hodge in the immediate aftermath of the 1997 Dearing Report, and of Barry Sheerman around the time of the 2003 White Paper and 2004 Higher Education Bill.

We have also benefited from colleagues and events in other countries, including many useful conversations with Bruce Chapman and Gary Hawke. I am grateful for spells as academic visitor at the University of Melbourne and the Australian National University, and for assistance from colleagues at the IMF, while visiting their Fiscal Affairs Department, on the intricacies of national income accounting.

We are also grateful for financial support to the Suntory-Toyota International Centre for Economics and Related Disciplines at the LSE; to the Esmée Fairbairn Charitable Trust for financing much of our work in 1989 and 1990; and to British Petroleum for financing work on widening access which included the research with Jane Falkingham on simulating different loan schemes. Much of our work on either side of the publication of the Dearing Report in 1997 was supported by two grants from the Nuffield Foundation.

Thanks are due also to Meghnad Desai and Neil Gregory who first suggested this book, and to John Ashworth, Gyula Gilly, Adrian Hall, Hugh Macadie, Erika Papp, Gus Stewart and Colin Ward for helpful comments on drafts of Chapters 1 and 16.

Our final thanks are to our wives, Gill and Louise, who have been argumentative, opinionated, exasperated (fortunately not with us), and unfailingly supportive. Over the years, the duo turned into a quartet.

Nicholas Barr
London
June 2004

References

Barr, Nicholas (1987), *The Economics of the Welfare State*, London: Weidenfeld & Nicolson, and Stanford, Calif.: Stanford University Press.

Barr, Nicholas (ed.) (2001), *Economic Theory and the Welfare State, Vol. I: Theory, Vol. II: Income Transfers, and Vol. III: Benefits in Kind*, Edward Elgar Library in Critical Writings in Economics, Cheltenham and Northampton, Mass.: Edward Elgar.

Barr, Nicholas and Low, William (1988), *Student Grants and Student Poverty*, Welfare State Programme, Discussion Paper WSP/28, London: London School of Economics.

Blaug, Mark (1970), *An Introduction to the Economics of Education*, London: Penguin.

Friedman, Milton (1955), 'The Role of Government in Education', in Solo, A (ed.), *Economics and the Public Interest*, New Brunswick, NJ: Rutgers University Press, pp. 123–44.

Friedman, Milton (1962), *Capitalism and Freedom*, Chicago: University of Chicago Press, Ch. 6, pp. 85–107, reprinted in Barr (2001, Vol. III, pp. 547–69).

Glennerster, Howard, Merrett, Stephen and Wilson, Gail (1968), 'A Graduate Tax', *Higher Education Review*, Vol. 1, No. 1, pp. 26–38, reprinted in Barr (2001, Vol. III, pp. 570–82), and in *Higher Education Review*, Vol. 35, No. 2 (Spring), pp. 25–40.

Peacock, Alan and Wiseman, Jack (1962), 'The Economics of Higher Education', *Higher Education: Evidence – Part Two: Documentary Evidence*, Cmnd 2154-XII, pp. 129–38. London: HMSO, 1963.

Prest, Alan (1962), 'The Finance of University Education in Great Britain', *Higher Education: Evidence – Part Two: Documentary Evidence*, Cmnd 2154-XII, pp. 139–52. London: HMSO, 1963.

Robbins, Lionel C. (1980), *Higher Education Revisited*, London: Macmillan.

UK Committee on Higher Education (1963), *Higher Education* (The Robbins Report), Cmnd 2154, London: HMSO.

UK Department of Education and Science (1987), *Higher Education: Meeting the Challenge*, Cmnd 114, London: HMSO.

Copyright acknowledgements

The authors and publishers wish to thank the following for permission to reproduce previously published material in this book:

The cartoon on the cover was originally published in 'Baker's Time Bomb Defused', *Times Higher Education Supplement*, 19 May 1995. Reprinted with the kind permission of David Parkins.

Excerpts from Barr, Nicholas, *The Economics of the Welfare State*, first edition. Copyright © 1987, 1993, 1998, 2004 Nicholas Barr. Used with the permission of Stanford University Press, www.sup.org.

'Eight Votes for a Voucher System', Nicholas Barr, 13 September 1988, the *Guardian*, © Guardian.

'Student Loans Made Easy', Nicholas Barr, first published in *The Times*, 28 July 1988, p. 29.

Nicholas Barr, 'The White Paper on Student Loans', *Journal of Social Policy*, Vol. 18, No. 3, pp. 409–17, 1989, © Cambridge University Press, reprinted with permission.

'Baker's Proposal: A Better Class of Drain', Nicholas Barr, first published in the *Independent*, 22 June 1989.

Nicholas Barr (1991), 'Income Contingent Loans: An Idea Whose Time has Come' in G.K. Shaw (ed.), *Economics, Culture and Education*, Chapter 13, Aldershot, UK and Brookfield, USA: Edward Elgar, pp. 155–70.

Nicholas Barr, 'Alternative Funding Resources for Higher Education', *Economic Journal*, Vol. 103, No. 418 (May), © Blackwell Publishing Ltd.

'Baker's Time Bomb Defused', Iain Crawford and Nicholas Barr, first published in *The Times Higher Education Supplement*, 1176, 19 May 1995 pp. 14–15.

'A Loan Source of University Income', Iain Crawford and Nicholas Barr, first published in *The Times Higher Education Supplement*, 1259, 20 December 1996, p. 11.

'Education Funding, Equity and the Life Cycle' in *The Dynamic of Welfare: The Welfare State and the Life Cycle*, Falkingham and Hills, © Pearson Education Limited.

'Opportunity Lost', Nicholas Barr and Iain Crawford, 2 September 1997, the *Guardian*, © Guardian.

'A Better Class of Students', Nicholas Barr and Iain Crawford, 9 September 1997, the *Guardian*, © Guardian.

'Universities in the First Division', Nicholas Barr and Iain Crawford, 16 September 1997, the *Guardian*, © Guardian.

Chapter 1

Higher education in Britain, 1987 to 2004

The spark that generated this book was a 1987 White Paper, *Higher Education: Meeting the Challenge* (UK Department for Education and Science 1987), which strengthened central government control of universities in England and Wales almost to the point of nationalising them. The problem was never one of academic freedom (as our noisy campaign demonstrates), but of the economic freedom of universities. Our initial motivation was our view that the academic response to the White Paper was supine, and that academics themselves should be taking a lead in reform.

The story since then can be divided into three parts.

- The late 1980s, a time of innovation, saw the passage of the Education Reform Act 1988, which strengthened central planning of higher education, and further legislation which introduced Britain's first large-scale student loan scheme. The chapters in Part 1 argue that central planning was the wrong direction, and that, though it was right to establish loans, the scheme introduced was the wrong one both in terms of design and because it did nothing to improve the funding of higher education.
- It was therefore predictable that funding problems would recur. As a result, the Dearing Committee was set up in 1996 and published its Report in 1997. The chapters in Part 2 discuss this period. Their main argument is that the recommendations of the Dearing Report (flat fees, covered by a better-designed loan) were coherent, albeit cautious, but that the government's response (income-tested fees unsupported by a loan entitlement) muddied the waters. Once more, an opportunity to solve the problems of higher education finance was lost.

- The chapters in Part 3 discuss a major push by government in the early 2000s, culminating in the 2004 Higher Education Act, which introduced variable fees fully covered by a student loan. The last few chapters take a supportive view of these reforms.

Part 1 Introducing student loans

The landscape in the late 1980s

We started from shared and strongly held views about the 'What' of higher education (i.e. its objectives), and the 'How' (i.e. the way higher education should best be organised).

The chapters in Part 1 are based round two objectives – expansion and access. In the late 1980s, the UK had one of the lowest participation rates in higher education (about 14 per cent) of any advanced industrial country. Expansion was necessary, first, as a national response to technological innovation, which has increased the demand for highly skilled people and reduced the demand for the less skilled. In addition, alongside broader arguments about personal development, education and training improve a person's life chances. The argument is not specific to higher education, but applies to post-secondary education more generally.

Improving access to higher education for people from poorer back-grounds, was (and remains) necessary to rectify the strong socio-economic gradient in university attendance, both to enhance social justice and because no country can any longer afford to waste talent.

Our concentration on these objectives in no way denies that universities also have wider purposes. Academic freedom and the pursuit of knowledge are important for their own sake; and universities contribute to the transmission of values, rooted in a country's history and culture. Research should be pluralist not only within each country but also internationally, not least because the questions asked by researchers and the approaches taken to answering them will differ across countries. Thus the finance of higher education should nurture teaching and research capacity, not only in the USA but also in the wider Europe, Asia and more broadly.

Our second starting point was the view that higher education is not a suitable case for nationalisation. University education is not like school education. First, there is an age gradient in the extent to which participants are well informed. School children, especially young ones, are not well informed, nor necessarily are their parents. These problems are a central reason why the state should provide the bulk of finance for school education and, separately, should be the major provider. The argument crops up throughout the book (for fuller discussion, see Barr 2001a, Ch. 11; 2004). In contrast, consumer choice – and hence market forces – is useful for higher education, where students are generally better informed than any central planner. Second, and reinforcing these arguments, there is a diversity gradient. It is right that, especially at primary level, schools should offer a fairly standard package of knowledge and skills and also – and critically important – attitudes and values (e.g. respect for diverse views).[1] But the older a child gets, the greater the case for diversity to reflect differences in interests and abilities, an argument that is at its strongest in higher education, and is further strengthened by the growing diversity of knowledge.

This analysis simultaneously argues for state school education and against central planning of higher education. Our advocacy of regulated market forces in higher education is thus rooted in the economics of information, not in ideology. We both strongly support state school education and the National Health Service.

Our initial premise was that denationalising universities meant that they would have to become less dependent on public funding. Various sources of private finance (discussed in Chapter 7), include family support, contributions from employers and university endowments. But it was – and remains – our view that the only large-scale and sustainable source of income for universities derives from their core services, teaching and research. We focused particularly on the former, for which the logic of denationalisation was clear:

- To increase their independence, universities would need to be able to earn money by charging fees.
- But a requirement to pay fees from family resources would unquestionably harm access, a non-negotiable objective for us both.
- Thus fees would have to be covered by a student loan, but loans with mortgage-type repayments would themselves harm access.
- What was needed, therefore, was a system of loans with income-contingent repayments (i.e. repayments calculated as $x\%$ of earnings until the loan had been repaid). As discussed in the first (Barr 1987) edition of *The Economics of the Welfare State* (see the extract in Chapter 2), the major advantages of income-contingent loans are twofold: they protect individuals from a heavy repayment burden during times of low earnings, thus minimising deterrents to access; and, if well designed, they ensure that a high fraction of total borrowing is repaid.

As well as assisting the autonomy of universities, the case for student loans emerged also from chronic underfunding of higher education as a whole – a recurring theme in subsequent chapters.

Our early work therefore included fees as part of the overall strategy, but concentrated on designing a student loan scheme, which (1) had income-contingent repayments, (2) was easy to administer and (3) did not substantially raise public spending, any increase being an anathema at a time when the Thatcher administration was in its pomp.

1 For fuller discussion of the role of education in transmitting attitudes and values, see Barr (2001a, pp. 161–4).

Chapter 2 1987 *Income-contingent loans: a central theme*

We have argued for many years, and others before us (Friedman 1955; Peacock and Wiseman 1962; Prest 1962; Glennerster *et al.* 1968) that student loans should have income-contingent repayments collected alongside income tax or social security contributions, until the borrower has repaid what he or she borrowed. Since the point is fundamental and one of the two central themes of this book, it is worth explaining why (for fuller discussion see Barr 2001a, Ch. 12).

A conventional loan is a useful benchmark. The loan (say to buy a house) will have a fixed duration (say 25 years) and a positive interest rate. Monthly repayments are determined by three variables: the size of the loan, its duration and the interest rate. Other than adjustments because of changes in the interest rate, monthly repayments are fixed.

Buying a house is a relatively low-risk activity:

(1) The buyer generally knows what he is buying, having lived in a house all his life.
(2) The house is unlikely to fall down.
(3) The real value of the house will generally increase.
(4) If income falls, making repayments problematic, he has the option to sell the house.
(5) Because the house acts as security for the loan, he can get a loan on good terms.

For all these reasons, the private sector provides home loans, with little role for the state beyond regulating financial markets.

The contrast with lending to finance a university degree is sharp. First, though many students are well informed, those from poor backgrounds might not be, potentially violating (1) in the list above. In addition, borrowers face risk and uncertainty, which arise because (2), (3) and (4), though true for housing, are less true for investment in skills. A qualification can 'fall down', because a borrower may fail his exams, and thus ends up liable for loan repayments, but without the qualification that would have led to increased earnings from which to make those repayments. Second, even well-informed students face risk: though the average private return to investment in human capital is positive, there is considerable variation about that average. In addition, even the private benefits of education are hard to quantify, so that the borrower faces uncertainty as well as risk about the return to a particular qualification. Third (element (4)), someone who has borrowed to pay for a qualification and subsequently has low earnings and high repayments does not have the option to sell the qualification, further increasing the borrower's exposure to risk.

Lenders also face uncertainty. If I borrow to buy a house, the house acts as security. If I fail to repay, the lender can repossess the house, sell it and take what is owed. Loans are thus available on good terms.

An analogous arrangement with human capital would allow the lender, if I default, to repossess my brain, sell it and take what is owed. Since that is not an option, lenders for human capital have no security: they face uncertainty about whether I will acquire the qualification, and whether my subsequent earnings will allow me to repay. Because there is no security, adverse selection is a second problem, since the borrower is better informed than the lender whether he or she aspires to a career in accountancy (a 'good' risk from the lender's point of view) or in acting.

The resulting inefficiencies are major. On the demand side, (1) some borrowers, particularly from disadvantaged backgrounds, may be badly informed about the value of a degree, not least because of a lack of family university experience, and (2) all borrowers face risk and uncertainty, both about the return to their investment and because they cannot sell the qualification should their income turn out subsequently to be low. The resulting borrowing will be inefficiently low.

The problem is accentuated on the supply side. Lenders face uncertainty about the riskiness of an applicant and therefore charge a risk premium. A risk premium assessed by a well-informed lender is efficient (e.g. higher car insurance premiums for bad drivers). But lenders are not well informed about an applicant for a student loan. Thus risk premiums will be inefficiently high, further reducing the amount of borrowing. Additionally, lenders face incentives to cherry-pick, i.e. to find ways of lending only to the best risks, analogous to incentives to cream skimming that face private medical insurers. One way to do so is to lend only to students who can provide security, for example, a home-owning parent. Once more, the resulting borrowing will be inefficiently low.

Conventional loans are also inequitable. The various efficiency problems impact most on people from poorer backgrounds, women and ethnic minorities, who may be less well-informed about the benefits of a qualification and therefore less prepared to risk a loan. In addition, these groups tend to have a less well-established credit record. They are therefore less tempting to lenders and thus likely to be on the wrong end of cherry-picking.

Income-contingent repayments exactly address these problems. Designed explicitly for that purpose, they have a profound effect on higher education finance in ways that are still not widely understood. Graduates with low earnings make low or no repayments; and people who never earn much do not repay. Separately, a larger loan (or a higher interest rate) has no effect on monthly repayments, which depend only on the person's monthly income. Instead, a person with a larger loan will repay for longer.

Chapter 2 (originally published in the first (1987) edition of *The Economics of the Welfare State*) was Barr's first piece of writing about loans. At the time it appeared to have had little impact. But it later transpired that it had had a significant influence on the Wran Committee in Australia, which introduced their Higher Education Contribution Scheme in 1989.

The scheme included the first large-scale scheme of income-contingent loans with repayments collected by the tax authorities, which became an important weapon against British civil servants, some of whom cast doubt on the practicality of our proposals.[2]

Chapter 3 1988 *Setting universities free from central planning: a second central theme*

The issue in 1988 was how to fund universities without central planning. Barnes and Barr (1988), from which Chapter 3 is drawn, was our unofficial attempt to draft the relevant White Paper, hence the book's subtitle 'The Alternative White Paper'.

The first edition of *The Economics of the Welfare State* argued against vouchers for school education on both efficiency and equity grounds. John Barnes's proposal for what, in essence, was a voucher scheme for higher education therefore initially provoked suspicion. The writing in Chapter 3, however, shows a growing realisation that the analysis which argues against vouchers for school education simultaneously supports the approach for higher education for reasons which the chapter sets out:

- *Information.* Students are well informed, or potentially well informed; even before the Internet considerable information was available about different degrees and (in contrast with health care) prospective students have time to seek advice and to ponder their options.
- *Competition.* Vouchers (called bursaries in Chapter 3) are compatible with more or less competitive regimes. With a completely hands-off approach, universities attracting large numbers would flourish, those unable to do so would go to the wall. At the other extreme, governments could determine the number of vouchers for each subject and university, mimicking pure central planning. Thus the mechanism allows public policy to determine the degree of competition, including vouchers tied to particular universities or particular subjects. The mechanism is also compatible with different fee regimes: 'Finally, and of considerable importance, is the issue of whether institutions are completely free to set their own fee levels, whether fees may vary only within a given range, or whether fee levels will be centrally established for all institutions . . .' (this volume, p. 35), a paragraph that foreshadows the fierce debates about fee variability in 2004, discussed in Chapter 15.
- *Redistribution.* Vouchers can be designed to be strongly redistributive, for example paying larger vouchers to students from disadvantaged backgrounds. The idea is articulated more fully by Le Grand (1989).

2 Higher education owes a considerable debt to Meredith Edwards, a member of the Wran Committee, whose pre-existing reputation for ferocity played a large part in convincing the Australian tax authorities to acquiesce to the Committee's proposal for income-contingent loan repayments collected alongside income tax.

The argument against central planning as a suitable mechanism for higher education – the second fundamental element in our strategy – is worth spelling out in more detail. Again, it is helpful initially to take a contrary case as a starting point. Consider the following stylised facts about health care: consumers are imperfectly informed because health care is a highly technical subject; treatment frequently results not from choice but because of an external event, such as breaking a leg; and when treatment is needed, there is often limited choice about its type. Much of the efficiency case for publicly organised health care is based on these facts. With food, the story is different. We are generally well informed about what we like and its costs, hence we can do our own shopping. And though food is a necessity, there is considerable choice over how we meet those needs. These *technical* differences explain why we ensure access to health care by giving it to people (largely) free; with food, in contrast, we ensure that elderly people have access to nutrition by paying them a pension and allowing them to buy their own food at market prices.

Within this stylised context, the question is whether education is more like food or more like health care. School education is more like health care: small children are not well informed; the need for education is externally imposed by legal compulsion so that it is consumed by all young people; and, especially for younger children, the range of choice over curriculum is properly constrained. There are also equity issues if middle-class parents are able to do better for their children in a more competitive system of school education. Thus there is a compelling case for publicly funded school education.

Higher education, in contrast, is more like food. Students are generally well informed and can (and should) be made better informed. There is genuine choice about whether or not to go to university – it is precisely that fact that has made taxpayer funding of higher education so regressive. Finally, the choice of which subject to study and at which university is large and growing. On the demand side, therefore, it can be argued that students are well informed, or potentially well informed, and hence better able than planners to make choices which conform with their individual interests and those of the economy. Though that proposition is robust for the generality of students, there is an important exception: students from poorer backgrounds might not be fully-informed, with important implications, discussed below, for access in general and debt aversion in particular.

On the supply side, central planning of higher education, setting aside the question of whether it was ever desirable, is no longer feasible. In response to technological change, advanced countries increasingly have mass higher education, meaning more universities, more students and greater diversity of subject matter. Thus the myth of parity of esteem and relative parity of funding is no longer sustainable. In principle, differential funding allocations could be made by an all-knowing central planner, but the problem is too complex for that to be the sole mechanism: mass higher education requires a funding regime in which institutions can charge differential prices to reflect their different costs and missions.

Moving away from central planning does not mean, and should not mean, that government is marginalised. The important and continuing role of government emerges throughout the book. Its tasks include: (1) partially funding higher education, (2) organising student loans, (3) promoting access, (4) acting as regulator, not least to ensure quality, and (5) establishing a rational incentive structure. These roles are all picked up in Chapter 16.

Thus the approach allows intervention to foster both distributional and educational objectives. The system can be as redistributive as desired; and the degree of competition is a policy variable, with different answers possible for different subjects. The resulting system is efficient, because outcomes are determined not by a single, dominant – and often badly informed and ineffective – arm of government, but by the interacting decisions of students, universities, and employers, subject to transparent influence by government. Particularly with complex mass systems of higher education, this approach is more likely than central planning to achieve individual and national objectives.

The debate about vouchers is summarised in the newspaper article (13 September 1988) (pages 40–2 after Chapter 3), a debate with Professor Ted Wragg, who argued against free-market vouchers with minimal redistribution. The response agrees with his opposition to such a construct, but argues that the mechanism can be used in very different ways to achieve objectives about which we are in agreement.

Chapter 4 **1989** *A specific loan proposal*

Alongside the analysis of fees in a regulated competitive environment, we continued to work on the design of a student loan scheme. Chapter 4 (originally published in *Student Loans: The Next Steps*, Barr 1989) is our first fully-fledged proposal. The scheme had two primary characteristics. For all the reasons discussed above, it had income-contingent repayments. Second, we argued that those repayment should be collected as an add-on to National Insurance Contributions, an idea originally suggested to us by Mervyn King.

The basic idea was set out in the article in *The Times* (28 July 1988) (pages 60–2 after Chapter 4), and an embryonic version included in Barnes and Barr (1988, pp. 28–32). In July 1988 a group of us[3] met Robert Jackson, then the Higher Education Minister. Though he was guarded in what he said at the time, we subsequently learned that he had discussed the idea of income-contingent repayments with the Inland Revenue, who

3 John Barnes, Nicholas Barr, Iain Crawford and Tony Travers.

had been unenthused. Later that month we presented a short paper informally to Kenneth Baker, then Secretary of State for Education in the Conservative government, stressing collection via National Insurance Contributions.

A White Paper on student loans (UK Department of Education and Science 1988), published in November 1988 left open the repayment method, including mortgage repayments but also (Option D) an income-contingent arrangement.[4] The article in the *Financial Times* (16 November 1988) (pages 63–5 after Chapter 4) offered a preliminary assessment, including an early critique of interest subsidies, which were to be (and remain) a recurring theme.

The material in Chapter 4 was written to influence the debate about loan design, with the twin objectives of expansion and improved access. The proposal was deliberately a loan, in which repayments cease once the borrower has repaid what he or she had borrowed, rather than a graduate tax, where repayments continue till (say) retirement. The specific proposition was that an add-on to the National Insurance Contribution of borrowers of one-third of 1 per cent would repay an indexed loan of £1,000 at a 2 per cent real interest rate over 25 years.

There were both philosophical and pragmatic reasons for adding repayments to National Insurance Contributions. Student loans are a device for consumption smoothing, i.e. they allow a person to redistribute from his older to his or her younger self, in exactly the same way as pensions allow people to redistribute from their younger to their older selves:

> Student loans . . . are very much in keeping with the spirit of the Beveridge system, one of whose main purposes is to enable individuals to be self-sufficient over their lifetime as a whole, by redistributing from themselves at one stage in their life cycle to themselves at another. . . . Student loans are just an up-front pension.
>
> (this volume, p. 58)

In philosophical terms, therefore, the use of National Insurance Contributions to collect loan repayments is entirely appropriate and has a resonance that is appealing.[5] The principle is not new: Chapter 2 points out that 'One of [the Yale student loan scheme's] most interesting features is that it provides a form of group insurance' (this volume, p. 30).

A second, and more pragmatic reason for suggesting the National Insurance mechanism was because it appeared to offer a way of circumventing the non-cooperation of the tax authorities.

---

4 The Government was clearly treading carefully. The White Paper was published the day after the US Presidential elections, ensuring that press coverage was limited.
5 The idea won an award from the Institute of Social Inventions in 1989.

Most of the features of the original loan have stood the test of time. The scheme:

- Included a real interest rate of 2 per cent.
- Had income-contingent repayments, but '[included] in the conditions of the loan a clause converting it into a mortgage-type debt upon emigration' (this volume, p. 50).
- Foreshadowed a changed balance between loan and grant to cover living costs.
- Included targeted interest subsidies, for example for people with caring responsibilities. 'It would be possible . . . partly or wholly to forgive the loan, either for labour market reasons, e.g. to persuade engineers to stay engineers, or for distributional reasons, e.g. for nurses or primary school teachers' (this volume, p. 55).
- Discussed loans deriving from private funds, including a new type of financial asset, 'analogous to the secondary market in mortgages. . . . The asset opens up the (not wholly fanciful) prospect of the National Union of Mineworkers' pension fund owning a stake in the long-term prospects of graduates; retired miners would be living off the sweat of young graduate city analysts' (this volume, p. 56). This foreshadowed the sales of two tranches of student debt in the later 1990s.

Chapter 5 1990 *The government loan scheme: a critique*

Since the 1988 White Paper on student loans left open the possibility of income-contingent loans, our initial approach was supportive. On 19 June 1989, Kenneth Baker, announced a scheme with mortgage-type repayments to be administered by the banks. At that point the gloves came off. The immediate response was an article in the *Independent* (22 June 1989) (pages 75–6 after Chapter 5). Toward the end of the piece is a passage that is pure Crawford:

> [T]hough the banks will administer the scheme, the money they lend is Treasury money. So the Government is paying banks to lend students the Government's money. It then pays the banks up to £60 a year for each student to try to get it back; and, if the banks, fail, the Government stands the loss, but still pays the banks for trying.

Chapter 5, originally published in the *Journal of Social Policy* in 1989, is a fuller commentary, which can also be read as a summary of the early story. The opening part establishes the aims of policy, in particular expansion and improved access; offers a critique of the system of student grants, i.e. tax-funded student support to help meet living costs; and discusses the different types of loan scheme. It then assesses the government's proposals. The first criticism is the high cost of the scheme, which absorbs resources that should be used for expansion and improved access. A second major criticism, with both efficiency and equity implications, is the interest subsidy. The proposal was that students would pay no interest, but the loan would be indexed, i.e. a zero real rate of interest:

> This represents an average interest subsidy of between 2 and 3 per cent. Like all blanket subsidies, it causes inefficiency and wastes public expenditure by spraying subsidies over those who do not need them. The incentive is for the best-off students to borrow the maximum . . . and put the proceeds into privatisation flotations. Much better to have no interest subsidy, and to use the saved resources to pay larger grants to poorer students so that they needed no loan, or only a small one.
>
> (this volume, p. 70)

The final part summarises the National Insurance Loan proposal.

To complete the chronology, the government's intention was that the banks would administer student loans, to which end negotiations continued throughout 1989. The banks decided that it was too risky in terms of relations with their best potential customers to run student loans as individual banks, and therefore set up an arms-length subsidiary, the Student Loans Company. Eventually, the banks decided to pull out altogether, at which point the government took over the embryonic Student Loans Company.

It is an interesting historical footnote that if the government had intended from the first to run the loan scheme itself, it would probably not have set up a separate loans administration, and most certainly not one in that form. At the time, we criticised the arrangements as being unnecessarily costly in administrative terms.[6] We were wrong. After a shaky start, the Student Loans Company developed a highly efficient administration; and the existence of an independent student loans administration turned out to have significant advantages in both educational- and financial-market terms. If the tax or social security authorities run student loans (which on the face of it seems the obvious way to run an income-contingent scheme) they will regard the collection of educational data as outside their remit, to the detriment of research on how to improve the system.[7] In addition, the tax authorities are not equipped to act in financial markets, for example to raise capital for student loans or to organise debt sales. What is needed is an institution with an educational remit but also the capacity to act in financial markets. The Student Loans Company can operate on both fronts.

6 'The Government is behaving just like its predecessors: faced with an ill-conceived loss-making enterprise, it is proposing to nationalise it' (Barr 1990).

7 The Education Department in New Zealand has complained about the reluctance of their tax authorities (which administer student loans) to collect data on educational outcomes.

Chapter 6 1991 *Pulling the arguments together*

The period from 1988–90 was one of intense activity on the higher education front. The Education Reform Act 1988 strengthened central planning of higher education; and the legislation on student loans introduced the right principle but the wrong loan scheme. Having spent a lot of time on policy, it seemed a good idea to write a reflective piece pulling together the academic arguments. Chapter 6, written for a Festschrift for Mark Blaug published in 1991, was the result. The opening section summarises the British debates of the 1960s and 1970s, including a history of the idea of income-contingent student loans. The next section summarises the economic analytics. The third part discusses the implications for loan design, including (section 3.3) principles for student support. The fourth section summarises the then state of play in a number of countries.

Conclusion to Part 1 *Marking our scorecard*

Subsequent events confirm the long lag between the development of analytical solutions and their implementation. Later chapters contain very little that is new in terms of policy design. The chapters in Part 1:

- Stress the centrality of income-contingent repayments, introduced in Britain in 1998.
- Stress variable but regulated fees, foreshadowed in England for 2006.
- Attack blanket interest subsidies, which continue to be a fiscal black hole.

Other predictions about which we were right were that:

- Mortgage-type loans would not be sustainable.
- The 1990 loan scheme would not solve the funding crisis it was intended to address.

Not all our arguments were right, however. The administrative costs of the student loan scheme were not as high as we predicted, not least because the Student Loans Company came to be run as a tight ship. For this and other reasons, we were wrong to oppose the establishment of a separate student loans administration.

Part 2 The chickens come home to roost: the Dearing Report

Having lost the late 1980s policy debate, we suspended campaigning until such time as the issue once more became politically salient, and each pursued other activities. In Barr's case this included two years working for the World Bank on reforming welfare states in the former communist countries of Central and Eastern Europe, a considerable source of insight into the central planning of UK higher education. Crawford's main activities were as Head of Public Relations at the London School of Economics, hence with direct experience of central planning at the sharp end.

Chapter 7 1993 *Alternative funding sources for higher education*

Given the prediction that the 1990 arrangements would not solve the funding crisis, we continued to work on ways of bringing in more resources. Chapter 7, originally published in the *Economic Journal* in 1993, summarises the state of play at the time and then (Table 7.1) sets out a taxonomy of funding sources. A central conclusion is that 'funding should not rely excessively on any one source. This is not a very dramatic conclusion, but non-economists seem to have a strong (and usually inappropriate) attraction to corner solutions' (this volume, p. 89).

Though private funding for teaching can come from various sources, the paper argues that the only large-scale and equitable source is the student's future earnings, i.e. loans, and concludes:

> As a response to the trade-off between size, quality and public expenditure, countries like Britain and Australia, with substantially tax-funded systems, are seeking to introduce more private funding. . . . Any move away from tax funding, however, must rest on a loan scheme which (*a*) does not deter access and (*b*) brings in private funds. Loans, from both an efficiency and an equity perspective, are thus the key to reform.
>
> (this volume, p. 112)

Periodically, we would lob a rock into the pond to keep income-contingency in play. The 1995 article 'Baker's Time Bomb Defused' (pages 114–17 after Chapter 7) – accompanied by the cartoon on the cover of this book – started by diagnosing the problem:

> Kenneth Baker, the former education minister, started the clock on what, in his memoirs, he genially referred to as his time bomb for the Treasury [when he] set the goal of doubling the participation rate. . . .
>
> His reference to time bombs refers to his recognition that he was proposing to double the undergraduate system with no mention of additional resources. . . .
>
> It is true that an undergraduate student loan system was introduced, but any savings that this scheme may eventually produce will arrive long after the bomb has exploded.

The article proposed that the National Insurance Loan scheme should be introduced initially for postgraduate students, both to pilot the idea and because the politics of loans for postgraduates (who had – and have – little support) would have been particularly favourable.

A further article 'A Loan Source of University Income' (pages 118–19 after Chapter 7), published in 1996 explored in more detail a mechanism for the private finance of student loans, based on Crawford's insight about the proper ownership of the Student Loans Company (this was part of our realisation that an independent student loans administration was not the mistake we had initially supposed). Specifically, the proposal was that the Student Loans Company should be owned by the universities collectively, making it unambiguously a private-sector institution, and hence easier for student loans to be classified as private spending:

> The proper owners . . . are the . . . universities. They are uniquely placed to own the SLC because they alone face a double market test. Students are their main business and therefore universities' priority is to get them the best deal. They also face a financial market test; since the price at which student debt can be privatised is higher the more credible the repayment mechanism.

The proposal was motivated in part by the need to strengthen loans by bringing in private finance, but also had implications for one of our other agenda, university independence: 'If universities own the SLC they become central participants instead of powerless spectators in talks about their future.'

Chapter 8 1995 *Education and the life cycle*

Chapter 8, originally published in 1995, reports simulations of the operation of the National Insurance Loan proposal, and illustrates the role of loans as part of redistribution over the life cycle (one of the key elements of *The Dynamic of Welfare* from which the chapter is drawn). The work is based on LIFEMOD, a micro simulation model developed by the Welfare State Programme at the London School of Economics, and on joint work with Jane Falkingham, one of LIFEMOD's creators (Barr and Falkingham 1993).

The chapter explores how the National Insurance Loan scheme would perform in comparison with (1) the government scheme (see Figure 8.3); and (2) a graduate tax or employer user charge (Table 8.4), and concludes that, depending on the real rate of interest charged, around 90 per cent of all lending to men would be repaid and about two-thirds of lending to women (Tables 8.2 and 8.3). Later work (Barr and Falkingham 1996) subjected these results to additional sensitivity tests and concluded that, taking men and women together, even under pessimistic assumptions, between 70 and 80 per cent of all lending to students would be repaid.

Chapter 9 1997 *Evidence to the Dearing Committee: funding higher education in an age of expansion*

Because of the incentives to expansion in Baker's time bomb, student numbers increased rapidly over the early 1990s. Predictably, therefore, the funding crisis bubbled back towards the top of the agenda, and became politically sensitive. The appointment of the Dearing Committee in mid-1996, to review the finance of higher education, was motivated by the funding problem; given the political sensitivity of the issue, the Committee was told to report in July 1997, later than the latest possible date for a general election. It is not unfair to regard the timing, if not the existence, of the Committee as a cynical plot between government and opposition to get higher education off the election agenda, a plot in which they were abetted by a compliant university sector.

We were invited to give several pieces of evidence to the Committee. Chapter 9, published in *Education Economics* in 1998, is a revised and slightly shortened version of our main submission.

The first part of the chapter, harking back to Chapters 3 and 4, maps out the implications of the expansion to a mass system; in particular (1) the need for a wide-ranging loan system, and (2) price differentiation and a relaxation of central planning. The rest of the paper maps out both elements in some detail, with particular discussion of how the loan scheme would work – on the grounds that a good loan scheme was the essential key to unlocking a wide array of reforms.

Chapter 10 1998 *The Dearing Report and the Government's response: a critique*

A Labour government was elected on 1 May 1997 after 18 years in opposition. The Dearing Report (UK National Committee of Inquiry into Higher Education 1997a, b) was published at 11 a.m. on 23 July 1997. Its key recommendations were (1) to replace mortgage loans by income-contingent loans: (2) to introduce flat fees of £1,000 per year, irrespective of subject or university, *but* fully covered by an income-contingent loan: and (3) to keep maintenance grants, which covered part of the living costs of students from poorer backgrounds.

The government responded at 3 p.m. on the same day with proposals that differed significantly: (1) the tuition fee was to be upfront (i.e. not covered by a loan), but (2) was to be income-tested so that students from poor backgrounds did not pay. The cost of the fee remissions was to be recouped (3) by abolishing the maintenance grant, replacing it by a loan. Thus the proposals replaced an income subsidy (the maintenance grant) by a price subsidy (fee remission for students from poor backgrounds).

The time around publication was hectic. Barr was in Australia, at a conference which was a precursor to the West Committee (the Australian equivalent of Dearing discussed in Chapter 11), Crawford was in London to advise the Committee of Vice-Chancellors and Principals (CVCP) and to talk to the media. The email interchange is vivid.

Crawford to Barr, 30 July 1997

I now think that it is worse than at first sight. Try this:

1) no increase in public funds
2) no increase in family contribution, statement by [Education Secretary] Blunkett points out that contribution to fees offset by extra maintenance loan
3) all loans charged to [public spending], confirmed by [Education Department] to CVCP.

Effect of 1–3 no increased resource whatsoever. Money moved from pot to pot in a zero sum game. Why, I ask myself, bother at all?

The above is the basis of my view expressed to CVCP who are somewhat shocked . . .

Barr to Crawford, same date

The key analytical flaw is the use of a *price* subsidy for *equity* reasons. I spent two years explaining this to governments in Central and Eastern Europe, and did not expect to have to explain it to the government of an OECD country. . . .

Gill [Mrs Barr] did a rant over the phone last night about how wrong it was to face students with debt, i.e. making them feel indebted. She reminded me that the whole *purpose* of income-contingent repayments is to take away the feeling of indebtedness. Thus it was a major blunder politically (quite apart from other reasons) by Blunkett to rush in precipitately on publication day, before any of the details of income-contingent repayments had been worked out. [Waiting] . . . would have enabled Blunkett to:

- make loud noises about how low earners make low repayments and people with no earnings make no repayments;
- say things like: you can go to university free; you won't have to pay a penny; we have got rid of parental contributions; and we have increased living expenses to restore the erosion since 1979.

Leaping in as he did, none of that was possible. Thus not surprising that – as Gill reported – someone in Any Questions talked about fees as Labour's poll tax. All of this was totally unnecessary.

Chapter 10, published in *The Political Quarterly* in 1998 is our more considered response. An earlier and fuller version (Barr and Crawford 1997) was invited by the House of Commons Education Select Committee.

The adoption of income-contingent loans was great good news. Recommendation 78 of the Dearing Report – not least because of the Crawford strategy of assiduously making sure over the early 1990s that everyone was aware of the arguments – stated that, 'We recommend to the Government that it introduces, by 1998/99, income contingent terms for the payment of any contribution towards living costs or tuition costs sought from graduates in work' (UK National Committee of Inquiry into Higher Education 1997b, p. 310). The government accepted the income-contingent part of the recommendation without demur.

The other key building block in the Dearing recommendations was the introduction of tuition fees. Though the Report was carefully worded, recommendation 79 was for a flat fee of £1,000 per year, irrespective of subject or course. On one view, this was a careful stepping stone; on another, it could be criticised for moving too slowly, variable fees being the better option. The Report was undoubtedly important in that it established the principle of fees.

Debate on the Report, however, was largely sidelined by the government's immediate response. The worst that could be said of the Dearing Report was that it was coherent but cautious. The Government's response merited much heavier criticism, missing a golden opportunity in its honeymoon period to make serious progress on higher education finance. Centrally, the response ignored the recommendation that tuition fees should be deferred, i.e. covering by an income-contingent loan. Instead, fees were to be income-tested so that students from poor backgrounds were exempt; but where fees were payable, they were upfront.

Chapter 10 highlights a series of problems with the Government's response, of which two stand out. First, the reforms brought in no extra income for universities. The core of Crawford's insight in his email of 30 July was that:

> Public spending on higher education will not go up (the budget said so); parental contributions (i.e. private spending) will not go up (the Secretary of State said so); and loans to students (the other potential source of private spending) count in their entirety as public spending. If public spending is unchanged and there is no extra private spending, there is nothing extra for higher education . . . . [The recommendations] do not produce a brass farthing in the short run.
>
> (this volume, p. 177)

Thus, systematically and predictably, the reforms failed to resolve the funding crisis. Pointing this out from an early stage did not make us greatly popular with the government or the Education Department, nor with the Vice-Chancellors, who yet again adopted a compliant attitude.[8]

8 We are not alone in pointing to the failure of the university sector to fight its corner. A leading Vice-Chancellor remarked acidly at the time that there were 'not enough gentlemen to form a club and not enough guts to form a cartel'.

Second, the proposals did not help access, indeed put access at risk. The loan to cover living costs was too small; and the combination of inadequate loans and upfront fees increased reliance on parental contributions – a system widely known to work badly, and one with an adverse gradient in respect of gender and ethnicity.

To make matters worse:

> [a] further impediment to access is the incentive to discriminate against British students. A flat fee will continue the erosion of quality at the best universities, which face the biggest shortfalls in funding. British students could suffer in one of two ways. The quality of the best institutions might fall; though British students could still get places, the quality of the degree would be less. Alternatively, the best institutions will largely stop teaching British undergraduates (for whom they receive on average £4,000 per year) and will use the fees from foreign undergraduates (around £8,000 per year) to preserve their excellence. The government is considering trying to prevent British universities from charging additional fees to UK/EU students. . . . [This] ends up harming the very people it is aimed at helping.
>
> (this volume, p. 179)

A separate, more narrowly technical, strand in the argument concerns the treatment of student loans in the public accounts. At the time, public spending was still measured on a cash-flow basis. Thus public expenditure figures made no distinction between grants, which never came back, and loans which brought in a future repayment stream. We had pointed this out to the Dearing Committee (Barr 1997a), and the Report (recommendation 80) urged a more rational approach. Matters improved over the later 1990s as government moved to resource accounting, which divided spending on student loans into two elements: the fraction of lending that never comes back is rightly included in current public spending; the future repayment stream, in contrast, appears in the public accounts as a financial asset (see Barr 1997b). Remaining issues of public accounting are taken up in Chapter 16 (section 3.1).

The three central strands of our post-Dearing assessment – adequate income-contingent loans, sensible treatment of loans in the public accounts, and variable fees – are the basis of the trilogy of newspaper articles on pages 185–92 after Chapter 10.

As already mentioned, much of our work on the Dearing Report and government response was produced for the Education Select Committee, which at about that time began to develop its influential role in higher education finance (see Chapters 13–15).

Chapter 11 **1998** *An international view*

Similar ideas for similar reasons were bubbling up in other countries at about the same time. In Australia, the West Committee was considering problems akin to those in the UK. There was extensive communication between the two chairmen, Ron Dearing and Roderick West. Bruce Chapman, one of the architects of the 1989 Australian Higher Education Contribution Scheme gave evidence to the Dearing Committee, and Barr was invited to Australia to take part in some of the West Committee's deliberations. In recommending variable fees, their Report (Commonwealth of Australia 1997, 1998) was more radical than Dearing. Chapter 11, originally published in the *Australian Economic Review* in 1998, is a joint assessment of the two reports. In New Zealand, too, government was considering more radical options, including funding all tertiary education as part of a single system (New Zealand Ministry of Education 1998).

Sadly, none of the reforms came to fruition. The UK government's response, while making important gains, badly muddied the Dearing recommendations. The Australian government was unable to muster sufficient political support, and most of the West Committee reforms were shelved. In New Zealand, the opposition unexpectedly won the election in 1999 and, impaled by a manifesto commitment, introduced interest subsidies. In all three countries, more radical reform had to wait.

Conclusion to Part 2 *Marking our scorecard*

The 1998 reforms were important both because they established income-contingent loans and because they introduced the principle of tuition fees.

However, the government was woeful in explaining income contingency. Three factors (or a combination) offer a possible explanation. First, by responding so quickly, the government and the Education Department might not have fully absorbed the power of the idea. Second (and with hindsight), the government responded to Dearing in July 1997 at a time when the tax authorities had not yet agreed to collect loan repayments (which did not happen till November of that year), making it difficult to be too definite about details. Third, as a Labour government, newly in power after 18 years in opposition, there was a powerful reflex against appearing to introduce what might wrongly be represented as an increase in taxation. This failure threw away the opportunity to get across to worried students, parents and Parliamentarians that income-contingent loans were fundamentally different from conventional loans, such as credit card debt. That failure stored up trouble for the 2004 reforms.

Sadly, many of our diagnoses (see 'A view ahead' in Chapter 10, pp. 180 et seq.) were accurate.

- There was no loan to cover fees, which were an upfront charge.
- The loan to cover living expenses was too small to cover realistic living costs, aggravating student poverty.

- There was no extra money for higher education at the time.
- The blanket interest subsidy was enormously costly.
- The system discriminated against British students, especially at the best universities which were able to substitute overseas students.

In two areas, we would now write differently. We would no longer criticise the Dearing Report for recommending that grants be retained. It is true that income-contingent loans, if they are large enough to cover tuition fees and living costs, are all that is needed for most students. However, those students who are least well informed about higher education – precisely those for whom access is most fragile – might not be prepared to take out loans, even if income-contingent. Grants and other forms of assistance are necessary for that group. In addition, as mentioned in Chapter 10, financial support is necessary for 16–19 year olds, to encourage them to continue education beyond the minimum school leaving age.

Secondly, though we were right in diagnosing the issue of private finance as important, our understanding of how to craft student loans to ensure that they are classified as private spending was at the time still incomplete.

Part 3 Shifting tectonic plates: the 2004 legislation

Chapter 12 2000 *The benefits of education: what we know and what we don't*

The post-Dearing reforms were followed by a period of relative quiet, though the parts of government concerned with long-term strategy continued to pursue matters. Chapter 12 was part of a conference organised by HM Treasury in 2000 on what government might do to increase economic growth. The paper summarises the state of play on the question: 'What is the efficient amount to spend on higher education?'.

The paper's argument is twofold. First, because we cannot measure what we need to measure, the optimal size of the higher education sector cannot satisfactorily be quantified. The paper goes on to argue that the right approach when policy makers are thus imperfectly informed but consumers and producers are better informed, is to put into place a system in which all the stakeholders (students, universities, employers, government) can make their choices facing a budget constraint that minimises avoidable distortions, supported by a system of loans to foster consumption smoothing and tax-financed transfers to promote access.

Chapter 13 2002 *Evidence to the Education Select Committee 1: funding higher education, policies for access and quality*

The 1998 reforms, however, soon ran into trouble. The problems were those listed above:

- Upfront fees were a problem.
- 'Debt' was a problem: loans to cover living costs were too small, impaling students on credit card debt; and government continued to be woeful in explaining that student loan repayments were a payroll deduction like income tax, not credit card debt.
- Underfunding of universities – and hence quality – was a problem.

Not least for these reasons, the Prime Minister was given a hard time on doorsteps, especially about fees and debt, during the 2001 election campaign, and announced at the Labour Party conference later that year that there was to be a review of higher education finance.

The Education Select Committee saw this as an opportunity to gather evidence. Our work in responding to Dearing had mainly been jointly authored to bring together the economic analytics and the politics. We became aware, however, that joint writing could dilute the separate strength of the two sets of arguments, and decided this time round to write parallel pieces. Chapters 13 and 14, our submissions to the Select Committee in 2002, set out what we thought the Review ought to recommend.

One of the biggest changes since the late 1980s was the enormous expansion of higher education: participation tripled from 14 per cent of young people in 1989 to over 40 per cent in the early 2000s, though without much change in socio-economic mix.[9] Our objectives changed in parallel – from expansion and access in the earlier period to quality and access in the early 2000s, as manifested by the subtitle of Chapter 13.

The chapter starts by setting out the wide areas of agreement, both in diagnosis of the problem and in objectives. Having summarised the lessons from economic theory, it then gives a critique of existing arrangements, including a major attack on blanket interest subsidies. The paper concluded with a strategy with three legs:

- variable fees to address the quality issue;
- a wide-ranging system of income-contingent loans to provide consumption smoothing; and
- active measures to promote access, both by providing financial support and, through outreach to schools, by improving the information available to potential students.

Chapter 14 2002 *Evidence to the Education Select Committee 2*

Chapter 14 offers practical suggestions to help young people's cash flow, both by paying student loans monthly rather than once a term, and by

---

9 The main source of expansion according to John Ashworth, then Director of the LSE, was that the middle classes increasingly sent their daughters as well as their sons to university.

improving their financial education. Both were offered as desirable for their own sake and because, at little cost, they would improve the hostile politics of 'debt'.

Once more the Education Select Committee was playing a major role. Our oral evidence evoked none of the party political Punch and Judy that might have been expected, but a series of searching and serious questions. The Committee's Report was published in July 2002. To our considerable pleasure, recommendations 20 and 21 argued that the large amount spent on blanket interest subsidies should be spent on better-targeted measures to promote access.

> 20. It is clear to us that the current zero real interest rate for student loans subsidises those from affluent backgrounds while providing insufficient funds to those from poor or otherwise disadvantaged circumstances. . . .
> 21. It is our view that there is considerable scope for the development of models of student support which are based on adjustable interest rates. . . .
>
> (Education and Skills Committee 2002, p. 34)

The Report also recognised that funding both for universities and for students was inadequate, and devoted considerable attention to promoting access.

The Report took a dismissive view of the Education Department's arguments in support of the interest subsidy – see, for example, Recommendation 25. More generally, the failure of the Department (as opposed to Ministers) to take a lead prompted Crawford's suggestion that,

> like the Scots, why not move higher and further education to the Department of Trade and Industry? Universities are actually private-sector organisations, albeit usually not for profit, and the DTI may be better at understanding their problems and opportunities. Such a move might also reduce the education department . . . to a more manageable size.
>
> (Crawford and MacLeod 2002)

Our strong support for the role of the Select Committee and for the general thrust of their recommendations is in our article in the *Guardian* (16 July 2002) (pages 265–6 after Chapter 14) – after 15 years of argument, our first piece as witness for the defence rather than the prosecution. The tectonic plates were starting to shift.

By autumn 2002 the government's repeatedly postponed Review had still not appeared, but was being trailed for publication in November – at which point the Education Minister unexpectedly resigned, to be replaced by Charles Clarke. With hindsight it is clear that he and his advisers read the existing draft and were unhappy. In short order, he announced that publication would be postponed for two months. The article in the *Financial Times* (22 November 2002) (pages 267–8 after Chapter 14) was written to try to nudge policy in what we regarded as the right direction.

Chapter 15 2003 *The Higher Education White Paper: a critique*

The government's review was published as a White Paper (UK Department for Education and Skills 2003) in January 2003. In terms of the three legs of the strategy set out above:

- Leg 1: fees – the White Paper proposed variable fees up to a ceiling of £3,000.
- Leg 2: loans – the White Paper extended loans to cover fees.
- Leg 3: access – the White Paper restored grants.

The only missing element in our strategy was action to reduce the interest subsidy. Here the argument had been heard and understood; but it was felt that the reforms were already radical enough, and that reducing interest subsidies, notwithstanding the powerful arguments for doing so in terms of policy design, would have been politically a step too far.

The Education Select Committee went back into action to gather evidence on the White Paper, the intention being to help shape the eventual Bill. Chapter 15, originally published in the *Political Quarterly* in 2003, is a shortened version of evidence to the Select Committee (Barr 2003), offering strong support for the White Paper and suggesting ways of improving things further. The Select Committee Report (Education and Skills Committee 2003), while supportive of many parts of the White Paper continued to urge action on the interest subsidy.

The response of the university sector was mixed. The introduction of variable fees, by strengthening competition, has profound implications for the management of universities. Some institutions welcomed the new freedoms, analogous to countries like Poland and Hungary when the communist system collapsed. Others were not enthusiastic, seeing the new arrangements more as a threat than an opportunity, and hence favoured a continuing flat fee, albeit a higher one.

A Higher Education Bill was included in the Queen's Speech in November 2003, and was clearly going to be highly controversial. On the one hand, the proposals were socially progressive because they strengthened mechanisms to promote access, and economically progressive because they reduced the extent of middle-class subsidy. Our article in the *Guardian* (2 December 2003) (pages 283–6 after Chapter 15) was written with Labour backbenchers in mind, stressing that this was a policy of which any progressive politician should be proud. One counter-view was that higher education should be free, or at least that any charges should not be differentiated. This latter view argued that variable fees are morally repugnant *per se* and, separately, that they would impede access. An entirely different counter-view was the worry that the proposals would cost middle-class votes. These arguments are taken up in Chapter 15 and the surrounding newspaper articles. In political terms, the issue is part of the broader debate about how public services should be run. It is this latter aspect that explains much of the passion on both sides of the argument.

The Bill was published in January 2004, with Parliamentary managers predicting defeat. The Prime Minister, Tony Blair, in effect, staked his premiership on the reform. The article in *The Times Education Supplement* (23 January 2004) (pages 287–8 after Chapter 15), was written a few days ahead of a crucial Parliamentary vote to garner support, along with other writing, e.g. Barr and Crawford (2004).

During January the government made it clear that it was happy to compromise in terms of improving Legs 2 and 3 of the policy, but that variable fees under Leg 1 were non-negotiable, a stance that was both brave and – for all the reasons given above – correct. Key changes to the Bill included (1) an increase in the loan to cover living costs, reducing reliance on parents and/or credit card debt, and (2) an increase in the grant to cover living costs. Amidst a flourishing email traffic, these changes were all introduced in ways that supported the underlying strategy rather than diluted it. As a result, the Bill was in significant respects better than the White Paper. On variable fees, the government played political hardball, at one stage saying that if they lost the vote they would withdraw the Bill, rather than pass a bad scheme, leaving it to rebel backbenchers to explain to their constituents why they had voted down a Bill which abolished upfront fees and restored grants to cover a large part of living costs. In the event, the government won the critical Second Reading debate in the House of Commons by five votes, down from a nominal majority of 160.

To conclude, the proposals in the Bill can be summarised as follows:

- Universities can decide what fees to charge for each of their courses, up to a maximum of £3,000 per year.
- However, higher education is largely free for students: income-contingent loans are large enough to cover all fees and the greater part of living costs; and there are grants and other forms of support for students from poorer backgrounds.
- The bulk of the costs of higher education will be financed from general taxation; the rest will come from (mainly better-off) graduates through their income-contingent loan repayments.

Chapters 2–15 contain the core of our writing since 1987. Readers in a hurry can extract the central points of the story from Chapters 5, 10 and 15. Chapter 16 pulls together together the central lessons from economic theory and international experience, and sets out a strategy for financing higher education relevant to all the advanced countries in the wider Europe, North America, the Far East and Australasia, and to many middle-income developing countries.

References

Barnes, John and Barr, Nicholas (1988), *Strategies for Higher Education: The Alternative White Paper*, Aberdeen: Aberdeen University Press for the David Hume Institute and the Suntory-Toyota International Centre for Economics and Related Disciplines, London School of Economics and Political Science.

Barr, Nicholas (1987), *The Economics of the Welfare State*, London: Weidenfeld & Nicolson, and Stanford, Calif.: Stanford University Press.

Barr, Nicholas (1989), *Student Loans: The Next Steps*, Aberdeen: Aberdeen University Press for the David Hume Institute and the Suntory-Toyota International Centre for Economics and Related Disciplines, London School of Economics and Political Science.

Barr, Nicholas (1990), 'MacGregor's Loan Doubts Are Old Hat', *Guardian*, 30 January, p. 23.

Barr, Nicholas (1997a), 'Student Loans: Towards a New Public/Private Mix', *Public Money and Management*, July–September 1997, Vol. 17, No. 3, pp. 31–40.

Barr, Nicholas (1997b), 'Student Loans in New Zealand', in *Third Report: The Dearing Report: Some Funding Issues*, Vol. II, Minutes of Evidence and Appendices, House of Commons Education and Employment Committee, Session 1997–8, HC241-II, London: TSO, pp. 119–21.

Barr, Nicholas (2001a), *The Welfare State as Piggy Bank: Information, Risk, Uncertainty and the Role of the State*, Oxford and New York: Oxford University Press.

Barr, Nicholas (ed.) (2001b), *Economic Theory and the Welfare State, Vol. I: Theory, Vol. II: Income Transfers, and Vol. III: Benefits in Kind*, Edward Elgar Library in Critical Writings in Economics, Cheltenham and Northampton, Mass.: Edward Elgar.

Barr, Nicholas (2003), 'Financing Higher Education in the UK: The 2003 White Paper', House of Commons Education and Skills Committee, *The Future of Higher Education, Fifth Report of Session 2002–03, Volume II, Oral and Written Evidence*, HC 425-II, (TSO, 2003), pp. Ev 292–309. Available at: http://econ.lse.ac.uk/staff/nb.

Barr, Nicholas (2004), *The Economics of the Welfare State* (4th edn), Oxford: Oxford University Press, and Stanford, Calif.: Stanford University Press.

Barr, Nicholas and Crawford, Iain (1997), 'The Dearing Report, the Government's Response and a View Ahead', in *Third Report: The Dearing Report: Some Funding Issues*, Vol. II, Minutes of Evidence and Appendices, House of Commons Education and Employment Committee, Session 1997–8, HC241-II, London: TSO, pp. 88–103.

Barr, Nicholas and Crawford, Iain (2004), 'Why Nobody Need Lose in this System' *Guardian Jobs and Money*, 22 January 2004, pp. 8–9.

Barr, Nicholas and Falkingham, Jane (1993), *Paying for Learning*, Welfare State Programme, Discussion Paper WSP/94, London: London School of Economics.

Barr, Nicholas and Falkingham, Jane (1996), *Repayment Rates for Student Loans: Some Sensitivity Tests*, Welfare State Programme, Discussion Paper WSP/127, London: London School of Economics.

Commonwealth of Australia (1997), *Learning for Life: Review of Higher Education Financing and Policy: A Policy Discussion Paper*, Canberra: AGPS.

Commonwealth of Australia (1998), *Learning for Life: Review of Higher Education Financing and Policy: Final Report*, Canberra: AGPS.

Crawford, Iain and MacLeod, Donald (2002), 'Learn Now, Pay Later . . .', *Education Guardian*, 19 November.

Education and Skills Committee (2002), *Post-16 Student Support*, Sixth Report of Session 2001–2, HC445, London: TSO. Available at http://www.parliament.uk.

Education and Skills Committee (2003), *The Future of Higher Education*, Fifth Report of Session 2002–3, HC425-I, London: TSO. Available at http://www.parliament.uk.

Friedman, Milton (1955), 'The Role of Government in Education', in Solo, A. (ed.), *Economics and the Public Interest*, New Brunswick, NJ: Rutgers University Press, pp. 123–44.

Glennerster, Howard, Merrett, Stephen and Wilson, Gail (1968), 'A Graduate Tax', *Higher Education Review*, Vol. 1, No. 1, pp. 26–38, reprinted in Barr (2001b, Vol. III, pp. 570–82), and in *Higher Education Review*, Vol. 35, No. 2 (Spring), pp. 25–40.

Le Grand, Julian (1989), 'Markets, Welfare and Equality', in Le Grand, Julian and Estrin, Saul (eds), *Market Socialism*, Oxford: Clarendon Press.

New Zealand Ministry of Education (1998), *Tertiary Education in New Zealand: Policy Directions for the 21st Century*, White Paper (Nov.), Wellington: Ministry of Education.

Peacock, Alan and Wiseman, Jack (1962), 'The Economics of Higher Education', *Higher Education: Evidence – Part Two: Documentary Evidence*, Cmnd 2154-XII, pp. 129–38. London: HMSO, 1963.

Prest, Alan (1962), 'The Finance of University Education in Great Britain', *Higher Education: Evidence – Part Two: Documentary Evidence*, Cmnd 2154-XII, pp. 139–59. London: HMSO, 1963.

UK Department of Education and Science (1987), *Higher Education: Meeting the Challenge*, Cmnd 114, London: HMSO.

UK Department of Education and Science (1988), *Top-Up Loans for Students*, Cm 520, London: HMSO.

UK Department for Education and Skills (2003), *The Future of Higher Education*, Cm 5735, London: TSO. Available at: http://www.dfes.gov.uk/highereducation/hestrategy/.

UK National Committee of Inquiry into Higher Education (1997a) (the Dearing Committee), *Higher Education in the Learning Society: Summary Report*, London: HMSO.

UK National Committee of Inquiry into Higher Education (1997b) (the Dearing Committee), *Higher Education in the Learning Society: Report of the National Committee*, London: HMSO.

Part 1

Introducing student loans

Chapter 2

1987 Income-contingent loans: a central theme

Nicholas Barr (1987), *The Economics of the Welfare State*, Weidenfeld & Nicolson and Stanford University Press, pp. 354–7.

Loans versus grants for university education

It has been suggested that the British system of paying grants (i.e. gifts) out of tax revenues to students to finance their university education should be abolished and replaced by loans. One reason (see Farmer and Barrel, 1982) is the failure of the grants system to remove all financial barriers to university attendance, partly because inequalities in school education cause a disproportionately high attrition rate among children from disadvantaged backgrounds, and partly because of the grants system itself. The latter reason sounds paradoxical. The argument is that the reduction in the real value of the student maintenance grant by nearly 20 per cent between 1963 and 1982 eroded the differential between the grant and juvenile earnings (which rose substantially); and that the means-tested parental contribution caused disproportionate problems for working-class students, and probably also for women. Both factors tended to reduce working-class applications (i.e. demand) to universities. Additionally, on the supply side, grants are costly, and university places therefore rationed by controls on public spending. These problems, it is argued, would be ameliorated by a system of loans.

The following discussion does not look at any specific proposals [. . .], but sets out in turn the general way in which loans operate; some examples from other countries; and the issues which divide their supporters and opponents. Under most loan schemes, actual or proposed, university education remains partially subsidised, either through low (or zero) fees and/or by a residual grant to all students or, in some schemes, only to students from disadvantaged backgrounds. The loan can come from the state (as in Sweden), or predominantly from private lenders such as banks or universities themselves (as in the USA), either with or without a state loan guarantee. Repayment can follow two generic models: the 'mortgage repayment' model (i.e. the individual repays what he/she has borrowed, plus interest); or the 'graduate tax' model (Glennerster, Merrett and Wilson, 1968), in which the individual pays a surcharge on income tax (i.e. repayments are related not to the size of the loan but to eventual income).

Thus the price of the loan can be commercial (rarely), or at a subsidised interest rate (usually), or income-related (often). The essence of the loans strategy is that individuals pay for the private benefits of their university education, but are subsidised to the extent of the external benefit conferred on others. This is a valid approach to efficient resource allocation only where *inter alia* consumers have perfect information about the long-run value of education, and where capital markets are perfect. Loans bring about the latter condition; whether the first holds sufficiently is one of the central issues in the loans versus grants debate.

Loans systems of different types work well in a number of countries. Farmer and Barrell (1982) cite two schemes of particular interest: the Swedish system, which is a large state scheme in a country with a socialist tradition (see OECD, 1980 and 1981), and a much smaller private scheme run by Yale University (see Nerlove, 1972 and 1975). The original Swedish system consisted of a grant topped up by a loan. In 1964 it was decided to switch the emphasis towards loans by the simple expedient of freezing the nominal value of the grant and allowing its real value to be eroded gradually by inflation. By 1978 the grant covered just over 10 per cent of the total cost of a university education. It was topped up with a loan from the state, available to all qualified high-school students; an element of positive discrimination was later built in; repayments are income-related. Under the Yale scheme students were grouped into cohorts; each cohort was *jointly* responsible for repaying its loan, and repayments were income-related so that those with below-average earnings after they left university repaid less than they borrowed, and vice versa. The resulting system was self-financing and generally experienced low default rates. One of its most interesting features is that it provides a form of group insurance, so that individuals who are poor or unemployed after leaving university are not burdened by large debts.

The issues which divide supporters and opponents of loan schemes are varied, complex and sometimes contradictory. A number of efficiency issues arise. First, what is the effect of loans on the quantity of university education consumed? It is argued that grants distort the individual decision to acquire a university education by making it too cheap, thereby (in the absence of a budget constraint limiting the number of university places) causing over-consumption. A subsidy may well be justified if university education creates external benefits but, so long as private benefits are positive, this is no argument for a 100 per cent subsidy; and if the screening hypothesis is true there might be no efficiency justification for any subsidy at all. Loan schemes, it is argued, avoid the tendency to overconsumption associated with grants. A logically incompatible view is that loans avoid *undercon-sumption*. Farmer and Barrell (1982) argue that the expense of the grants system has kept the university sector below its optimal size. Loans, they argue, relax the budget constraint, and so enable an expansion of univer-sity education at no additional public cost. Other writers argue that loans, by reducing public expenditure, enable taxes to be reduced with benefi-cial incentive effects. It should be noted, however, that a *public* loan scheme, even if self-financing in the long run, is likely to *increase* public spending in the short term, when the state will be issuing many loans and receiving few repayments.

A second set of issues concerns consumer sovereignty. Some writers argue that the need to repay loans would give students undue encour-agement to take 'vocational' subjects. The US and Swedish experience lends little support to this view. It is also argued that students who finance their own education through loans are likely to be more assertive in demanding the kinds of courses they want, including more flexible oppor-tunities for part-time study than currently exist at British universities.

A third efficiency (and equity) issue concerns the possibility that loans create a disincentive to women to acquire a university education, i.e. that women graduates burdened by repayments bring a 'negative dowry' upon marriage. Since women on average spend fewer years in the labour force than men they might be more reluctant to take out loans. This problem would be solved if repayments were income-related,[1] so long as the income in question was that of the woman herself rather than the joint income of husband and wife.

Loan schemes have two undoubted equity advantages: they solve the inequities arising from capital market imperfections; and they avoid the regressivity of the grants system resulting from differential consumption of university education by social class [. . .]. A third, and controversial, equity issue is whether loans contribute more than grants to equality of oppor-tunity. Farmer and Barrell argue from a socialist perspective that loans, by making it possible for the university system to expand, open up oppor-tunities for students from disadvantaged backgrounds, partly because more places in total would be available, and also because students no longer depend on parental contributions if they are not eligible for a full grant.

---

1 Though this might have efficiency implications.

But it does not follow that working-class take-up of university education would necessarily increase. The need to repay loans, even if repayments are income-related, and even if the loans are available on generous terms to students from poor families, might well increase inequality of university attendance by social class. It requires considerable optimism about one's future to take out a loan which, even if no tuition fees are charged, would amount at least to £7500 for a first degree. It might be advisable to introduce any UK scheme gradually, along Swedish lines, by freezing the nominal value of the current grant and allowing students to top it up with a loan as inflation eroded its real value (for a recent UK proposal see Glennerster and Le Grand, 1984).

Possible improvements within the existing system

The strategy of public production, regulation and finance [. . .], at least for school education, is common to all industrialised countries. The evidence on the efficiency of the British system is scant [. . .], so discussion of reform is concerned mainly with equity. The first issue is that imperfect information arises differentially by social class; partly as a result, the *quality* of school education varies with socio-economic status. Attempts to increase the information available to working-class parents are unlikely to have much impact. A more plausible approach, where disadvantage is concentrated by area, is to strengthen efforts to increase the resources available to primary and secondary schools, i.e. the Educational Priority Area strategy writ large.

The information problem is also one of the causes of the unequal distribution of the *quantity* of education. Again, efforts to improve information are unlikely to have much effect. Probably the most important inducement to children from poor families to stay at school until the age of 18 would be a grant, probably income-related, for those who remain at school after the minimum leaving age.

The regressivity of university finance has two roots: a system of grants financed out of tax revenues; and the fact that few children from a working-class background go to university. Loan schemes tackle the problem by altering the system of finance, which deals with the first root but not necessarily the second. Since low university attendance by working-class children is both inefficient (because it wastes talent) and inequitable, attempts to deal with the second root of the problem are desirable on their own account. This would involve improvements in the equity of the school system, both by equalising the quality of education and by income-related grants for 16- to 18-year-olds. Additionally, universities could make more strenuous efforts to recruit students from disadvantaged backgrounds.[2]

2 The London School of Economics has an experimental scheme whereby, in liaison with
  the Inner London Education Authority, it attempts to identify gifted children from

References

Barr, Nicholas (ed.) *Economic Theory and the Welfare State, Vol. I: Theory, Vol. II: Income Transfers, and Vol. III: Benefits in Kind*, Edward Elgar Library in Critical Writings in Economics, Cheltenham and Northampton, Mass.: Edward Elgar.

Farmer, M. and Barrell, R. (1982), 'Why Student Loans Are Fairer Than Grants', *Public Money*, Vol. 2, No. 1 (June), pp. 19–24.

Glennerster, Howard and Le Grand, Julian (1984), 'Financing Students', *New Society*, 13 December, pp. 421–2.

Glennerster, Howard, Merrett, Stephen and Wilson, Gail (1968), 'A Graduate Tax', *Higher Education Review*, Vol. 1, No. 1, pp. 26–38, reprinted in Barr (2001: Vol. III, pp. 570–82), and in *Higher Education Review*, Vol. 35, No. 2 (Spring), pp. 25–40.

Nerlove, Mark (1972), 'On Tuition and the Costs of Higher Education: Prolegomena to a Conceptual Framework', *Journal of Political Economy*, Vol. 80, No. 3, Part 2 (May/June), pp. 1178–218.

Nerlove, Mark (1975), 'Some Problems in the Use of Income-Contingent Loans for the Finance of Higher Education', *Journal of Political Economy*, Vol. 83, No. 1 (February), pp. 157–83.

OECD (1980), *Goals for Educational Policy in Sweden*, Paris: OECD.

OECD (1981), *Educational Reforms in Sweden*, Paris: OECD.

disadvantaged backgrounds. These children are encouraged to apply to the School, and may be offered a place conditional on lower 'A'-level marks than is the School's general custom. Once at the School they receive extra tuition. Several other universities have similar schemes.

Chapter 3

1988 Setting universities free from central planning: a second central theme

John Barnes and Nicholas Barr (1988), 'Some Specific Policy Proposals', in *Strategies for Higher Education: The Alternative White Paper*, Aberdeen University Press, Ch. 6, pp. 45–9.

The range of policy choices

Table 3.1 attempts to draw together the threads of earlier discussion by setting out schematically the main ingredients of the system and the more important policy choices which can be made within it. The first part shows how universities will be financed (via students, via government and from other sources); the second shows the extent to which institutions of higher education will (or will not) be subject to regulation, in particular with respect to student numbers, conditions of employment and to the level of fees they may charge.

Since universities will be financed mainly by students the main part of the table concerns their sources of income, namely state bursaries, loans, and the private sector. Bursaries can come not only from the DES [Department of Education and Science], but also from other state agencies, such as the police and the armed services. There are three policy decisions relevant to bursaries. First, their average size: should they cover only the average level of fees, or should they also make a contribution to the student's maintenance? Second, the variation in their size: bursaries would certainly have to be higher for science and medicine than for the arts; they could also be higher in the face of shortages in a particular skill; and they could be higher for students from poorer backgrounds. Third, would the bursaries be restricted either by subject (classics, Urdu), or by institution (e.g. usable only at Scottish universities)?

Loans [. . .] can be organised in two ways. Income-related loans will generally be state-run, with repayment via the tax system or via National Insurance Contributions. Alternatively, loans can be organised along mortgage lines by the state, by the private sector or by the two sectors in combination, with or without a subsidised interest rate. In either case repayment could be required in full, or could be remitted in whole or in part if a student subsequently went into a particular job or came from a particular background.

The third major source of student income is the private sector. The most common items under this head are the student's own earnings; the student's past saving or inherited wealth; bank overdrafts and credit cards; support in cash or kind from the student's family, including rent-free accommodation; finance from the student's university (e.g. a scholarship or payment from a hardship fund); finance from industry (e.g. a bursary from British Telecom); and finance from overseas.

Institutions of higher education will still receive some of their income directly from government. The DES may continue to pay a residual recurrent grant, at least for some universities, at least initially; the Department may also make ad hoc grants from time to time, e.g. for capital expenditure; and it might pay universities a per capita 'bounty' for students studying certain subjects or from a particular background. In addition, institutions are likely to receive at least some of their research funding from the Research Councils or a successor body and possibly also from specific research contracts direct from government departments.

Finally, institutions can derive income from a variety of other sources, such as their own entrepreneurial activity, sponsorship from industry and from fund raising, appeals and similar activities.

The last part of the table considers whether universities will be subject only to the constraint of their revenue-raising powers, or whether they will face additional restrictions. Degree structures, for the most part, will be left to institutions themselves to determine but subject to external inspection, not least for reasons of consumer information. Institutions should generally be free to determine student numbers, though possibly with restrictions as to the number of publicly-funded students any one institution might accept. They would also be free to set the terms and conditions of their employees, though government, if it wished, could impose restrictions, e.g. about minimum pension entitlement, or about the universities' freedom (or lack of it) to offer tenured contracts. Finally, and of considerable importance, is the issue of whether institutions are completely free to set their own fee levels, whether fees may vary only within a given range, or whether fee levels will be centrally established for all institutions of higher education.

Table 3.1 Organisation of higher education: the range of policy options

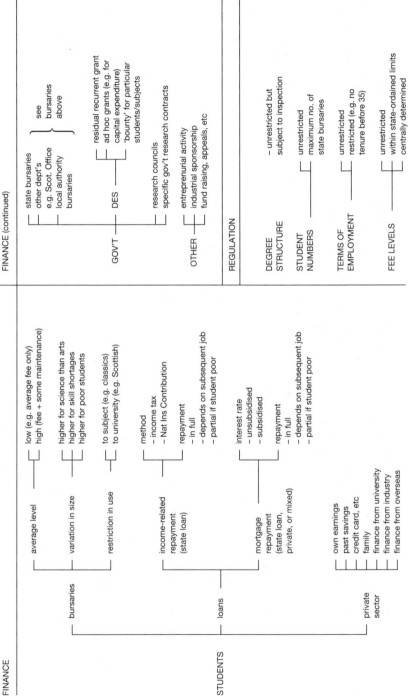

Different models of higher education

The options in the table make clear the diversity possible within the system proposed earlier. Two issues predominate: how competitive should the higher education system be; and to what extent should its finance be redistributive? Intervention can take two forms: it can influence the *allocation* of resources (e.g. by subject or institution) and/or their *distribution* (e.g. towards poorer students). The proposals [...] are thus compatible with movements along two axes, one running from planned allocation to market allocation, and the other from less egalitarian to more egalitarian. This section illustrates the range of possibilities through two schemes, one a largely free market system with maximum competition and little redistribution, the other with fairly substantial intervention both educationally and to enhance equality of opportunity.

A nightwatchman model

Universities in this case are free to set their own fee levels, and the only constraint imposed by government on state bursaries is their total number and their monetary value. If the government did not wish to influence students' choice of subject all bursaries would have the same value; and one possible value is that of the average university tuition fee. The total number of such bursaries would be established by reference to political views about the efficient size of the higher education sector and the need to contain public expenditure.

Students would fund their maintenance from private sources, which would include their own earnings; assistance from family; and private philanthropy, including scholarships offered by institutions of higher education. In the interests of improving capital markets the state would probably wish to institute a commercial loan scheme. The government could offer loans itself out of public funds, or could act as guarantor to private lenders such as banks and building societies. In either case it would be possible to subsidise the interest rate.

A scheme of this sort has no redistributive implications except to the extent that the fee bursaries and any interest subsidies are paid out of progressive taxation. Poorer students would have to do more paid work; or they would have to find assistance from private sources; or they would go to a cheaper institution; or they would not attend higher education at all.

Research would be funded by the universities themselves, partly by building up endowments and partly through research contracts from industry. In addition government might fund specific projects which it wanted undertaken.

An interventionist model

Government in this case has a 'hands on' approach. To influence the allocation of resources, some bursaries could be tied to vulnerable universities for reasons of regional balance, and others to subjects which the government wished to protect or promote. It might for example wish to protect certain arts subjects; or it might wish to encourage the expansion of a particular subject (e.g. engineering), to which end it could issue more and/or higher-valued tied bursaries.

The typical bursary would be large enough to pay tuition fees and to make a significant contribution to maintenance. Students with lower-income parents could receive a larger bursary. The total number and the size of bursaries would be decided on grounds of the efficient size of the higher education sector and also in terms of the needs of poorer students.

Students would be funded substantially by bursaries. The other main source of support would be a loan scheme with income-related repayments. Repayments would in any case be small for those who went into low paid jobs (nurses, primary school teachers), and hence would create little disincentive to going to university. It would, in addition, be open to government to exact smaller repayments from certain people (e.g. those going into certain jobs, or those coming from a particular background).

Such a scheme would be substantially redistributive. In a maximally redistributive scheme students from poor backgrounds would receive a bursary high enough to pay tuition and maintenance in full; and loans could be forgiven for those who subsequently went into (say) nursing.

Arrangements of this sort would increase the demand for higher education by poorer students. If it were wished in addition to operate on the supply side, universities could be paid a 'bounty' by government for any students from poorer backgrounds. A similar mechanism could be used for other groups which the government wished to encourage, e.g. mature students, or students studying a particular subject.

A further variant in this model concerns the ability of institutions to charge differential fees. Arguably, if the best institutions charge higher fees than others, the chances of students from poorer backgrounds will be restricted. To meet this point the government could establish fixed fees, with different levels for arts, science and medicine, leaving universities to compete in terms of quality of service and excellence of staff and teaching.

Alternatively, even in a maximally interventionist model, universities could be allowed to charge different fees (possibly within some range) with assistance for poorer students. Such assistance could take the form of higher bursaries, means tested on parental income; or there could be a higher 'bounty' to expensive universities for any poorer students they recruited; or the government could boost universities' scholarship funds (these methods are not mutually exclusive).

Research would be funded in part by higher education institutions themselves and by industry. Government in addition would fund research via specific research contracts and/or via the Research Councils or a successor body. It would also be possible for a residual recurrent grant to be retained both to fund research and to help reduce tuition fees.

We have two proposals to commend to the government, and to Vice-Chancellors and Principals, our academic colleagues, parents and students. First, we urge acceptance and speedy implementation of the specific National Insurance-based loan scheme set out earlier. Second, we recommend acceptance in principle of the system of financing and organising higher education for which this book has argued. Once the idea is accepted, a second stage is to debate the specific scheme to be implemented. At present we seek agreement only on the general system.

Nicholas Barr, 'Eight Votes for a Voucher System', *Guardian*, 13 September 1988, p. 23.

Eight votes for a voucher system

Nicholas Barr

Professor Wragg's article (Education Agenda, August 9) attacks so-called voucher finance (more accurately described as student bursaries) for higher education. He sets out problems which might arise if such a system were implemented in a short-sighted way. But that is not an argument against a properly organised system of bursaries. Taking Professor Wragg's criticisms in turn:

(1) The declining pool of 18-year-olds in the 1990s would lead to an unseemly scramble for voucher-bearing school leavers:

This would be a problem only if Government were to act stupidly by reducing funding in line with the declining number of 18-year-olds. If instead it continued to fund the same number of students as now, a larger proportion of 18-year-olds and/or a larger number of mature students could go into higher education and there would be no need for a scramble.

(2) Students would choose history in preference to physics:

If this is true, is it necessarily a problem? Industry and accountancy, for instance, seem to value history degrees highly. But if the Government or industry thinks it is a problem, the solution is to give more and/or larger bursaries to physics students, as the Government does currently to encourage teacher training in some subjects.

(3) There would be a huge growth in accounting departments:

This assumes that those who run universities will act stupidly and will expand on the blind assumption that the higher demand for accounting degrees will last for ever. They are much more likely to act intelligently, and make long-run commitments to expansion only when it is clear that there is a long-run increase in the demand for the subject.

(4) Unused engineering labs will stand as empty mausoleums:

As in the previous paragraph, empty buildings will be a problem only if those who run universities act short-sightedly. This is the decision faced by any firm when it considers whether to build a new, specialised factory, a decision which most firms seem to manage fairly well. Is Professor Wragg really claiming that planning by the University Grants Committee has been a total triumph?

(5) A voucher scheme would reduce choice, just as competitive super-markets stock only a small number of popular lines:
The analogy with supermarkets is false. It is true that some goods can be produced economically only on a large scale (which is why people do not have a family steel mill at the bottom of their garden).

Other goods, such as water colour paintings, are inherently small scale. In other cases the technology is flexible: clothes *a la* Christian Dior are small scale, clothes *a la* Marks and Spencer large scale; either makes economic sense and clothing, in consequence, is highly diverse. Higher education is like clothes. It can accommodate large first-year courses in economics, physics and French, and small, specialist courses. Harvard University has a (small) department of Celtic studies.

(6) Students will be disappointed because they will not be able to find a place on the most popular courses:
This is eminently true under the present system. Bursaries, by giving institutions of higher education more flexibility, will reduce (but never wholly remove) disappointed students.

(7) Excess demand will lead to 'topping up payments' which would be 'good news for the well-heeled but not so for the underprivileged':
This assertion assumes that the scheme cannot be redistributive. But a system of bursaries can give substantial assistance to poor students (as a personal view I would never support a scheme that did not do so). It is perfectly possible to give larger bursaries to students from poorer backgrounds. It is also possible to pay a *per capita* 'bounty' to universities for particular kinds of students (e.g., those from a poorer background) and such an offer could be more generous for the best universities. The idea that vouchers cannot be strongly redistributive is, quite simply, wrong.

(8) Finally, schemes based on bursaries protect the independence of universities by making them dependent on many consumers, not primarily on one: This is a point which Professor Wragg largely brushes to one side.

Professor Wragg, in short, is attacking a straw man. His views are based on two assumptions. The first is that those managing universities will act stupidly and short-sightedly. But why should they not act sensibly? For that matter is Professor Wragg really claiming that central planners under the present system have shown great wisdom and foresight?

His second assumption is that the system of bursaries will do nothing to protect either poorer students or less fashionable subjects. It is, of course, possible to have a wholly laissez-faire voucher system, with possible ill-effects of the kind Professor Wragg identifies.

But (and this is the heart of the argument) schemes of this sort do not have to be laissez-faire. It is equally possible to have an interventionist system which protects subjects like classics, which gives larger bursaries to students doing nursing than to students of management, and which is strongly redistributive towards student from poorer backgrounds.

Chapter 4

1989 **A specific loan proposal**

Nicholas Barr (1989), 'National Insurance Based Loans', in *Student Loans: The Next Steps*, Aberdeen University Press, Ch. 5, pp. 52–66.

1 The basic idea

Different types of income-contingent loan schemes

Student loans must have income-related repayments [. . .]. Thus it is vital to choose Option D (UK, 1988, para 3.15). Loans of this type can vary along two dimensions. They can be organised via *income tax* or via *National Insurance Contributions* (NICs). There is a strong presumption that administrative costs are minimised when a small scheme (i.e. student loans) is 'piggy-backed' onto a larger one like income tax or the National Insurance system.

The second dimension is whether the scheme is organised as a loan or as a graduate tax. Under a loan scheme the student repays what he/she has borrowed until the loan (plus interest) has been paid off, at which point repayment ceases. With a graduate tax repayments are for life, or until some predetermined date such as the age of retirement. Graduate taxes thus redistribute from rich graduates to poor; pure loan schemes do not. Each approach is internally consistent; either is possible, and either can be supported; but it is important not to muddle the two.

Though these ingredients can be put together into different packages, the scheme suggested here is very specific: it is a genuine loan scheme with repayments organised via NICs.

Loans to replace parental contributions

The starting point is to phase out parental contributions. The method is best shown by example. The full London grant in 1989/90 is £2650. Students would still be assessed for a parental contribution; however, they would be told that they could now take out a loan equal to the assessed parental contribution, up to a maximum of £1325 (i.e. half the grant). The decision whether or not to take out a loan would be the student's (i.e. there is nothing compulsory about the scheme). The effect would be to abolish at a stroke all assessed parental contributions of less than half the grant. And for the best-off parents it would halve the parental contribution, with the promise of total abolition once the scheme was fully in place.

Alternatively, since students need a boost to their incomes, it would be possible to adopt the above procedure with two changes: some parental contribution would still be required; and students could be allowed to borrow so as to take their total income to (say) £500 above the current full grant, thus raising their total income by about 20 per cent.

Repayment would be via an additonal NIC paid by all individuals who had taken out a loan. For the majority of graduates this would be through the Class I employee contribution. For the self-employed the addition would be applied to the Class IV contribution (but would not be eligible for the Class IV partial tax relief). The calculations in section 2 all relate to the Class I contribution. As a later policy option there could be an additional employer NIC for students graduating after September 1990.

It is worth pointing out immediately the appropriateness of the National Insurance system for collecting repayments, not just because it is administratively cheap, but also because student loans, in that they enable students to redistribute over their lifetime, are very properly part of the Beveridge set-up (a point discussed further in section 8). In addition, no new precedent is created as regards hypothecation: National Insurance Contributions are themselves hypothecated; and hypothecation of some of the resulting revenues already takes place, e.g. the contribution from the National Insurance Fund to the National Health Service. Nor is any administrative precedent raised. Section 6 suggests that graduates pay a slightly higher rate of NIC; the administrative mechanism is exactly the same as for individuals who are contracted out of the state earnings-related pension scheme (SERPS), and therefore pay a lower contribution over certain income ranges.

The source of funds should be the private sector to the maximum extent possible so that Treasury funds can be used to expand higher education. Ways of achieving this are discussed in section 3.

Administration could be public or private. The disbursement of loans could be organised by central government (the DES or the Department of Social Security (DSS)) or by local authorities (as the grant is currently). Alternatively the distribution of loans could be organised in the private sector by banks or by higher education institutions. Section 6 discusses how these arrangements could be administered.

The system set out in this chapter is very flexible. The various options are described in section 7, though many will not be relevant at the time the scheme is implemented, but could be set in place later. [. . .]

2 The arithmetic of the scheme

The arithmetic is very hopeful. Table 4.1 shows the extra NICs necessary to repay £1,000 over 10, 15, 20 and 25 years at different rates of interest, assuming that the average earnings of all graduates over their working life are around the national average. The calculations are simple. A loan of £1,000 can be repaid over 25 years at a 2 per cent rate of interest with annual repayments of £51.22. If average earnings are £12,000, an extra contribution of 0.43 pence in the pound will yield £51.22.

For reasons of efficiency and also to prevent the arbitrary redistributive effects of inflation, the loan should be indexed; and there should be no substantial interest subsidy. The desirability of both features was argued earlier. It is worth reminding ourselves that what is being proposed is a genuine loan and not a graduate tax. The loan scheme, of itself, is distributionally neutral; distributive goals are achieved more effectively by giving disadvantaged students a larger grant so that they do not need a loan, or require only a small one [. . .].

Since a degree is a lifelong investment it should be possible for an individual to spread repayment over a long period. Given the repayment mechanism there is no argument against the standard 20 to 25 years involved in house purchase (another durable investment).

This points towards a loan in which the principal is indexed to changes in the price level, with a 2 or 3 per cent interest rate and repaid over 25 years. If we assume that (a) the base for NICs and (b) earnings both keep pace with inflation we can ignore inflation and use the figures in Table 4.1.

Table 4.1 Additional National Insurance Contribution (pence per £1) per £1000 borrowed[a,b]

Interest rate	10 years	15 years	20 years	25 years
0 per cent	0.83	0.56	0.42	0.33
2 per cent	0.93	0.65	0.51	0.43
3 per cent	0.98	0.70	0.56	0.48
5 per cent	1.08	0.80	0.67	0.59

Notes:
a Per £1000 borrowed; compound, monthly repayments, loan indexed to changes in retail prices.
b The calculations assume that the average earnings of graduates is £12,000 per year (i.e. about the national average).

Alternative methods of calculating repayments

Method 1 makes direct use of Table 4.1. An indexed loan with a 2 per cent interest rate can be repaid over 25 years by an extra NIC of 0.43 pence in the pound per £1,000 borrowed.

This, however, is a very conservative figure. Historically earnings and the base on which NICs are paid have both risen in real terms by 2 per cent a year or more. It follows that a repayment of x per cent of earnings will rise in *real* terms (i.e. over and above the rate of inflation) by 2 per cent a year or more. Method 2 makes use of this fact. If we expect earnings to rise by 2 per cent each year we can use the top line in Table 4.1. In other words, a repayment of 0.33p per pound with real income growth of 2 per cent will yield as much over 25 years as would a repayment of 0.43p (in the second line of Table 4.1) with no growth in real income. An indexed loan of £1,000 can thus be repaid over 25 years by an extra NIC of 0.33 pence.

It is highly plausible for at least three reasons to predict that a graduate's real earnings will rise on average by at least 2 per cent per year: earnings overall will rise because of economic growth; the earnings of individual graduates will rise with promotion; and the earnings of graduates will rise as skilled labour becomes increasingly scarce for demographic reasons.

Some possibilities

Using the growth-based figure (Method 2) of 0.33 pence, half the grant for a three-year degree could be replaced by an extra NIC of 1¼ pence; in the long run, *75 per cent of the London grant could be replaced by an extra NIC of 2 pence in the pound*. If this were shared between the graduate and his/her employer, each would pay an extra penny in the pound. For non-London students the figures would be even lower.

3 Private-sector start-up funds and the role of industry

Start-up funds

Any loan scheme will run a deficit in its early years, when students are borrowing but not yet repaying to any great extent. One of the great advantages of the NI scheme [...], is that it can be introduced at low public-expenditure cost through the use of private-sector funds to start the scheme.

With secure repayments, banks would be more than prepared to lend to students and, as argued earlier, this should be possible under Ryrie rules without a 100 per cent guarantee. The possibility of the banking sector as a source of funds is realistic in this case precisely because banks are not called on to collect repayments.

A second and additional source of private-sector funds is a user charge on those who employ graduates (an increasingly scarce resource in the 1990s), through an additional employer NIC of 1p in the pound for anyone graduating after April 1990. Depending on the precise assumptions about the number of graduates each year and their average earnings, the yield in the first full year could be between £12 and £14 million. In the second year, with a second cohort of students, the yield would at least double, and so on. If the charge were levied in respect of all students graduating after April 1990, the yield of the employer contribution would rapidly become substantial.

The importance of private-sector funds

In terms of economic theory it should not matter from which sector students borrow. Suppose it is efficient to expand higher education, and that students borrow from public funds. If additional public borrowing 'crowds out' private investment, it will only be less-efficient private investment which is crowded out – a result which is itself efficient (see Buiter, 1985).

That theoretical conclusion, however, is valid only in a world where both government and taxpayers are wholly rational and have perfect knowledge about the future. Neither is true. Treasury funding requires that taxation is higher than would otherwise be the case, with possible disincentive effects; and higher public spending may have adverse effects in financial and foreign-exchange markets. If students borrow from private funds, no issue of taxation or incentives arises – we do not, after all, argue that the large and growing mortgage debt discourages work effort.

There are also political issues. To the extent that the loan scheme is privately funded, there is no need for a battle between the DES and the Treasury every time it is proposed to extend the scheme to a new class of student. More fundamentally, there is virtually unanimous support for the principle of academic freedom, and considerable support for the view that excessive reliance on Treasury funding threatens that freedom (Robbins himself warned against the dangers if universities received more than half of their income from government sources). It follows that the use of private-sector loan funds, by diversifying the sources of funding, contributes to the independence of higher education, an outcome which is all the more desirable given the conflict within government described earlier.

Thus there are powerful arguments in both economic and political terms for the use of private-sector funds. The resulting savings in public expenditure are huge. Under the NI scheme public spending is nearly £600 million lower than the White Paper scheme in 2005, and the cumulative public-expenditure savings exceed £18 billion. Why does this matter? It matters, first, because the use of private-sector funds on this scale releases public-sector resources which could be used, at least in part, to expand higher education. This is an area in which a properly-organised partnership between government and the private sector can be fruitful.

Second and separately, the loan scheme could expand easily to meet growing student demand. If banks receive a secure return at close to a market interest rate they will be content for the scheme to grow, just as mortgage lending has been able to grow over the years without any worries about its implications for public spending. The scheme suggested here has the same possibilities for expansion.

Expansion possibilities

If the loan scheme in the long run halves the taxpayer cost of student maintenance this does not mean that we can double the number of students with no increase in public spending; such an argument ignores the cost to the taxpayer of running universities and polytechnics, which would rise if student numbers increased.

The logic of expansion at a constant level of public spending is as follows. If the loan system saves £350 million per year [. . .], that amount can be spent each year on expansion without raising public spending. Expenditure on higher education other than on student maintenance is currently about £2.4 billion; if half of the maintenance grant remains, total public spending on higher education is around £2.8 billion. £350 million is about 12½ per cent of expenditure on universities and poly-technics, so that savings from the loan system could finance an increase in places of that magnitude with no net addition to public spending; if the unit of resource (i.e. real expenditure per student) were allowed to decline (drawing a veil over whether or not that would be a good idea) expansion could be greater.

There could be further expansion if the loan were allowed to exceed half the grant. Suppose that in the long run the loan replaced 75 per cent of the grant, and was repaid by an extra penny in the pound each for graduate and employer. The resulting savings are £525 million per year, enough to finance a 20 per cent increase in student numbers.

The role of industry

We saw earlier that the three main groups who benefit from higher educa-tion are the students themselves, their employers and society at large through the external effects of education. Thus there is a case on efficiency grounds that employers should make a continuing contribution to higher education – a case which is strengthened by demographic prospects.

The possibility of industry contributing some of the start-up funds has been discussed already. A different role (and the two roles could be operated consecutively) is through an additional employer NIC, say of an extra penny in the pound. It might be desirable to impose such a charge irrespective of the graduate's loan status.

The additional contribution is efficient in two ways. First, it forces employers to face the costs of the trained brainpower they hire (given the demographic prospects, an increasingly scarce resource). It might be argued that the employer contribution will be passed on to the consumer in (very slightly) increased prices. That, too, is efficient: it makes consumers face the costs of the scarce resources involved. It is efficient if a poor coffee harvest drives up the price of coffee; and it is efficient if employers, and through them consumers, pay higher prices after a poor brain harvest.

The additional employer contribution also helps to minimise an important market failure. When the government seeks contributions from industry for City Technology Colleges, individual firms are reluctant to contribute because they can see no individual benefit. Each firm has an incentive to be a 'free rider'. The additional employer NIC entirely avoids the free-rider problem: a firm pays what is, in effect, a user charge, and pays it only for those graduates who are contributing to its profits, and whom it wishes to continue to employ.

It will, no doubt, be argued that such a contribution will reduce the competitiveness of British industry. There are at least two responses. First, the imposition is considerably smaller than that imposed on banks by the White Paper. Second, the additional contribution, since it goes back into higher education, is productive. The additional employer contribution, in short, is efficient in both static and dynamic terms. In addition, an extra 1p employer NIC, if levied only up to the upper earnings limit,[1] will cost the employer no more than £170 per year; the sums involved are thus small and unlikely to cause dissension in the ranks.

4 Costs and savings

Costs arise in principle in three ways: through default, through write-offs and through emigration. Defaults and write-offs were discussed earlier. All that need be added is that the scheme proposed here is *not* a graduate tax but a genuine loan scheme (see section 1 for the distinction). The solution to leakages, therefore, is not to try to recoup them from richer graduates, but to finance them (either in full, or sharing the risk with the private sector) out of general tax revenues.

Turning to emigration, the first solution is to note that an extra NIC of 1¼p will not *cause* graduates to migrate,[2] so that it would not be costly to ignore emigration and include it in write-offs. The second solution is to include in the conditions of the loan a clause converting it into a mortgage-type debt upon emigration, enforced through foreign courts if desired (this is the only solution offered by the White Paper scheme). A third and more stringent form of enforcement, unique to the NI scheme, notes that it would be possible to attach the past contributions or future benefits of a defaulting emigrant. If this were done (and it can be argued that it is not necessary) the only people to escape would be emigrating 21 year olds who never returned. Again, the public-expenditure cost is likely to be small.

For all the reasons discussed here and earlier, the long-run, steady-state savings of the scheme are enormous compared with the White Paper scheme. These savings allow expansion in the 1990s when it is needed most, and by the early 2000s could be large enough to offer in addition net savings in public expenditure.

5 Incentive issues

In principle, income-related repayments avoid the 'spikes' discussed earlier. NICs do not wholly avoid the problem, however, because there is a small 'spike' at the lower earnings limit.[3] This is unfortunate but not devastating. Though the problem is unavoidable, it is vastly smaller than the 85 per cent 'spike' in the White Paper scheme.

Apart from the 'spike' at the lower earnings limit, the extra NIC of 1¼p is small enough to avoid labour supply disincentives; all that is happening, after all, is that graduates are giving up part of the 2p income tax cut of the 1988 budget.

If 75 per cent of the maintenance grant were replaced by a loan, the extra contribution would be only 2p for a three-year degree, or 1p each for the graduate and his/her employer. Even if the incidence of the employer contribution were substantially on the graduate there is no evidence of any substantial disincentive; and for graduates above the upper earnings limit, the extra NICs take the form of a lump-sum tax, whose distortionary effect is minimal.

As a separate point, NI-based loans, in contrast with mortgage-type loans, do not distort the choice of degree subject or subsequent job.

Finally, note that the proposals in this chapter do not depend at all on present institutions, and would carry over very easily to any conceivable reform of NICs short of their total abolition.

6 Administration

Administration would be simple because input would be necessary on only two occasions: when the extra NIC is 'switched on' when the student takes out a loan; and, years down the road, when it is 'switched off' when the loan has been repaid.

Cumulation during student days

All students have a National Insurance number or could easily get one.

Administrative model 1

At the end of each academic year the lending institution (see below) would make a return to the Department of Social Security (DSS) of the student's total borrowing during the year. A 'flag' (see below) would be put against the student's NI number. This deals automatically with students who do not complete their degree (to avoid incentive problems, failure to complete a qualification is *not* a reason for forgiving the loan).

Students in this model would pay extra NICs on earnings whilst a student. This is administratively simple but not ideal from a policy viewpoint. It would be desirable, if an administratively easy way could be found, of suspending the extra NIC until after graduation.

Administrative model 2

In this case, the lending institution keeps cumulative records of the student's borrowing and makes the return to DSS only at the end of his/her student days. This automatically postpones payment until after graduation. It would, however, require a mechanism to deal with students who did not graduate.

The lending institution

In principle students could borrow from central government (DES or DSS) or through local government, as currently with the maintenance grant and fees. Or the disbursement of loan funds could be by higher-education institutions, who already distribute scholarship and hardship funds, and who will be in charge of running the Access Funds. The argument of section 3, however, is that the needs of expansion are best served through the use of private-sector funds; thus students borrow from banks, who would be repaid from the yield of the extra NICs.

It is worth clarifying what is possible and what is not. Discussion earlier argued against a loan scheme in which the private sector was responsible both for disbursing the loans and for collecting repayment. But repayments collected by employers through the National Insurance system are the key ingredient which makes private-sector participation genuinely possible.

Administrative action 1: switching on

At the end of each academic year the lending institution would report to DSS the student's NI number and the amount he/she had borrowed during the year. Alternatively (and from the point of view of DSS simpler), there could be one cumulative return at the time the student graduated.

DSS would put a 'flag' against the student's NI number. The simplest method would add a suffix G to the NI number of all students who had borrowed (henceforth for short graduates', taken to include students who did not graduate). There is an exact analogy with those who currently contract out of the state earnings-related pension, and the administrative mechanism would be exactly the same. Any person with the G suffix would pay extra NICs of (say) 1¼p in the pound irrespective of the amount borrowed, and the repayment period would vary.

During repayment

The employer already makes an annual return to DSS for each employee. *The arrangements suggested here require no extra information to be transmitted.* The DSS computer already keeps individual cumulative account of contributions; it would be a simple programming job to extend the computerised record to include the cumulative loan repayment.

The channelling of the repayments from DSS to the banks could be done in a number of ways. Much the simplest is to aggregate the loans of each bank. Under both the White Paper and the NI schemes, banks do not have the option of refusing loans to any student who qualifies. In consequence, there is no need for banks to keep records on individual loan accounts; instead, banks and the DSS could deal in aggregates.

The way in which this works is best shown by example. Suppose that there are only two banks, each of which cumulates its total lending to students. If bank A has lent a total of £200 million and bank B £100 million, bank A would be entitled to two-thirds and bank B to one-third of the revenue from the extra NIC (boosted from general tax revenues to deal with leakages, as discussed earlier). These sums could be paid by the DSS either to banks A and B directly, or the entire proceeds of the additional NICs could be paid to banks through the clearing mechanism.

From the graduate's point of view, repayment is on a strictly individual basis, with repayment ceasing once the loan plus interest has been paid off; but all repayments are put into a single pool, of which each lending institution receives a proportionate share. This procedure has no efficiency costs and offers enormous administrative simplification.

The fact that banks all draw proportionately from a common repayment stream might make it appear that they are not really lending to individuals at all, but to the government. If so, might such an arrangement fall foul of the Ryrie rules? There are two responses. First, as discussed earlier, the Ryrie rules are relevant only to the extent of any Treasury guarantee; if banks receive a guarantee of up to 10 per cent of outstanding loans, then this is the maximum potential public expenditure.[4] Second, it can be argued that banks are not lending to government, but investing in graduates. Discussion of this latter view is taken up in section 7.

It would, of course, be possible to work on an individual basis, under which the NICs of each graduate were credited to his/her individual loan account. To achieve this, the graduate's bank account would be 'tagged' by his/her NI number, which would serve as the link whereby the DSS computer could talk directly to banks' computers. Such an arrangement is entirely possible, but would involve development of the necessary software; it might also require additional investment in computer capacity. Neither cost is trivial. It should be noted, however, that both take the form of a one-off, start-up cost; once the initial investment is made, the system thereafter would be relatively cheap to run.

Administrative action 2: switching off

When the student has repaid the loan the DSS computer will so signify. At that stage the employer will be notified that the G suffix has been deleted.

Several points are worth repeating. There are only two administrative episodes; switching on and switching off. In between, everything works automatically using existing computerised administrative machinery and procedures. There is a sharp contrast with, say, mortgage interest relief pre-MIRAS,[5] where tax codes had to be changed every time the interest rate changed (in 1977/8 I had *five* PAYE codes – see Barr, 1977).

Other than switching on and switching off, student loans would not be organised by government at all: the loan would be issued by the banking system; and repayments would be administered by the employer as part of the existing collection of NICs. The only exception is the self-employed, for whom the detailed arrangements via the Class 4 contribution remain to be worked out. All in all, the proposed arrangements are very substantially a private-sector scheme, the desirability of which was discussed in section 3.

7 Longer-run possibilities

The initial scheme should be simple. The idea, however, is very flexible, and could be extended in the long run in all sorts of ways. Some are listed here to illustrate the point; none is essential to the scheme.

The balance of loan and grant

In the longer term loans could replace more than the parental contribution up to half the grant. The White Paper talks of a long-run balance of 50 per cent grant and 50 per cent loan. Once the loan scheme was in place and bedded down, both technically and in terms of people's perceptions, the loan element could perhaps be increased, with the grant increasingly taking on the function of ensuring a level playing field between different types of student [. . .]. This would be relatively easy with the scheme suggested here, very difficult from every point of view with repayments organised along the lines of Option A [mortgage repayments].

The balance could be shifted much more easily if repayment were shared between graduates and employers. A contribution by employers to higher education is highly desirable on efficiency grounds [. . .]; and the National Insurance mechanism offers an administratively easy way of bringing this about. As we have seen, 75 per cent of the London grant could be replaced by an extra penny each for the graduate and his/her employer, and less for the non-London grant.

Longer degrees and postgraduate qualifications

It would be speculative at this stage to delve too deeply into these matters. But using the growth-based calculation in section 2, an extra NIC of .33p will repay £1,000 over 25 years; thus a loan equal to half the (non-London) grant for a four-year Scottish degree would require an extra NIC of 1.4p. A loan equal to half the London grant over five years (e.g. for medical students) would require an extra 2.1p. Or suppose a student took out a loan for half the grant for a three-year degree, plus a full grant for a postgraduate year; again, the extra NIC would be 2.1p. A loan to cover the full London grant for a three-year degree plus a three-year PhD requires additional NICs of around 5p. For all sorts of reasons it would be necessary to place a ceiling on the total amount of additional NIC to which any student could make him/herself liable. What this shows is that the loan scheme *can* be extended to longer periods of study. Whether it *should* be so extended is a matter of policy. It might, for instance, be decided that doctors should not have to incur a substantially larger loan than other students, in which case they could be given some extra grant-type support, possibly from the Department of Health and Social Services.

Home responsibility protection

Consider the case of a woman who graduates aged 21, marries and has children without going into the labour force. Under the scheme as it stands, interest on her loan continues to clock up. If she joined the workforce aged 35 (which demographics will make very desirable) she might be in a position where she could never repay in full. If this outcome were thought undesirable for reasons of incentives or of equity, existing home responsibility protection could be extended to the interest component of the loan.[6] This would have the effect of 'stopping the clock', and the person concerned would join the labour force at 35 in exactly the same position as if they had joined at 21. For a student borrowing half the non-London grant at a 2 per cent interest rate, the implied subsidy would cost around £65 per person per year. Since it is part of existing home responsibility protection, such payments should come from the National Insurance Fund rather than from general tax revenues.

Forgiving the loan

It would be possible within the scheme partly or wholly to forgive the loan, either for labour market reasons, e.g. to encourage, engineers to stay engineers, or for distributional reasons, e.g. for nurses or primary school teachers. The mechanism could be used to give appropriate incentives: for instance repayments could be suspended (but not forgiven) for the first five years; thereafter 20 per cent (or 10 per cent) of the loan could be forgiven for each further year of service. The entire loan would thus be written off after ten or 15 years.

Accelerated loan repayments

It bears repetition that this is a genuine loan scheme in which no student repays more than he/she has borrowed. It would therefore be both possible and easy for any student to repay early if he/she so wished; and it would be open to government to give an inducement to early repayment were this thought desirable. Equally, employers could pay off a graduate's loan as a 'golden hello', though it is more likely that they would do so only after the graduate had worked for, say, five years (i.e. a golden glad-that-you-stayed).

A new type of financial asset

It was suggested in section 6 that though the NICs of individual graduates could be channelled back to their individual loan accounts, it would be administratively vastly cheaper if each bank aggregated its student lending and received a proportionate share of total graduate repayments. Thus if bank A had made half of all outstanding student loans it would be entitled to half of the yield of the extra NICs.

Bank A thus has a claim on half of the yield of (say) 1¼ per cent of an earnings stream which will rise over time in line with the increase in real graduate earnings. This claim is a financial asset which can be sold. Depending on the precise way in which repayments are calculated, the asset can represent an equity stake in graduates. Harking back to the earlier discussion, financial markets have not in the past been willing to make long-term loans to students because the loan is unsecured. A theoretical way of giving banks security is to legalise slavery; an equity stake in graduate earnings achieves exactly the same result.

The new financial asset is analogous to the secondary market in mortgages. It has several advantages. It deals with banks' reluctance about having too much long-term debt by giving them the option to have as much or as little long-term involvement in student loans as they want. Pension funds, in contrast, want long-term assets, but the government is currently not selling long-term gilts in any quantity. Viewed as national investment, the asset is efficient given the demographic prospects; and from the viewpoint of individual saving, it is safer than buying cocoa futures.

The asset opens up the (not wholly fanciful) prospect of the National Union of Mineworkers' pension fund owning a stake in the long-term prospects of graduates; retired miners would be living off the sweat of young graduate city analysts. From one viewpoint, this achieves the Tory dream of a shareowning democracy; from another it achieves a socialist dream of the young and rich supporting the elderly and less well-off; from another it would alleviate conflict over pay differentials.

8 Advantages of the scheme

Many of the advantages have emerged at least implicitly during earlier discussion, but it is useful to list them systematically (see also the comments by Lords Beloff and Halsbury (*Hansard* (Lords), 9 November 1988, cols 640 and 642).

The strategy for expansion and access

The strategy has two principles. First, start-up funds should come from the private sector, and the saved public expenditure used to expand the system; this contributes to access on the supply side. Second, loans with income-related repayments do not discourage prospective students, thus addressing access on the demand side. Further demand-side policies would be additional assistance for 16–19 year olds, and phasing out the parental contribution. The scheme (unlike mortgage-type arrangements) makes a very substantial contribution to access and expansion.

Efficiency

The expansion of higher education can be supported in *efficiency* terms, given demographic trends, the single European market and the technological developments underlying the move towards a knowledge-based society. A related advantage is that the scheme can readily be extended to new classes of student, thus avoiding a battle between DES and the Treasury every time expansion is proposed.

Additionally, since the extra NIC is small, job choice is not distorted and labour-supply disincentives are minimal; for those above the upper earnings limit the additional contribution is equivalent to a lump-sum tax, and therefore does not distort job choice or labour supply at all.

Since there is little escape from NICs, repayment can be spread over an extended period, but early repayment is possible. The result, given that something close to a market rate of interest is charged, is to minimise distortions to intertemporal choice.

Cost

The scheme saves public expenditure from the very first year and is cheap to administer. Defaults are minimal; emigration leakages can be kept small; and the unpaid loans of the low paid (estimated earlier at about 8 per cent of outstanding loans) are likely to be a declining cost given demographic trends.

Administrative costs will also be small. DSS will have to switch on the additional NIC and, years later, switch it off. In between, administration for the great majority of graduates will be by the employer. The scheme is flexible, and can have additional features added in later years without causing major administrative burdens during the transition.

In terms of defaults, loans written off and administrative costs the scheme is cheaper than the White Paper proposals by amounts which run into hundreds of millions of pounds per year.

Equity

The scheme is not only efficient and cheap. It is also fair, and seen to be so. It is a loan, not a graduate tax, and so no-one repays more than he/she has borrowed. Equally, however, no-one repays more than they can afford: the unemployed make no repayments, nor do parents working in the home; and graduate nurses make only small repayments, at least early in their career. In the longer term there are options for home responsibility protection and forgiveness of loans in less well-paid jobs.

Legislative implications

A small but highly important point is that the scheme might well require no additional legislation save a few extra clauses in the 1990 Finance Bill.

Advantages relative to collection via income tax

The arguments in favour of a loan as opposed to a graduate tax have already been made. In addition, the use of NICs rather than income tax to collect repayments has several advantages.

Since it is earnings which are increased by a degree, it is right that repayment should be based on earnings rather than total (earned plus unearned) income; NICs achieve this automatically.

Second, the upper earnings limit has the major advantage, as mentioned already, that for those above it the extra contribution has all the characteristics of a lump-sum tax.

The upper earnings limit also automatically solves the 'Mick Jagger problem'. If repayment were, say, an extra 2p on a former student's marginal rate of income tax, Mick Jagger (one and a bit years as an LSE undergraduate) could end up single-handedly providing maintenance for the entire UK undergraduate population. Depending on one's viewpoint this is inequitable; it also gives strong incentives to emigration.

NICs are hard to evade; what is more the individual has no incentive to evade since contributions carry entitlement to future benefits.

The use of the National Insurance mechanism also lends itself easily to an employer contribution, a highly desirable policy in efficiency terms, and one which is easy to administer.

Finally, since NICs are levied strictly on an individual basis, the 'negative dowry' problem is solved automatically.

Some of these features could be managed under income tax, but, they would require a lot more administrative input. They happen automatically with the National Insurance mechanism.

Compatibility with the idea of National Insurance

The use of the National Insurance system in this context offers considerable reinforcement to the contributory principle.

Student loans, upon reflection, are very much in keeping with the spirit of the Beveridge system, one of whose main purposes is to enable individuals to be self-sufficient over their lifetime as a whole, by redistributing from themselves at one stage in their life cycle to themselves at another. That is what the National Insurance retirement pension does. Student loans are precisely another such case. The student needs access to his/her future earnings; private capital markets are not able for technical reasons to supply such loans [. . .]; thus an arrangement which uses the National Insurance mechanism is *efficient*. Student loans are just an up-front pension.

Political dimensions

Who are the winners and losers? Most graduates will be worse off by about a penny in the pound. *That is the worst loss that will be sustained by anyone.* When students ask why they should pay for something which they have hitherto had free, there are two answers: first, a good loan system will increase their current income; second, and much more important, their additional NICs enable them to share the wealth by improving access for the next generation of students.

This brings us to the winners. They are, first, students currently in poverty because of unpaid parental contributions. Second, are prospective students who do not go into higher education because they know that their parents will not pay their contribution. Under the scheme proposed here, parental contributions can largely be abolished for many parents, and halved instantly for the richest. The scheme thus offers a genuine prospect of Parents Lib; for many students it will also be Students Lib. The scheme will therefore be popular with students; for largely the same reasons, it will also be popular with parents; and, by offering secure repayments at close to a market interest rate, it will be popular with banks.

Finally, and most important of all, are the biggest winners – those many students who currently are unable to get into higher education because places are so scarce.

Notes

1 Upper earnings limit for National Insurance: once an individual's income has reached the upper earnings limit (£325 per week in 1989/90) no additional National Insurance Contribution is levied.

2 Thus the moral hazard problem associated with mortgage-type loans (i.e. the incentive they give borrowers to default) is avoided.

3 No National Insurance Contributions are levied below the lower earnings limit. . . . As a result of the changes in the March 1989 Budget, once that limit is exceeded, NICs are payable at 2 per cent of total earnings below the lower earnings limit (£43 per week in 1989/90). An increase in earnings from £42.99 to £43.01 therefore makes the individual liable for NICs of 86 pence (i.e. 2 per cent of £43), thus facing him/her with a 'spike'. Earnings in excess of £43 per week pay NICs at 9 pence in the pound. Thus for weekly earnings of £43 per week or more, an individual's NIC is 86 pence plus 9 per cent of earnings above £43.

4 Treasury officials in private have confirmed that there is no case for applying the Ryrie rules to total student borrowing, but at most to that proportion which is guaranteed.

5 Mortgage Interest Relief at Source: under MIRAS I pay my building society £75 for each £100 in interest I owe; the building society receives the remaining £25 directly from the tax authorities. Thus there is no need to change a person's tax code if the mortgage interest rate changes.

6 An individual who works in the home looking after young children or the disabled is automatically entitled to home responsibility protection, whereby he/she is 'credited' with National Insurance contributions. Thus years for which home responsibility protection is received count as full contribution years for entitlement to benefits such as the National Insurance Retirement Pension.

References

Barr, Nicholas (1977), 'PAYE Codes in 1977–8', *British Tax Review*, No. 6, pp. 321–4.
Buiter, W.H. (1985), 'A Guide to Public Sector Debt and Deficits', *Economic Policy*, November.
UK (1988), *Top-Up Loans for Students*, Cm 520, London: HMSO.

Nicholas Barr, 'Student Loans Made Easy', *The Times*, 28 July 1988, p. 12.

Student loans made easy

Nicholas Barr

The White Paper on financing students in higher education has once again been delayed, mainly, it appears, because the Treasury and the DES cannot agree on how student loans can be introduced within existing public expenditure limits. Students, in consequence, will continue to be inadequately funded by the grant system and will have no systematic access to borrowing.

What is needed is a way forward which achieves the Government's educational objectives without higher public spending. The answer lies in a system of loans repaid via national insurance contributions.

The mechanics of the scheme are simple. Students take out loans from the state, which they repay in the form of a graduate addition to the national insurance contribution (NIC). To ensure that this involves no increase in public expenditure, the starting point is to set the level of next year's student grant in the usual way and, initially, to keep in place the system of parental contributions.

In addition, two changes would be announced: that henceforth 10 per cent of the grant, the percentage rising over time, will be repayable via the extra NIC; and that the parental contribution will be phased out as rising repayments make it possible to do so without increasing public spending. The system thus costs the same as current arrangements for about three years, at which point repayment revenues start to come in.

This approach is feasible for quite a modest increase in NICs. Consider a loan scheme designed initially to replace the parental contribution. To achieve this, a typical student would now require a loan of about £2,800 over a three-year degree. A 2.5 per cent additional NIC for someone earning £15,860 a year (the current upper earnings limit for NICs) yields about £400 which, at a 10 per cent interest rate, repays a £2,800 loan in 12 years. Parental contributions can thus be abolished at no public cost via a 2.5 per cent additional NIC for the typical student, and pro rata more or less for those with larger or smaller loans. Once the system is well established, it can be extended to cover a larger proportion of the grant.

The scheme has major advantages over the current system and also over the various loan schemes already considered. The inefficient and greatly disliked parental contribution would be phased out, a popular move with parents and also with students. The phasing out can be achieved without any increase in public spending, and the process could be accelerated as public expenditure constraints permitted, if the Government so wished.

There are other advantages. Since the student benefits from having a degree it is right that he or she should contribute towards its costs. Repayments based on national insurance are related to the student's subsequent income; thus a graduate nurse pays back very little, at least early in her career. This feature should be crucial to the wider political acceptability of any substantial reliance on loans.

The scheme causes no major administrative problems. It will be cheap to implement and bad debts are minimized (defaulting would certainly be considerably, less than with commercial loans). The scheme requires only the insertion of the relevant clauses into the Finance Bill, not separate legislation.

Finally, the use of the national insurance mechanism is highly appropriate. The former student is paying for part of his or her degree, and so repayment properly takes the form of a contribution, which is an important aspect of national insurance. The resulting system is also a form of group insurance: the risk of borrowing to finance a degree is taken on by the generation of graduates as a whole, rather than by individual students, who are protected against unemployment and other contingencies. Since there are technical problems with private insurance for some risks (e.g. unemployment) it is *efficient* for the state to organize student loans this way.

An obvious question is why students should not be financed by commercial loans repaid like a mortgage. There are two arguments against mortgage-type repayments as the primary source of undergraduate finance. First, many students would be unable to obtain a long-term loan from a bank or building society. The solution is for the state to guarantee the loan. But Treasury rules require the *whole* of the guaranteed sum to be added to public expenditure (hence, it appears, the DES problems with the Treasury).

Even were this difficulty to be resolved, the fundamental criticism of commercial loans is that they waste talent, since many students from poorer families would be discouraged from going to university. Borrowing to finance a degree is much more risky than borrowing to buy a house: the prospective student is by no means sure what he is buying; there is a substantial risk (or at least a perceived risk) of failing the degree outright; and many students are far from clear what return the degree might bring. These problems apply with particular strength to children from less privileged backgrounds. Income-related payments thus accord with the Government's objective of encouraging inter-generational mobility.

The scheme is also compatible with the Government's desire to keep taxes low. For those above the upper earnings limit, the extra contribution is equivalent to a lump-sum tax, with the efficiency advantage of not distorting the choice between jobs.

The Government, in conclusion, should recognize the advantage and the political popularity of NIC-based repayments; the opposition parties should drop their resistance to any sort of loan scheme; and the Treasury and DES should take up these proposals as a basis for a mutually acceptable accommodation.

> Nicholas Barr, 'Student Loans: Disentangling the Myths of the White Paper', *Financial Times*, 16 November 1988, p. 29.

Student loans: disentangling the myths of the white paper

Nicholas Barr

It is important to disentangle the myths from the realities of last week's white paper on student loans:

Myth 1: Last week's publication is a white paper. It is not. It is a green paper: in key areas it simply sets out the options without choosing between them. A crucial unmade decision is what the repayment mechanism should be. Another is the role of the private sector. It is also far from clear how the parental contribution will be indexed.

Myth 2: The white paper reduces access because loans deter potential students (the Jack Straw argument). Loans raise not a two-way, but a three-way debate between grants, mortgage-type loans, and loans with income-related repayments. The Jack Straw argument is true of mortgage-type loans (Options A, B and C in the white paper), but not of loans with income-related repayments (Option D). International experts are unanimous that income-related repayments are the only correct approach to undergraduate loans. The choice of Option D is therefore critical.

Myth 3: The white paper increases access (the Kenneth Baker argument). The only way to improve access is to have more places in higher education. In the white paper scheme students borrow ultimately from public funds. Thus the Treasury pays student fees, the maintenance grant and also the loan. There are no public expenditure savings until 2002 (Annex E), and thus no early possibility of the large-scale expansion to which Education Ministers seem genuinely devoted.

The scheme raises the living standards of students inside the system, but does little for outsiders who are unable to get in because the system cannot expand. This is an avoidable problem.

Myth 4: Loans are expensive in public expenditure terms. The initial deficit, though inevitable, need not be financed from public sources. One private source is the banking system. Long-term unsecured student loans, however, are risky (hence the private sector has never offered them on any large scale). A Treasury guarantee is required, which is costly in public expenditure terms, as demonstrated by high default rates in the

US. A Swedish royal commission on their (private sector) loan scheme concluded that it would have been cheaper to give the students the money.

A more promising possibility is a user charge for employing graduates (an increasingly scarce resource in the 1990s), through an additional employer National Insurance Contribution of 1p in the pound for anyone graduating after April 1989. The charge would not at first finance all net outgoings. But the yield in the first full year would be £12m to £14m, in the second year (with a second cohort of students) at least double that, and so on. If the charge were made from April 1989 the net public sector cost of the scheme could be zero by 1994 (and with a 2p charge by 1992). The public savings could be used to expand the system.

Myth 5: Cuts in public spending are necessary because of the ageing population. The proportion of elderly people is rising, presaging high costs of pensions and health care. Thus, it is argued, we should cut public spending elsewhere, including education. Matters are more complex. What is needed is to cut consumption today, thereby freeing resources for investment in technology and in human capital, both of which will increase output in the future. There might be a case for cutting public and private consumption, but none whatever for cutting investment in either sector. The education system should be expanded precisely because of demographic change, to avoid what in the past has been called an 'investment gap.'

Myth 6: A well-constructed loan scheme needs an interest subsidy. The white paper charges no interest but indexes the principal. This implies a real rate of interest of zero. The long-term real interest rate approximates the rate of economic growth: that is about 3 per cent. Implicit in the white paper, therefore, is a long-run interest subsidy of 3 per cent, which is inefficient and wasteful of public expenditure because it is poorly targeted. Well-off undergraduates are given an incentive to borrow up to the maximum and put the money into privatisation flotations.

Myth 7: The white paper is distributionally neutral. Parental contributions will not be frozen unless the formula by which the contribution is calculated is fully indexed to changes in earnings. The biggest beneficiaries will be the best-off parents (who pay the highest contributions) and students with the largest unpaid parental contributions (students with well-off parents). On both counts the measures are carefully targeted on Tory parents whose uprising scuppered Sir Keith Joseph's 1984 attempt to impose parental contributions on tuition fees.

The losers are students with the largest social security receipts, who lose more benefit than they gain from the loan facility. This is not an argument against organising student support so as to avoid the social security system. But the change is parsimonious.

The best features of the white paper are that income-related repayments remain on the agenda and the fact that loans will be indexed.

Its strategic weakness is access. Several solutions are on offer. My preferred one is two-pronged. First, the National Insurance system could be used to collect a small user charge from employers for all new graduates. The crucial virtue of this approach is to reduce the Treasury cost of the loan scheme to zero within three or four years of its introduction. The saved public resources could and should be devoted to enlarging the higher education sector. And, on the demand side, loan repayments must be income-related, so that students from disadvantaged backgrounds are not deterred With that package (which is eminently possible within the framework of the white paper) Kenneth Baker and his higher education minister Robert Jackson really *would* increase access.

Chapter 5

1990 **The government loan scheme: a critique**

Nicholas Barr (1989), 'The White Paper on Student Loans', *Journal of Social Policy*, Vol. 18, No. 3, July, pp. 409–17.

Background issues*

The White Paper, *Top-Up Loans for Students* (UK, 1988) announced that the publicly-funded student maintenance grant would be partly replaced by a loan. Though many aspects will be decided only after further consultation, the outline proposal is the following. Students will borrow up to £420 in the first year. No interest will be charged, but the loan will be indexed to the rate of inflation (that is, if prices double the student will repay twice the nominal amount he/she borrowed). The grant will be frozen, and as prices rise the loan element will rise until students are supported 50 per cent by the grant and parental contribution and 50 per cent by the loan. In consequence, the parental contribution is frozen but not abolished. The key element which has yet to be decided is how repayments should be arranged.

---

* This review draws on earlier work (Barr, 1987 and 1989; Barr and Low, 1988; and Barnes and Barr, 1988). Professor Mervyn King suggested the use of the National Insurance mechanism for student loans, and many people have contributed to the proposals, most particularly John Barnes and Iain Crawford. None of them should be implicated in remaining errors.

The loans controversy can be divided into three questions:

(1) Should there be a loan system at all? (Answer, yes).
(2) If so, what *type* of loan scheme? (Answer, one in which repayments are related to the individual student's subsequent income).
(3) Has the White Paper any merit? (Answer, not as it stands, but with some modification it could do a great deal for access and expansion).

This section outlines the aims of higher education policy, since the White Paper should be judged by the extent to which it contributes to their achievement; it then discusses the British grants system, whereby students are maintained at taxpayer expense to an extent which is unusual by international standards. The second part of the paper criticises the weaknesses of the White Paper and the third part shows how its proposals could beneficially be amended.

The aims of higher education

Three aims predominate: access, expansion and efficiency. Improving access is crucial for two reasons: because of the class bias in participation in British higher education; and because the UK has much the smallest higher education sector of any developed economy (UK, 1988, Chart F).

Expansion (the second aim) is therefore vital. It improves equality of opportunity, because increased access is possible only if there are more places in higher education. It is necessary also for efficiency, given increasing international competitiveness (a process which will intensify after 1992), and also for demographic reasons, since the proportion of elderly people is rising, presaging high costs of pensions and health care. For both reasons, expansion of education at all levels is needed now.

Efficiency relates first to the size of the higher education sector. Though no definitive answer is possible, the previous paragraph suggests that the system should be larger than currently, possibly considerably larger.

A separate question is how the costs of higher education should be shared. Again, no quantitative answer is possible. But higher education has three sets of beneficiaries: the students themselves (higher earnings, greater job satisfaction and more generally); industry, through a more productive labour force; and society as a whole, represented by government, through the external benefits of education. It is therefore both efficient and fair that costs should be shared between the students, their employers and the taxpayer.

A fourth aim is rather different: any proposal for expansion should not involve substantial additional public spending. It can be argued that this has nothing to do with efficiency, but is a politically imposed objective. Whether or not this is the case, a cautious approach to public expenditure is a key attribute of any policy which lays claim to realism.

The grant system

Unfortunately, the grant system is not a good way of achieving these aims. The system pays UK students a grant (paid out of taxation) which historically was sufficient to support a student fully. Students with better-off parents do not receive the full grant, the shortfall being made up by a parental contribution (for an institutional summary, see UK, 1988, Annex A). Though the system worked well in its early days (the 1960s), its increasing problems are well-known and well-documented (Barr and Low, 1988; Cornish and Windle, 1988).

First, the grant has not kept pace with inflation, and therefore frequently fails to keep individual students out of poverty. It is now officially admitted that the full grant is too low to support a typical student (UK, 1988, para. 2.15); and many students do not receive even that parsimonious amount because about half of parents who are supposed to pay a contribution pay less than the assessed amount. As a result, one student in 13 in 1982/3 remained below the poverty line even when income from all sources was included (Barr and Low, 1988, Table 6).

Though many students are poor, their parents, typically, are not. Compared with the population at large, students are twice as likely to come from families in the top 40 per cent of incomes, and over three times as likely to come from families in the top 12.5 per cent. The President of the National Union of Students (Sherlock, 1988) defended the grant system as 'an integrated, targeted student finance system'. That is correct. It is targeted with considerable precision on the middle class. To those who follow the literature on such matters (Goodin and Le Grand, 1987) this comes as no surprise.

The third problem with the grant system is its cost. The UK taxpayer makes the largest contributions per student to maintenance (as distinct from fees) of any country (UK, 1988, Chart 6). The system is thus costly in public spending terms. This fact more than any other has restricted the size of the higher education sector. It is not overstating the case to say that the grant system, far from increasing opportunity, is the single greatest impediment to access and expansion.

It follows that any attempt to solve the student maintenance problem by raising the value of the grant and increasing the number of grants on offer would not only be hideously expensive (around an extra £1.5 billion per year – three times what is currently spent on the grant), but would further worsen the class gradient. To spend such a huge sum on grants would be to pour more money on the insiders, at the expense of the many bright outsiders who are currently unable to find a place, or who are discouraged by the shortage of places from ever applying. It is not wholly fanciful to say that students who defend the grant system are behaving exactly as Marx predicted the ruling elite would behave in defence of its privileges. The loan scheme outlined later is designed specifically with outsiders in mind.

Different types of loan scheme

The way out of these problems is at least partially to switch to loans. The importance of choosing the right loan scheme, however, cannot be over-stated. It is surprising the extent to which most people still see the issue as a two-way debate between grants and loans. In reality, it is a three-way debate between grants, mortgage-type loans (which are organised like a mortgage or conventional bank loan) and loans with repayments related to the graduate's subsequent income, for example in the form of an extra penny or so on his or her rate of income tax or National Insurance Contribution.

Mortgage-type loans (Option A in para. 3.15 in the White Paper) would be disastrous for access. They discourage applicants (reducing access on the demand side), and are costly in public spending terms thus ruling out expansion (and so reducing access on the supply side). For fuller discussion of the deficiencies of loans of this type, see Barr (1989, Chapters 3 and 4).

Loans with income-related repayments (Option D, para. 3.15) are the way forward, a view held almost unanimously by international experts and by all political persuasions (for an excellent article from a socialist perspec-tive, see Farmer and Barrell, 1982). Lord Robbins (1980, p.35), in discussing a proposal for such loans by Alan Prest, wrote that 'it is a matter of regret to me, personally, that I did not at the time [of the Robbins Report] sufficiently appreciate the advantages of the Prest scheme'.

Loans of this sort can vary along two dimensions: repayments can be organised via *income tax* or *National Insurance Contributions*; and they can be organised as a *loan* or a *graduate tax*. Under a loan scheme a student repays what he or she has borrowed until the loan (plus interest) has been paid off, at which point repayments end. With a graduate tax, repayments are made until (say) the age of retirement. A graduate tax thus redistributes from rich graduates to poor; a pure loan scheme does not. Both approaches are internally consistent; either is possible, and either can be supported; but it is important not to muddle the two.

Criticisms of the White Paper

Space precludes discussion of many of the detailed criticisms of the White Paper. This section concentrates on its strategic flaws.

Costs

The running costs of the White Paper scheme are of four types and are huge. First, repayments are to be collected by banks. Under Option A, the mortgage-type repayments would be suspended if a graduate's income fell below 85 per cent of average income. The administration of this threshold would require banks to replicate many of the functions of the Inland Revenue. A Swedish government committee recently concluded that their (private sector) loan scheme cost more to administer than was collected in repayments. Under Option A a similar result is entirely predictable.

Other running costs include defaults (fraudulent non-repayment) and write-offs (graduates who do not earn enough fully to repay their loan). The White Paper allows for a default rate of 10 per cent and *in addition* a write-off rate of 15 per cent. Thus it is assumed that 25 per cent of loans will never be repaid. A further cost is the interest subsidy of 2–3 per cent implicit in the White Paper (discussed further below). As a result of these costs, the White Paper scheme does not save any money, even in the long run.

Access and expansion

Access and expansion are clearly ruled out. Option A would harm access by accentuating the class gradient in higher education. Option D, if properly implemented [. . .] does not discourage applicants. However, access cannot be improved without additional places – and expansion is ruled out in the short run because students borrow Treasury funds, and in the long run by the huge running costs of the scheme. The White Paper, in short, replicates the worst mistakes of the grant system.

Efficiency

A major aspect of efficiency is the incentive effects of the 85 per cent threshold below which repayment is suspended. If a graduate's repayment was, say, £400 per year, a small increase in earnings could take him or her across the threshold, bringing a liability for a large repayment. This 'spike' in the tax structure would be an additional manifestation of the poverty trap. Though the White Paper tries to mitigate the worst effects by talking of 'a tapering scale of repayments' where income is only a bit above the threshold (para. 3.15), the effect of the 'spike' is predictable. There will be an incentive for (particularly) women to work part time, at least until the age of 50 (the age at which the unpaid loan is written off). This is simultaneously socially undesirable and singularly inept in the face of demographic pressures to maximise labour force participation.

A second problem of both efficiency and equity is the White Paper's proposal to index the loan to the rate of inflation, but not to charge any interest. This represents an average interest subsidy of between 2 and 3 per cent. Like all blanket subsidies, it causes inefficiency and wastes public expenditure by spraying subsidies over those who do not need them. The incentive is for the best-off students to borrow the maximum they are allowed and put the proceeds into privatisation flotations. Much better to have no interest subsidy, and to use the saved resources to pay larger grants to poorer students so that they needed no loan, or only a small one.

The running costs of the scheme have already been discussed. The combined costs of default, write-offs, the interest subsidy and administration eat up all the savings. It would be cheaper simply to give the students the money. This is a classic example of Okun's leaky bucket. Because of the huge expense involved, the White Paper fails to address access and expansion: it therefore does nothing to improve equality of opportunity; and given demographic pressures the result is also inefficient.

The political context

The White Paper was eventually published after two-and-a-half years and many postponements, and when it finally came it was fundamentally flawed. Both facts are explained by a major and (at the time of writing) unresolved battle within government. The Department of Education and Science (DES) wants access and expansion; in contrast, it is increasingly clear that the Treasury is not concerned with either aim, but almost exclusively with meeting the nation's need for skilled personnel through central control of higher education and manpower planning. The DES and Treasury aims are wholly incompatible – the one adheres to the Robbins principle, the other abandons it. The Archangel Gabriel could not write a White Paper to achieve both. Hence the delay, and a scheme (the result of Treasury pressure) which does virtually nothing for access and expansion.

What is good about the White Paper?

Not all the news is bad. The White Paper foreshadows three Access Funds, each of £5 million per year for undergraduates in higher education, for postgraduates and for students in further education, respectively. These take the form of discretionary bursaries to assist students in financial difficulties. Their effect is to supplement institutions' existing hardship funds; a welcome feature is that the funds are to be administered by the further and higher education institutions themselves, rather than by central or local government.

The most important good point of the White Paper is that it is sufficiently broad to accommodate a scheme of the sort described below, which really would enhance access and allow expansion. Such a scheme would fit in under Option D (para. 3.15) which allows for loans with income-related repayments. It would also be possible, within the White Paper framework, for students to borrow from private-sector funds to pay for the loans, and to use the Treasury contribution to the loan scheme (£850 million in the years up to 2002 according to Annex E) to enlarge higher education. The best bit of the White Paper, in short, is that it does not rule out a good scheme.

A strategy for access and expansion

The strategy for achieving expansion and improved access rests on two principles.

(1) On the supply side, the funds for student loans should come from the private sector. The savings in public spending which the loan scheme

makes possible should be used to create more places. Thus resources are diverted from student maintenance (especially that of better-off students) into expansion.

(2) On the demand side, access is addressed in three ways: by having loans with income-related repayments (so that applicants are not deterred); by offering additional assistance to students aged 16–19 (thus improving access at the point where many young people from the lower socioeconomic groups drop out); and by phasing out the parental contribution, the failure of which is itself a bar to access.

The following scheme, in which the grant is partly replaced by a loan, conforms with these principles.

Repayment

Students borrow from banks (thus bringing in private-sector resources) and repay through an additional National Insurance Contribution (NIC) paid by all individuals who have taken out a loan. The additional NICs are channelled via the Department of Social Security computer back to the lending institutions. The loan scheme *per se* is distributionally neutral, distributive goals being achieved more effectively by giving disadvantaged students a larger grant so that they do not need a loan, or require only a small one. This type of arrangement received broad endorsement from the Vice Chancellors in their response to the White Paper (CVCP, 1989, para. 11).

The arithmetic of the scheme is very hopeful. On plausible assumptions an indexed loan of £1,000 could be repaid over 25 years at a 2 per cent rate of interest by an extra NIC of 0.33 pence. Thus half the London grant over a three-year degree could be replaced by an extra NIC of 1.25 pence in the pound, so that a student could borrow half the grant and pay NICs at 10.25 pence in the pound rather than the 9 pence which most people pay (and even less for non-London students).

Social policy aspects

First, and most obviously, no one will repay more than they can afford. Individuals who are unemployed make no repayments; and a graduate nurse pays back very little, at least early in his or her career. Mature students make repayments on the same basis as everyone else; it might be, given that they start repaying later, that they never repay in full. In all such cases, the loan fund is reimbursed out of general tax revenues.

Second, since NICs are charged on a strictly individual basis, there is no question of a 'negative dowry' in which one person is responsible for his or her partner's loan.

It would be possible after a period of years to forgive the loan for some groups, for example, nurses or primary school teachers. It would also be possible to extend home responsibility protection to the interest component of loan repayments for any graduate who worked in the home looking after children or a disabled person. This would mean, for instance, that a woman entering the labour force for the first time aged 40 would be in exactly the same position vis-a-vis her loan as she was when she graduated.

A further possibility is to use the employer NIC to repay part of the student's loan, thus providing a ready mechanism for industry to contribute to the costs of higher education.

Administration

The scheme will have low administrative costs because student loans are 'piggy backed' onto NICs. Extra administrative input would be needed on only two occasions: when the additional NIC is 'switched on' at the time the graduate first joins the labour force; and, years later, when it is 'switched off' when the loan has been repaid.

In addition, defaults and write-offs will be low. NICs are hard to evade, so that defaults will be minimal. Write-offs will be small, in part because most graduates will make at least some repayments, and because demographic factors will create pressures for increased labour force participation.

Advantages

The scheme has many major plus points and no substantial losers.

* It allows substantial saving in public expenditure, and therefore makes possible an immediate expansion of higher education.
* The savings in public expenditure are large, up to £300 million per year by 2005, and around £350 million per year in the long run. It is thus possible to have expansion in the 1990s and also Treasury savings in the early 2000s, when the demographic crunch comes.
* The scheme enables parental contributions to be phased out as the loan is phased in, and some of the saved public expenditure can be devoted to improving access at the 16–19 year level.
* The scheme is fair, and will be seen to be so. No one repays more than they have borrowed, and with income-related repayments no one repays more than they can afford.
* The use of the existing National Insurance mechanism makes the scheme cheap to administer. It also offers an easy way for industry to contribute to the costs of higher education.
* The scheme is flexible and readily extensible to new classes of student, including part-time students and those currently eligible only for non-mandatory awards; and it allows policy options such as loan forgiveness and home responsibility protection.
* The scheme accords well with one of the key Beveridge principles. It helps individuals to be self-sufficient by enabling them to redistribute

to themselves at different stages in their life cycle. This is exactly what retirement pensions do – student loans can be thought of as an up-front pension.

• Finally, the scheme can be accommodated within the White Paper framework under Option D. This is the route which the Government should follow.

References

A.J.L. Barnes and N.A. Barr (1988), *Strategies for Higher Education: The Alternative White Paper*. Aberdeen University Press for the David Hume Institute and the Suntory-Toyota International Centre for Economics and Related Disciplines, London School of Economics.

N.A. Barr (1987), *The Economics of the Welfare State*, Weidenfeld & Nicolson, London, and Stanford University Press, Stanford, CA.

N.A. Barr (1989), *Student Loans*: The Next Steps, Aberdeen University Press for the David Hume Institute and the Suntory-Toyota International Centre for Economics and Related Disciplines, London School of Economics.

N.A. Barr and W. Low (1988), *Student Grants and Student Poverty*, London School of Economics, Welfare State Programme, Discussion Paper No. 28.

J.W.P. Cornish and R.E. Windle (1988), *Undergraduate Income and Expenditure Survey*, 1986/7, Research Services Limited, London.

CVCP (1989), *The Response of the Committee of Vice-Chancellors and Principals to the Government's White Paper 'Top-Up Loans for Students'*, CVCP, London.

M. Farmer and R. Barrell (1982), 'Why student loans are fairer than grants', *Public Money*, 2:1, June, pp. 19–24.

R.E. Goodin and J. Le Grand (1987), *Not Only the Poor: The Middle Classes and the Welfare State*, Allen & Unwin, London.

L.C. Robbins (1980), *Higher Education Revisited*, Macmillan, Basingstoke.

M. Sherlock (1988), 'Baker's Loans', *The Guardian*, 15.11.88.

UK (1988), *Top-Up Loans for Students*, Cm 520, HMSO, London.

Nicholas Barr, 'Baker's Proposal: A Better Class of Drain', *Independent*, 22 June 1989, p. 21.

Baker's proposal: a better class of drain

Nicholas Barr

Kenneth Baker, Secretary of State for Education, is right to argue that student support should include loans, but completely wrong in the loan system he is proposing. His scheme will work, but only if vast and unnecessary amounts are spent on administration and defaults.

In Monday's statement to the House of Commons, he claimed agreement with the banks over the administration of student loans 'subject to the satisfactory outcome of the contractual negotiations'. That claim is true only in the sense that I might have agreed to buy your house provided we can agree on the price. Mr Baker has nailed his political reputation to the mast, and the banks are now in a position to drive a hard and expensive bargain.

Loans are to be administered by a new agency jointly owned by the participating banks, under contract to the Government. Though this looks like a market body, it is in reality a private-sector, publicly funded quango. 'The Government will meet the costs of detailed preparatory work,' Mr Baker said, '. . . the range of costs [being] from £8.3m to £11.5m.' In addition, the Government 'will fund the company for the administrative costs of the scheme'.

Mr Baker announced annual operating cost of between £10.4m and £14m, or between £8 and £12 per borrower per year, adding that he was 'glad to say that these are many times smaller than the amounts I have been reading about in the Press over the last few months'.

The £8–12 figure is technically correct but highly misleading for three reasons. First, it takes no account of the overhead costs of establishing the system. Second, it omits important continuing costs, including depreciation on overheads and cost of debt collection – an odd omission in what is, in effect, a debt collection agency.

Third, and most important, Mr Baker's figure is for 1995, only five years after the scheme is due to start. At this stage, most of those involved will still be receiving loans and, for them, administration will be cheap. Only a few students will have left college and started to repay their loans. But the major costs of a loans scheme arise out of collecting repayments.

For the typical student, repayment will take about 15 years, and it could take up to 25. So the numbers who have to be chased for repayments will roughly double every three years until around 2008. By choosing 1995, Mr Baker is taking the one year when administrative costs are most heavily biased towards the cheaper cases – students receiving rather than repaying loans.

Properly taking account of all these factors, using standard accounting conventions, raises costs considerably. Various internal bank estimates suggest a conservative range of £50–£60 per account per year, or up to £900 to administer repayments over a 15-year period. Cumulating over all students, administrative costs once the scheme is mature are likely to be £150m a year.

The estimates of administrative costs presented to Parliament are thus highly misleading. To them must be added the costs of the subsidy arising because no interest is charged (another £150m a year once the scheme is mature) and those of defaults and write-offs (a plausible estimate, based on last November's White Paper on student loans, is £130m a year).

The Government scheme, once it is mature, will therefore cost more than £400m a year to run, considerably more than the £230m savings claimed in the White Paper. If, instead, employers were to collect repayments through the national insurance system, the loan scheme would be some £350m a year cheaper to run. And, since repayment would be secure, students would be able to borrow the banks' money, thus privatising the scheme beyond anything that the Government has dreamt of.

The proposed system is not only hugely and unnecessarily expensive; it is also unfair, with repayment, as Mr Baker put it, 'on the basis of equal amounts, adjusted annually for inflation'. In other words, except where repayment is suspended for low-earning graduates, repayments will be organised like a mortgage or bank overdraft, creating a major deterrent for students from poor backgrounds.

Finally, and in many ways worst, though the banks will administer the scheme, the money they lend is Treasury money. So the Government is paying banks to lend students the Government's money. It then pays the banks up to £60 a year for each student to try to get it back; and, if the banks fail, the Government stands the loss, but still pays the banks for trying.

Mr Baker's statement set out a better class of drain down which to tip large volumes of taxpayers' money. If the Government is not prepared to adopt a better loans scheme, it would be cheaper to give the money away.

Chapter 6

1991 **Pulling the arguments together**

Nicholas Barr (1991), 'Income-contingent Student Loans: An Idea Whose Time Has Come', in G. K. Shaw (ed.), *Economics, Culture and Education: Essays in Honour of Mark Blaug*, Edward Elgar, pp. 155–70.

1 The historical backdrop

1.1 Introductory matters

This paper tells a story with three elements. First is the development of a set of coherent theoretical propositions, emanating in part from the Robbins Report (1963), which underpin the intellectual case for income-contingent student loans. Second is the story of how long it took and how much campaigning until their gradual implementation in the late 1980s. Third, and by way of a grace note (perhaps a disgrace note), is how the British government, in introducing an ill-conceived loan scheme in 1990, missed a golden opportunity to take the Robbins proposals a large step forward.

Section 1 summarizes the history of the student loans debate in Britain. The relevant economic theory is discussed in section 2, and its implications for policy design in section 3. Section 4 looks at loan schemes, actual or proposed, in Sweden, Australia, New Zealand and the USA, and describes recent British developments.

Funding for higher education derives from five broad sources: from government in the form of grants or scholarships:[1] from the student him/herself, largely out of future income; from the student's family; from the private sector, for example, contributions from industry; and from private charitable foundations. Though all these sources are discussed, the main emphasis is on the second, and in particular on income-contingent loans, that is, a loan whose repayment takes the form of x per cent of the individual borrower's subsequent annual income. This type of loan is in sharpest contrast with loans organized like a mortgage or bank overdraft, with repayment in fixed instalments over a fixed period.

Loans can cover the cost of tuition fees, living costs or both. Where tuition is tax-funded (as in much of Western Europe) loans are mainly for maintenance; in the USA they are for either or both. For economic purposes what matters is the total cost of higher education, and the assistance available to students in meeting that cost; little distinction is therefore made between tuition and maintenance costs.

1.2 Debates in the 1960s and 1970s

The British higher-education debate

It can be argued that higher education owes a great deal to Sputnik 1, which motivated additional educational spending on both sides of the Atlantic. In Britain there were also worries about poor economic performance. Both factors lay behind the appointment of the Robbins Committee in February 1961. In welcoming the publication of its Report, Sir Eric Ashby (1963) wrote:

> [it] is long overdue. It is at least a generation since we came to realise that Britain's stability in peace and safety in war depend on experts. We have created a world which cannot be run without graduates.

The Robbins Report should be read alongside the Anderson Report (UK 1960), which consolidated earlier arrangements by introducing a system of a mandatory, tax-funded maintenance grants, means-tested on parental income. The Robbins Committee's (1963: para. 31) conclusions rested on a number of principles of which, for present purposes, the most important was that:

> [t]hroughout our Report we have assumed as an axiom that courses of higher education should be available for all those who are qualified by ability and attainment to pursue them and who wish to do so.

Access to higher education, in other words, was a prime objective. In pursuit of that objective, among others, the Committee recommended *expansion* of higher education, from about one in twelve of 18-year olds to about one in six by 1980.

Among the written evidence to the Committee were the first two UK proposals for income-contingent student loans. Peacock and Wiseman (1962: para. 33) argued for:

> government or government-assisted . . . loans to students . . . at sub-sidised rates of interest and with fairly generous repayment terms. The loans could be paid off in the form of deductions through [income tax].

Prest (1962: 147) advocated publicly-funded loans to students:

> on condition that they enter into a contract to repay a specified propor-tion of their lifetime earnings to the government.

> [T]he obvious [repayment] mechanism is to gear this in with an indi-vidual's income tax payments, a fixed proportion of income being paid each year to amortise the original advance. (148)

The idea was picked up in the Report, which acknowledged several advantages of loans, not least that tax-funded grants tend to be regressive, since higher education is disproportionately used by students from higher-income backgrounds (for the complexities underlying that argument, see Blaug 1982). The major worry about loans was their incentive effects, in particular the deleterious effects on access.

> On balance we do not recommend immediate recourse to a system of financing students by loans. At a time when many parents are only just beginning to acquire the habit of contemplating higher education for . . . their children . . . *we think it probable that it would have undesirable incentive effects*. (Robbins Report 1963: para. 47, my emphasis).

The market-versus-the-state debate

The loans issue arose also in the broader debate about the proper role of government. In a general defence of the market mechanism. Friedman (1962) considered the government's role in vocational and professional training. He accepted the capital market imperfections discussed in section 2.2 in particular the riskiness of student loans (for example, the absence of any security). He (1962: 103) pointed out that:

> [t]he device adopted to meet the corresponding problem for other risky investments is equity investment plus limited liability on the part of shareholders. The counter-part for education would be to 'buy' a share in an individual's earning prospects; to advance him the funds needed to finance his training on condition that he agree to pay the lender a specified fraction of his future earnings.

On that basis he (1962: 105) advocated loans from government, in return for which,

> [t]he individual ... would agree to pay to the government in each future year a specified percentage of his earnings in excess of a speci-fied sum for each $1,000 that he received. ... The payment could easily be combined with payment of income tax and so involve a minimum of additional administrative expense.

These early student-loan proposals derived from the benefit principle (he who benefits should pay). A different approach starts from a predis-position towards free, tax-financed education, abandoning that model only because of its regressiveness when applied to higher education. Glennerster, Merrett and Wilson (1968: 26) point out that:

> in the United Kingdom, higher education is now financed as a social service. Nearly all the costs are borne out of general taxation. ... But it differs radically from other social services. It is reserved for a small and highly selected group. ... It is exceptionally expensive. ... [And] education confers benefits which reveal themselves in the form of higher earnings. A graduate tax would enable the community to recover the value of the resources devoted to higher education from those who have themselves derived such substantial benefit from it.

The conclusion is that the benefit principle and the ability-to-pay approach, despite their very different starting points, lead to identical policy prescriptions.

Subsequent history of the student loans debate in Britain

The idea of income-contingent loans slowly entered the academic litera-ture. Blaug (1966) stressed again the distinction between mortgage-type and income-contingent loans, and made the link with the broader issue of the finance of all post-school education.

The early 1970s saw various proposals. It is rumoured that Margaret Thatcher, whilst Secretary of State for Education, brought a proposal to Cabinet which was summarily rejected by the then Prime Minister, Edward Heath. Outside government, Mark Blaug devised an income-contingent scheme for postgraduate students. It can be argued that this was the obvious way to begin: the numbers involved are smaller; mass access is less of an issue; and there is arguably less disincentive effect and less political oppo-sition. The scheme, nevertheless, sank almost without trace (perhaps again the Prime Ministerial veto). A third proposal, by Maynard (1975) looked at loans in the broader context of the funding of higher education.

The election of a Labour government in 1974 effectively ended any likelihood of loans in the short run. The emphasis of higher education policy was to pursue expansion and improved access through the existing system of tax-funded maintenance grants, though public spending cuts after the 1976 economic crisis ruled out any success.

The major event of the later 1970s on the loans front was Lord Robbin's conversion. In an article in the *Financial Times* (reprinted in Robbins, 1980: 35) he expressed regret that at the time of the Committee he had not sufficiently appreciated the advantages of income-contingent loans.

With the election of a Conservative government in 1979, loans came back on to the political agenda. The academic background was set by writers like Woodhall (1982). Keith Joseph, then Secretary of State for Education, was committed to the policy, supported by politicians such as Rhodes Boyson. Any explanation of why no scheme was implemented can only be speculative. Three possible reasons suggest themselves: the high up-front-taxpayer cost of a loan scheme in its early years (coupled with a government committed to public spending cuts); the administrative difficulties cited by the Inland Revenue whenever the scheme was mooted; and the political dangers of reducing a middle-class perk.

The upshot is that by the early 1980s, though there was no political consensus, agreement outside the ranks of politicians was widespread. According to Blaug (1980: 45):

> virtually every advocate of student loans in Britain (Alan Peacock, Jack Wiseman, Alan Prest, Sir Charles Carter, Gareth Williams, Ernest Rudd, Anthony Flew, Donald Mackay, Michael Crew, Alistair Young, Arthur Seldon, Lord Robbins and Mark Blaug) . . . favours an income-related loans scheme. . . .

As discussed in section 4, similar debates were also a recurrent theme in other countries.

2 Analytics

2.1 The theoretical case for subsidizing higher education

The funding paradox

Higher education faces a painful and unavoidable tension. Large taxpayer-subsidies for tuition fees or maintenance can lead to supply-side constraints because of the desire to contain public spending. Where qualified students have no automatic entitlement to a place in higher education (for example, Britain), the constraint takes the form of a view (typically by the Treasury) about student numbers. The result can be a high quality system, but one which turns away at least some qualified applicants. In countries where students have a right to a place, the impact of cost containment is mainly on quality. With less public funding per student (for example, USA), there are no externally imposed supply-side constraints. However, unless limited taxpayer funding is sufficiently redistributive, students from lower-income backgrounds will be deterred from applying.

Thus high subsidies can harm access on the supply side but their absence can harm it on the demand side. This is the dilemma which a well-designed loan system should alleviate. To address the problem, two issues require discussion: does higher education have any benefits in production terms (the so-called screening issue)?; and if so, does it create benefits over and above those to the individual recipient (the externality issue)?

The screening problem

The investment case for higher education rests on the (usually unstated) assumption that it causes increased productivity. The screening hypothesis argues that education is *associated* with increased productivity, but does not *cause* it (the large literature on this and other aspects of the education literature is surveyed by Blaug (1976, 1985)).

The distribution of earnings depends on factors like sex, race, family circumstances, natural ability and the quantity and quality of education (Blaug 1970: 32–46). The screening hypothesis is a special case which argues, first, that education beyond a basic level does not increase individual productivity and, second, that firms seek high-ability workers but are unable, prior to employing them, to distinguish them from those with low ability. The problem is analytically identical to adverse selection in insurance markets, or more generally to 'lemons' (Akerlof 1970), in the sense that one side of the market has more information than the other. Individuals therefore have an incentive to make themselves distinctive by some sort of signal (Spence 1973; Varian 1984: ch. 8). According to the screening hypothesis, higher education fills exactly this function: it gives a signal to prospective employers, which it is in the *individual's* (though not necessarily in society's) interests to acquire. Just as an individual's good health may be due more to a naturally strong constitution than to medical care, so, according to this view, is productivity the result of natural ability rather than post-primary education.

There are various counter-arguments. Wherever higher education overlaps with professional training (for example, in medicine), there is a direct contribution to productivity. The strong form of the hypothesis also assumes that there is only one type of job. In practice, skills and job characteristics are heterogeneous, so that it is necessary to match workers and jobs, giving education an additional social return as a matching device.

Whether there is *some* validity in the hypothesis is an empirical matter. The verdict is undecided and likely to remain so, since individual productivity is determined in part by unmeasurable influences like natural ability and family background. Attempts to quantify the determinants of productivity which omit the unmeasurable factors are statistically flawed.[2]

A different argument for investment is higher education as a hedge against technological dynamism. Specific skills may become redundant in the face of technological progress, but higher education gives people *general* skills and can therefore be viewed as an investment which saves the resources which would otherwise have to be devoted to retraining labour whose skills had been made redundant by changing technology.

There is a genuine investment argument for higher education – but it must be made with circumspection.

Externality arguments

Higher education has at least one strong external benefit. By raising a student's earnings, it increases his/her future tax payments, in the absence of any subsidy, an individual's investment in a degree would confer a 'dividend' on taxpayers in the future. This is inefficient, in that investment in higher education would be inefficiently small, and is therefore the minimum case for a subsidy. This line of argument can be used as a justification for subsidizing *any* type of investment which raises future income: that is precisely what usually happens through the tax system, at least so far as business investment is concerned.

Does higher education create external benefits over and above this tax dividend? It is part of the conventional wisdom (Le Grand and Robinson 1984: 64–6) that it does. *Cultural benefits* arise out of shared experiences and common values. *Production benefits* arise if education not only makes someone more productive but also contributes to the productivity of others (if colleagues learn the same word-processing package they contribute to each other's productivity as well as to their own).

These effects, however, can go both ways. Higher education encourages questioning attitudes and so, it might be argued, can create negative cultural benefits (Grosvenor Square, Paris and Berkeley in 1968). If higher education unduly raises expectations, the result could be individuals who are discontented with their job, with possible ill-effects on their productivity.

These arguments are intended merely as a caution against blindly *assuming* that higher education creates external benefits. If there are potential costs as well as benefits, the issue must be resolved empirically. Again, however, measurement problems make a definitive answer impossible. The heart of the difficulty is that education might raise not only individual earnings (which can be measured), but also job satisfaction and enjoyment of life generally (which cannot). Estimates of the private rate of return to education are suspect because, of necessity, they omit all non-money returns. Estimates of the social rate of return are doubly suspect: they omit non-money returns and (since no other procedure is possible) they also ignore the screening problem.

The externality justification for subsidizing higher education is strong in presumptive terms, but wholly satisfactory empirical verification is still lacking. Because of the 'tax dividend' point there is an unarguable efficiency case for *some* subsidy, but it is not possible to show how much.

Whatever the size of the external benefit, higher education also confers private benefits on individuals: thus it is efficient that they (or their families) should make a contribution. Two questions arise: what is the efficient and equitable size of that contribution?; and what form should it take? We have seen that no quantitative answer is possible to the first question. On the second, as discussed in section 3.1, it is possible to be rather more definite.

2.2 *Capital market imperfections*

When the Robbins Report (1963: para. 647) argued that student loans would discourage applicants, it implicitly assumed loans organized like a mortgage or bank overdraft, with repayment in equal annual instalments, possibly with some mitigation at low incomes. Such loans create problems on both sides of the market.

Demand-side-problems

Mortgage-type loans are risky from the individual student's viewpoint and so are likely to deter applicants, particularly from disadvantaged backgrounds. This is inefficient because it wastes talent, and inequitable because it reduces intergenerational mobility.

It is sometimes argued (Department of Education and Science 1988: Chart J) that people from lower socioeconomic groups will borrow to buy a house, so why not to buy a degree? Apart from the tax advantages, when someone buys a house (a) he knows what he is buying (since he has lived in a house all his life); (b) the house is unlikely to fall down; and (c) the value of the house is likely to go up. When people borrow for a degree, (a) they are not fully certain what they are buying (particularly if they come from a family with no graduates); (b) there is a high risk (or at least a high perceived risk) of failing the degree outright; and (c) not all degrees carry a high rate of return. More generally, though the *average* private return to a degree is positive (Department of Education and Science 1988: Annex D), there is a considerable variance around it. For all three reasons, borrowing to buy a degree is considerably more risky than borrowing to buy a house, and the risks are likely to be greater for people from poorer backgrounds and for women.

Supply-side problems

Long-term loans are risky also to the lender. There is no collateral (contrast the case of lending for house purchase). If the legalization of slavery is ruled out, the private sector will make long-term unsecured loans only with a government guarantee; and that guarantee will be costly (see the discussion of US default rates in section 4.4). A second form of risk to the lender is asymmetric information, in that students are better-informed than lenders whether they aspire to careers in arbitrage or the arts.

Because the guarantee is expensive, total lending will be strictly policed, creating the sorts of supply-side constraints discussed earlier. There are also high administrative costs, particularly for more risky students. Lending institutions have to keep detailed records of each borrower. The cost of chasing repayments is also substantial, the more so because the loan is unsecured.

3 Implications for policy design

3.1 Forms of student loan

Types of repayment

The fact of the matter is that private financial markets for long-run student loans do not work very well; if they did, such loans would already be on offer, as with loans for house purchase. For precisely the reasons just discussed. Friedman stressed the riskiness to both lender and borrower, and pointed to equity finance as a private-sector device for dealing with such problems.

The analogy with equity finance leads naturally to income-contingent loans. The graduate does not make fixed annual repayments; instead, the lender is entitled to a share of the graduate's subsequent earnings, analogous to dividend payments. The argument thus leads to a system in which the graduate pays the lending institution a fraction of his/her income – that is, income-contingent repayments.

As discussed in section 1.2, the graduate tax approach, though drawing its main inspiration from egalitarian objectives, leads to precisely the same result. The first conclusion, and a very firm one, whether one starts from the benefit principle or from ability to pay, is that loan repayments should be a fraction of the individual graduate's subsequent income.

Subsidies for loans

Almost all loan systems are subsidized, creating a mixture of loan and implicit grant. Though the intuitive appeal is understandable, intuition in this case should be resisted. The resulting system is inequitable because the subsidy is generally regressive and usually large (for estimates in a US context, see Johnstone 1986: ch. 6). In equity terms it makes more sense to charge a market or near-market interest rate, and channel the saved resources into redistributive grants or scholarships.

Interest subsidies are also inefficient, first, if the interest rate bears on a student's choice between supporting him/herself by current earnings or out of future earnings. Second, the interest subsidy gives an incentive to borrow an inefficiently large amount, if only to benefit from the difference between the subsidized and the market interest rate. There is one counter-argument. If some students (particularly from poorer backgrounds) over-estimate the degree of risk, there might be an efficiency case for subsidy (see Williams and Gordon 1981). Again, however, such students might more effectively be encouraged into higher education by giving them a larger grant.

Even without the incentive to excessive borrowing, subsidized loans are expensive, creating supply-side constraints: either the amount each student can borrow is rationed; or the number of student places is restricted.

The role of private funds

Under appropriate conditions (market or near-market interest rates, secure repayment and/or government guarantee), the private sector would be prepared to lend the money students borrow, and to expand the system to meet demand, as with house purchase. What, if any, are the arguments in favour of loans from private-sector funds?

In theoretical terms it should not matter from which sector students borrow. Suppose it is efficient to expand higher education and that students borrow from public funds. If additional public borrowing crowds out private investment, it will only be less efficient private investment which is crowded out – a result which is itself efficient.

That theoretical conclusion, however, is valid only under stringent assumptions: in particular, government and taxpayers must be rational and well-informed about the future. Neither is true. Public funding requires that taxation is higher than would otherwise be the case, with possible disincentive effects; and higher public spending may affect financial and foreign-exchange markets. If students borrow from private funds no issue of taxation or incentives arises – we do not, after all, argue that the large and growing mortgage debt discourages work effort.

There are also political issues. There is virtually unanimous support for the principle of academic freedom, and considerable support for the view that excessive reliance on public funding threatens that freedom (Robbins himself warned against the dangers if universities received more than half of their income from government sources). It follows that diversifying the sources of funding contributes to the independence of higher education.

3.2 Other aspects of student support

Student loans are only one aspect of funding. This section briefly discusses other sources.

The role of tax-funded grants and scholarships

Though most countries have maintenance grants of some sort, it is questionable whether heavy reliance on grants is the most efficient or equitable form of support. The much-vaunted UK system shows the potential pitfalls. Public spending constraints led to erosion of the basic grant, a problem exacerbated by the failure (discussed below) of many parents to contribute to student support. In consequence, some 8 per cent of students in 1982–3 were below the official poverty line (Barr and Low 1988: Table 6). But though many students are poor, their parents are usually well-off. UK students disproportionately come from better-off families (ibid: 51–9). Grants are also expensive in public-expenditure terms and so exert downward pressure on the size of the system.

The role of compulsory family support

Student support in most countries relies heavily on parents. When education was a concern mainly of the social élite, this approach was both natural and appropriate. The reliance on *compulsory* parental support is open to question today, when higher education is both a mass phenomenon and an economic necessity.

The arguments in favour of parental contributions are, first, that they save public spending thus allowing a larger higher education sector. Second, since parental support is generally means tested (see Johnstone 1986: 145–53) it can be argued that they are equitable. Third, students cannot easily borrow from the private sector; but parents can borrow, and so parental contributions can be thought of as an indirect form of private-sector loan. Parental contributions, on this view, are an inter-generational attempt to correct a technical failure in capital markets. A counter-argument is that a well-constructed loan scheme is a more efficient and equitable way of correcting the market failure.

There are other counter-arguments. Parental contributions may constrain the system because attempts to enlarge it by increasing parental contributions can lead to a revolt amongst middle-class parents (as happened in Britain in 1985). Parental support can also be patchy: this is the case in the UK (Barr and Low 1988), though anecdotal evidence suggests that it works better in other countries.

This is not an attack on the idea of parents helping their children, merely on the idea of building a system of student support on the *assumption* that parents will contribute. With a well-constructed (for example, not heavily subsidized) loan system, students and their parents can make their own choices; parents who wish to help their children can do so; and children whose parents refuse have other options.

The role of employers

Since employers benefit from the education of their employees, it is efficient for at least two reasons that they contribute to its costs. It forces them to face the costs of trained manpower (given the declining number of younger workers, an increasingly scarce resource). It might be argued that the employer contribution, whatever form it takes, will be passed on to consumers. That, too, is efficient: it makes them face the costs of the scarce resources involved. It is efficient if a poor coffee harvest drives up the price of coffee; and it is efficient if employers, and through them consumers, pay higher prices after a poor brain harvest.

An employer contribution also helps to minimize an important market failure. Employers resist making donations on any substantial scale to education and training because the resulting graduates might subsequently work for another firm. Each firm thus faces an incentive to leave educational donations to other firms, that is, a free-rider problem. One solution is a user charge, possibly in the form of an additional payroll tax for each graduate employed. An employer thus pays only for graduates who are currently contributing to his profits and whom he finds it worthwhile to continue to employ. Given the free-rider problem it is no surprise that industry nowhere contributes on more than a trivial scale.

3.3 Principles

This section draws together the implications of the theory for policy design in the form of a set of propositions.

(a) Higher education creates a 'dividend' for future taxpayers, and possibly also other external benefits (though the latter cannot be quantified), thus giving an efficiency case for taxpayer support. But there are also major private benefits, so the individual student should meet part of the costs of higher education.
(b) There is a case for shifting the emphasis of support from the family to the individual student. It is both inefficient and inequitable that students should be compelled to depend on their families; students should have the option of borrowing against their future earnings.
(c) Since taking a degree is risky, student support mechanisms, for both efficiency and equity reasons, should offer protection against risk both to the individual borrower and to the lender.

Proposition (a) implies a shift, in at least some countries, away from grants; proposition (b) suggests at least a partial shift away from compulsory reliance on parental contributions. The two together point towards loans, but proposition (c) implies that loans should not leave the individual student carrying all the risk. Hence:

(d) Loan repayments should be related to the subsequent income of the individual student and, where necessary, should be government guaranteed.

(e) There are strong arguments for the retention of some grants. Their main function, however, should not be *general* student support, but to bring about a level playing-field between different groups of students. There should be a larger grant for students from disadvantaged backgrounds (possibly starting at the minimum school-leaving age). Such a policy can be justified on equity grounds; there is also an efficiency argument for doing so if students from poorer backgrounds overestimate the degree of risk of doing a degree.

(f) In the absence of strong *efficiency* reasons, loans should not be heavily subsidized: the same is true for equity reasons. Loans are a device for giving students access to their future earnings. Distributional goals should generally be pursued explicitly through grants.

(g) Since employers are one of the main beneficiaries, it is efficient that industry contributes to the cost of higher education. Such a contribution should take the form of a payroll tax, rather than reliance on voluntary donations, which face free-rider problems.

What is needed, in conclusion, is a balance between grants, loans and parental support, a balance which will change over time and across countries. This is not a very dramatic conclusion: but non-economists seem to have a strong (and usually inappropriate) attraction to corner solutions.

4 Policies in different countries

4.1 Sweden

Sweden was early in the loans game (1965), was prepared to learn from experience and ended up with a system which conforms more than most with the seven propositions just outlined (for a survey, see Morris 1989). The 1965 measures were intended to expand higher education in the face of public-expenditure constraints, and to equalize participation rates across socioeconomic groups. The package provided support at 140 per cent of the official subsistence level, comprising a grant (25 per cent of the total) and a tax-funded loan. The grant was fixed in nominal terms, so that the loan became more important over time. Means testing against parental income was abolished.

After a two-year grace period, an individual's first repayment was his total debt divided by the repayment period (normally the number of years to his 51st birthday). Thereafter the nominal annual repayment was increased each year by the rate of inflation. The system was thus a publicly funded mortgage loan with a zero real interest rate. In 1975 the interest rate was changed from the rate of inflation to a (generally higher) nominal rate of 4.2 per cent.

By the early 1980s (a) inflation had eroded the fixed grant so that the loan element had increased to 94 per cent of student support; indebtedness for a three-year degree could reach £12,000. In addition, (b) there was increasing complaint that student support was inadequate. There was also (c) a reversal of the earlier improvement in the social composition of students. Because of worries that (c) was causally related to (a) and (b), a review of student support was established, leading to reform in 1989.

The main characteristics of the 1989 reforms were:

(a) Total student support was increased by about one-fifth, from 140 per cent of subsistence to 170 per cent.

(b) The grant element was increased from under 6 per cent to about 30 per cent of the total and was indexed, thus restoring a stable relativity between grant and loan.

(c) Repayment terms were tightened somewhat: the grace period was reduced, and the interest rate set at half the market rate (generally higher than the previous rate of 4.2 per cent).

(d) Loans are no longer funded from taxation, but out of borrowing by the National Debt Office; only the interest subsidy and written off loans are a budgetary charge.

(e) Repayments are 4 per cent of gross income two years earlier.

The reforms explicitly or implicitly acknowledge a number of lessons:

(a) *Interest subsidies*   The extent to which loans are subsidized has been steadily decreased by reducing the grace period and by gradual increases in the interest rate.

(b) *The balance between grant and loan*   There was general agreement that the balance had tipped too far towards loans, acknowledging the need for multiple sources of support.

(c) *Parental contributions*   Means-testing against parental income was abolished in 1965, and against a spouse's income in 1982.

(d) *Private funding*   Loans continue to be publicly funded, but the 1989 transfer of loans to the government loan account is at least a step in the right direction.

(e) *Income-contingent repayments*   Large loans with mortgage-type repayments were associated with lower participation by the lower socio-economic groups. The 1989 reforms therefore introduced explicit income-related repayments.

In 1965 Sweden had a publicly funded mortgage-type loan with heavy interest subsidies. Twenty five years later it had a much less heavily subsidized income-contingent loan scheme which allowed the possibility of partial private funding.

4.2 *Australia*

The Australian government appointed a Committee on Higher Education Funding in 1987, with terms of reference which made explicit mention of expansion and improved access. The Committee's Report (Australia 1988) (the Wran Report) was published in May 1988 and, as amended, took effect in January 1989 (for an analysis, see Chapman 1988; Chapman and Chia 1989).

The core of the reform package was a Higher Education Contribution Scheme, whereby students became liable to a contribution which is intended to be about one-fifth of the average tuition fee (that is, the contribution does not vary across subjects). Students have the option of paying the contribution on enrolment (at a 15 per cent discount). Otherwise the contribution is paid out of a loan at a zero real interest rate. Repayment is suspended for individuals with annual earnings below the national average. Thereafter, repayment is 1 per cent of taxable income, rising to 2 per cent and, at the highest incomes, to 3 per cent, collected through the tax system.[3]

Though often represented as a tax, the scheme is properly thought of as a loan for two reasons: it is voluntary in the sense that the fee charge can be paid upon enrolment; and the additional contribution is 'switched off' once the charge has been paid. Several points are noteworthy. The revenue from the scheme will finance expansion of higher education. Repayments are based on individual ability to pay, explicitly to avoid compromising access. Though the contribution is argued to be more equitable than the previous tax-funded system, the change should not be overstated: the effect of the interest subsidy is to reduce the contribution from 20 per cent of average tuition costs to closer to 10 per cent (see Hope and Miller 1988).

The Australian scheme, in short, is a tax-funded income-contingent loan scheme with subsidized interest rates, designed with the explicit aims of expansion and improved access.

4.3 *New Zealand*

The Report of the Working Group on Postcompulsory Education and Training (1988) (the Hawke Report) echoed earlier concern of the Report of the Universities Review Committee (1987) over New Zealand's low enrolment in higher education, and its underfunding. The Hawke Report considered, *inter alia*, how to pursue expansion and improved access without increased public spending. One of its main conclusions (para 3.10) was that

> [t]he most attractive way of obtaining private funding . . . is that recommended by the recent Wran Committee in Australia.

> The Working Group, with the exception of Treasury, favours [the scheme] being seen as a means of acquiring additional resources for [higher education].
>
> The particular merits of the Wran proposals are that it provides for funding for students independently from their family . . . while ensuring that repayments are required only when they have income levels which enable them to be sustained.

The Hawke Report went beyond the Wran Report in one important respect: it rejected interest subsidies. It proposed a real interest rate of about 3 per cent except for individuals caring for children, who would pay a zero real interest rate (that is, in the latter case real debt would not increase during time out of the labour force). The Report estimated that a user charge of 20 per cent of average tuition costs at a 3 per cent real interest rate could be repaid by a contribution of about 3 per cent of taxable income.

The Hawke proposal was thus a tax-funded income-contingent scheme without substantial interest subsidy, intended to encourage expansion without harming access. Though endorsed, with modifications, by government (New Zealand 1989: section 3.5), the scheme was not implemented. The New Zealand government failed to follow Australia's example by imposing the collection of repayments on the tax authorities. When the tax authorities demurred, the government turned to the banking sector. The banks, however, were reluctant to become involved, not least because the government was not prepared to give an unconditional guarantee to bank loans, whilst still requiring the banks to lend to all qualified applicants. In September 1989 they pulled out and the scheme was shelved. Three months later, as discussed shortly, exactly the same thing happened in Britain.

4.4 USA

The problems of student loans in the USA are well-known. Five stand out (see Reischauer 1989: 34–42).

(a) *Complexity* It is unduly kind to talk about a loan 'system': '[t]he complex range of grants and loans from federal, state and campus sources is a major administrative problem for most institutions. Students seldom understand all that is available' (Department of Education and Science 1989: para 123).
(b) *Mortgage-type repayments* apply almost without exception.
(c) *Interest subsidies* are pervasive.
(d) *High default rates* The largest scheme (Stafford Student Loans (formerly Guaranteed Student Loans)) gives a federal guarantee to loans to students by banks. The banks therefore have little incentive to chase

defaulters. The result, in combination with the absence of any mechanism for suspending repayments when income is low, is high default rates (USA 1988: 1–118).

(e) *Cost* The combined effect of interest subsidies and defaults is that the system is very costly and of only questionable benefit in encouraging participation from the lower-income groups (Bosworth, Carron and Rhyne 1987: ch. 6).

During his presidential campaign, Michael Dukakis proposed a new scheme (*New York Times*, 8 September 1988, A1 and B11, and Editorial, 11 September). Students would borrow from banks; the federal government would guarantee the loan. Repayment would be a percentage of the individual student's subsequent income, collected alongside the social security contribution. It was claimed that this 'Pay As You Went' scheme would save public money, be equitable, administratively simple and have few defaults. The scheme went down with the Dukakis campaign.

Reischauer (1989), in what he describes 'as a first cut at a new approach', offers a much more fully articulated social insurance approach to student-loan policy. Students would borrow from a federal trust fund, it being left open whether the funds would be federal or private. Repayment, in the form of an addition to withholdings under the Federal Insurance Contributions Act (FICA), would be a percentage of the individual's income, varying with the amount borrowed. The loan would bear a positive real interest rate. Reischauer argues that real repayments are largely unaffected by fluctuations in nominal interest rates, since such fluctuations generally reflect the rate of inflation which in turn is captured by the buoyancy of wages; thus higher inflation causes higher interest rates, but also, through higher wages, leads to higher repayments. In the basic model it is assumed that repayment will be over an entire working life. Reischauer calculates that under those circumstances a 1 per cent additional contribution would repay a loan of $4,000.

The scheme is an income-contingent loan scheme with no substantial interest subsidy, and with the possibility of private-sector funding. Its main difference from the schemes discussed earlier is that the additional contribution is not 'switched off' once the loan has been repaid, thus introducing redistribution within cohorts of students. The use of the social security mechanism is a major administrative simplification, not least because of its well-defined and already-measured tax base (an option not available in Australia and New Zealand, which have no explicit social security contributions).

4.5 Britain

This section picks up the British story from section 1. It is more personal than the others since, with help and encouragement from Mark Blaug,

Alan Peacock and others, I spent much of 1989 opposing an ill-designed government loan proposal and advocating an alternative.

The government loan scheme

This (Department of Education and Science 1988) was published (on the day after the US presidential election, ensuring muted coverage) with the stated objective of reducing the taxpayer cost per student. Under the proposals, students take out a loan to supplement the maintenance grant; the grant is frozen until student support comprises 50 per cent grant and parental contribution, and 50 per cent loan. The loan bears a zero real interest rate, and is repaid in (usually) ten instalments (that is, mortgage-type repayments), suspended for those earning below 85 per cent of the national average. Students borrow Treasury money, but in the original proposal both the issuing of the loan and the collection of repayments were to be administered by the banks.

The scheme has strategic flaws. First, mortgage-type loans are likely to harm access. Given the discussion in section 2.2 there is no need to labour the point. Secondly, the original proposal was that students borrow Treasury money, with repayment collected by the banks. Both legs were misspecified. If students borrow Treasury money, there is no public expenditure saving in the short- or medium-term: and the administrative costs of a completely new repayment system run by the banks are very high, eroding most of the long-term savings. The Government admitted (*Hansard*, WA, 24 July 1989, col. 441) that the scheme produces no cumulative net saving for at least 25 years; even that figure is a gross underestimate, in that it omits any interest charge on the cumulative deficit over those years. Thus the scheme yields no savings for a long time, and hence frees no resources for expansion; at the same time it risks harming access. Even in its own terms the White Paper fails to achieve any desirable objective.

Nor was it liked by the banks, both because they were not prepared to assume the administrative costs associated with a completely new repayment mechanism and because they were concerned about relations with their prospective best customers. For both reasons the banks contemplated participation only if repayments were collected by an arms-length institution, the Student Loans Company, owned jointly by the banks, whose costs would be met by government. The result was one of those peculiar animals designed by a committee – a private-sector publicly funded QANGO (see Barr 1989b).

In December 1989, however, after a year of discussion with government, the banks pulled out. The Government decided to press ahead by running the Student Loans Company itself, thus duplicating what the tax/social security authorities do already. As a companion-in-arms put it, the Government behaved just like its predecessors: faced with an ill-conceived loss-making enterprise, it nationalized it. The scheme took effect in October 1990.

The national insurance loan scheme

An alternative proposal (Barnes and Barr 1988; Barr 1989a) was designed with the explicit objectives of expansion and improved access. Its key characteristics are:

(a) The loan would bear a real interest rate of 3 per cent.
(b) Repayment would take the form of an addition to the individual's National Insurance Contribution (NIC); an indexed loan equal to half the maintenance grant could be repaid by a graduate with average earnings over 25 years by a 1 per cent addition to the NIC.
(c) The additional repayment would be 'switched off' once the individual had repaid the loan plus interest. Thus no one would repay more than he/she had borrowed.
(d) Because repayments (i) bear a realistic real interest rate, and (ii) are secure, it is possible for the money that students borrow (subject to a partial Treasury guarantee) to come from the private sector.

The scheme has various advantages:

(a) *Expansion and access* are enhanced. Income-contingent repayments do not discourage applicants; and low earners, women working in the home and unemployed individuals are automatically protected.
(b) *Administration* is simple and cheap because it 'piggy-backs' on to an existing system and uses a well-established tax base.
(c) *Security of repayment* Defaults are minimal: NICs are hard to evade; and, because they give title to future benefits, there is little incentive to evade. Security also facilitates repayment over an extended period, thus allowing a low repayment rate. Since the asset is long-lived, this arrangement is efficient. Secure repayment also facilitates private-sector funding.
(d) *Private-sector funds* The possibility of funding loans largely from the private sector opens up the possibility of *immediate* public-expenditure savings, thus freeing resources for expansion and proactive measures to improve access.

The scheme, in short, conforms with the criteria set out in section 3.3 (in many ways a tautologous observation, since it was designed to do so).

An obvious question is why the scheme was not adopted (an early version was in ministers' hands several months before the White Paper was published). A possible answer (though one which it has not proved possible to verify) is that the idea of using National Insurance has a public-sector ring to it which is ideologically unacceptable. As in New Zealand, the scheme lives to fight another day.

—— (1989). *Shifting the Balance of Public Funding of Higher Education to Fees: A Consultation Paper*, London: Department of Education and Science.

Friedman, Milton (1962). *Capitalism and Freedom*, Chicago. Ill.: University of Chicago Press.

Glennerster, Howard, Merrett, Stephen and Wilson, Gail (1968). 'A Graduate Tax', *Higher Education Review*, 1, (1).

Hope, Julie and Miller, Paul (1988). 'Financing Tertiary Education: an Examination of the Issues', *Australian Economic Review*, 4: 37–57.

Johnstone, Bruce (1986). *Sharing the Costs of Higher Education: Student Financial Assistance in the United Kingdom, the Federal Republic of Germany, France, Sweden and the United States*, New York: College Entrance Examination Board.

Le Grand, Julian and Robinson, Ray (1984). *The Economics of Social Problems*, 2nd edn, London: Macmillan.

Maynard, Alan (1975). *Experiment with Choice in Education*, London: Institute for Economic Affairs.

Morris, Martin (1989). 'Student Aid in Sweden: Recent Experience and Reforms' in *Financial Support for Students: Grants, Loans or Graduate Tax?*, ed. Maureen Woodhall, London: Kogan Page.

New Zealand (1989). *Learning for Life: 2. Education and Training beyond the Age of Fifteen*, Wellington: Department of Education.

Peacock, A. T. and Wiseman, J. (1962). 'The Economics of Higher Education', in *Higher Education: Evidence – Part Two: Documentary Evidence*, Cmnd 2154–xii, London: Her Majesty's Stationery Office: 129–38.

Prest, Alan (1962). 'The Finance of University Education in Great Britain', in *Higher Education: Evidence – Part Two: Documentary Evidence*, Cmnd 2154–xii. London: Her Majesty's Stationery Office: 139–52.

Reischauer, Robert (1989). 'HELP: A Student Loan Program for the Twenty-First Century', in *Radical Reform or incremental Change? Student Loan Policies for the Federal Government*, ed. Lawrence E. Gladieux, New York: College Entrance Examination Board.

Report of the Universities' Review Committee (1987). *New Zealand's Universities: Partners in National Development* (The Watts Report), Wellington: New Zealand Vice Chancellors' Committee.

Report of the Working Group on Postcompulsory Education and Training in New Zealand (1988) (the Hawke Report), Wellington.

Robbins, Lionel (1980). *Higher Education Revisited*, London: Macmillan.

Robbins Report (1963). *Higher Education:* Report of the Committee under the Chairmanship of Lord Robbins, Cmnd 2154, London: Her Majesty's Stationery Office.

Spence, Michael (1973). 'Job Market Signalling', *Quarterly Journal of Economics*, 87, (August): 355–74.

UK (1960). *Grants to Students* (the Anderson Report), Report to the Committee Appointed by the Minister of Education and the Secretary of State for Scotland, Cmnd 1051, London: Her Majesty's Stationery Office.

USA (1988). *Budget of the United States Government: Fiscal Year 1988, Appendix*, Washington D.C.: Government Printing Office.

Varian, Hal (1984). *Microeconomic Analysis* (2nd edn), New York: Norton.

Williams, Gareth and Gordon, Adrian (1981). 'Perceived Earnings Functions and Ex Ante Rates of Return to Post-Compulsory Education in England', *Higher Education*, 10. (2): 199–227.

Woodhall, Maureen (1982). *Student Loans: Lessons from International Experience*, London: Policy Studies Institute.

Part 2

The chickens come home to roost

The Dearing Report

Chapter 7

1993 Alternative funding sources for higher education

Nicholas Barr (1993), 'Alternative Funding Resources for Higher Education', *Economic Journal*, Vol. 103, No. 418, May, pp. 718–28.

I The backdrop[1]

This paper discusses the funding of higher education, starting (Section II) with the theoretical answers to a number of key questions. Section III sets out alternative funding packages, and Section IV considers recent developments in a number of countries. To make such a vast topic manageable, the paper is limited in several ways. It discusses the funding but not the production of higher education. It does not discuss the nature of the 'product', nor the specific issues raised by the funding of research. It looks only at advanced industrialised economies.[2] Finally, it attempts to be systematic in surveying broad options, but not in surveying countries.

Since policy can usefully be assessed only against stated aims, a word is needed about objectives. *Macro efficiency* aims relate to the total quantity of resources devoted to higher education, i.e. to the size of the sector. *Micro efficiency* is concerned with the division of total higher education

1 I am grateful to Mark Blaug, Bruce Chapman and Howard Glennerster for helpful comments on an earlier version. Remaining errors are my responsibility.
2 For discussion in developing economies see Albrecht and Ziderman (1992), Psacharopoulos and Woodhall (1985), and World Bank (1986).

resources between teaching and research and between different subject areas, and with the quality of the output and the extent to which it satisfies the demands of its three major constituencies, students, employers and government. *Equity* aims relate to the distribution of higher education by socio-economic group. Improving access for students from disadvantaged backgrounds depends on the organisation both of higher education and of the school system. Thus equity includes discussion of how resources should be divided between higher education, and policies to promote access earlier in the system.

UK policy is concerned particularly with macro efficiency (e.g. expansion of the higher education system) and with improving access. Other countries, such as the United States, with large systems and a fairly broad class composition, are more concerned with aspects of micro efficiency, most particularly the quality of education and its contribution to broader aims such as output growth.

These different concerns should not be surprising, since they follow fairly directly from the different nature of the two systems. Large taxpayer subsidies (for tuition fees and/or living costs) create supply-side constraints because of the desire to contain public spending. Where, as in Britain, qualified students have no automatic entitlement to a university place, the constraint takes the form of a view (typically by the Treasury) about student numbers. The result is a high-quality system, but one which (at least by admission standards in other countries) turns away qualified applicants. In countries where students have an entitlement (explicit or implicit) to a place, the impact of cost containment is mainly on quality. With less public funding per student, as in the United States, there are no externally imposed supply-side constraints. However, unless limited taxpayer funding is sufficiently redistributive, students from lower-income backgrounds will be deterred from applying. Thus high subsidies can harm access on the supply side, but their absence can harm it on the demand side. This painful tension highlights the need for a clear view of objectives and of a policy strategy to fulfil them.

II Economic theory

This section summarises the answers economic theory suggests to three key questions.

Should higher education be subsidised?

Should funding be primarily public, as in the United Kingdom till relatively recently, or substantially private, as is more the case in the United States? There is a strong presumption that higher education should be subsidised, but it is important to be clear about why quantification is problematic. The investment case for higher education rests on the (usually unstated) assumption that it increases individual productivity. The screening hypothesis argues that post-primary education is associated with increased productivity, but does not cause it (for surveys, see Blaug (1976, 1985)). The hypothesis argues, first, that education beyond a basic level does not increase individual productivity and, second, that firms seek high-ability workers but are unable, *ex ante*, to distinguish them from those with low ability. The problem is similar to adverse selection in insurance markets, or more generally to 'lemons' (Akerlof, 1970), in the sense that one side of the market has more information than the other. The validity of the hypothesis is an empirical issue which is undecided and likely to remain so, since individual productivity is determined in part by unmeasurable influences like natural ability and family background.

Alongside the screening arguments are questions about externalities. Though belief in the external benefits of education is widespread, again measurement problems make definitive answers impossible. The heart of the difficulty is the inability to measure the tendency for the education of individual A to increase B's productivity. Estimates of private rates of return are suspect because, of necessity, they omit non-monetary returns such as job satisfaction. Estimates of the social rate of return are doubly suspect: they omit non-monetary returns and (since no other procedure is possible) also ignore the screening problem.

There is one other potential external benefit. Unless the extreme version of the screening hypothesis holds, higher education raises a student's earnings and, thereby, increases his/her future tax payments. In the absence of any subsidy, an individual's investment in a degree would confer a 'dividend' on future taxpayers. This line of argument can be used to justify subsidising any type of investment which raises future income; that is precisely what usually happens through the tax system, at least so far as business investment is concerned. The 'tax dividend' point gives an efficiency case for some subsidy, but it is not possible to show how much.

Should higher education be centrally planned?

Should funds be allocated to institutions by government (the main channel in Europe), or via students and other consumers of higher-education services, as in the pure vouchers model and, up to a point, with private universities in the United States? A second, and related, question is whether there should be different answers for teaching and research. There are two strands to the argument: the bureaucratic nature of central planning; and the fact that there are better methods for allocating resources to higher education.

In Britain, the University Grants Committee (UGC), which until 1990 channelled public resources to universities, was increasingly criticised (Barnes and Barr, 1988, ch. 3). The core argument against central planning is that central monitoring of university activities requires large amounts of information: and that information is costly to acquire, can in many cases not be measured, and is often subverted by the individuals supplying it to the central planning authority.

Such costs might be inevitable if other solutions were less efficient. Though the matter is controversial, there are several reasons for believing that students and other demanders of higher education services (in sharp contrast with the case of school education) are better regarded as well-informed than ill-informed, making consumer sovereignty a useful instrument. Information is available, and more can be made available. The information is generally simple enough for the student to understand and evaluate. The student has time to acquire the information he/she needs, and time to seek advice. Finally, it should be noted that students make choices already.[3]

A separate issue is whether students are more capable than planners of making choices which conform with the needs of the economy? All the available evidence (Ahamad (1973); Gannicott and Blaug (1973); Psacharopoulos and Woodhall (1985, ch. 4)) highlights the failures of manpower planning. As an anecdotal example from Canada in the early 1980s, the graduates in greatest demand were those with degrees in philosophy, since one of the leading edges in information technology was 'fuzzy logic'. Philosophy departments in Britain at the time were under serious threat from the central planners.

A strong case can be made for a move away from central planning towards a suitably regulated market system for allocating resources towards and within higher education.

How should student loans be designed?

If there are to be student loans (as in an increasing majority of OECD countries) what is their optimal design? A key distinction is between *mortgage-type* loans, with repayment in fixed instalments over a fixed period, and *income-contingent* loans, whose repayment takes the form of x per cent of the individual borrower's subsequent annual income, making the repayment period endogenous. A second key issue is whether students borrow from the government or the private sector.

There are strong arguments for income-contingent repayments. They offer the borrower insurance against potential future poverty, a feature of greater relevance the higher the applicant's degree of risk aversion. With mortgage loans, in contrast, students bear a much higher fraction of the risk, thus deterring applicants, particularly from disadvantaged backgrounds (Bennett, Glennerster and Nevinson, 1992). This is inefficient because it wastes talent and inequitable because it reduces intergenerational mobility.

---

3 For further discussion, see Cave, Dodsworth and Thompson (1992), Johnes (1992) and various of the other articles in the same issue of the *Oxford Review of Economic Policy*.

Mortgage loans create problems also on the supply side. In the absence of slavery, lending for educational purposes is risky, since there is no security. The resulting capital-market imperfection leads to a shortage of loan capital for educational investment. The point is well-known. Friedman (1962) noted the riskiness of student loans and pointed out that

> the device adopted to meet the corresponding problem for other risky investments is equity investment plus limited liability on the part of shareholders. The counter-part for education would be to 'buy' a share in an individual's earning prospects [and] to advance him the funds needed to finance his training . . . (p. 103).

> The individual . . . would agree to pay to the government in each future year a specified percentage of his earnings in excess of a specified sum for each $1,000 that he received (p. 105).

Equity considerations, also of venerable pedigree, point in the same direction. Glennerster, Merrett and Wilson (1968, p. 26), starting from a predisposition towards tax-funding, point out that higher education, though publicly funded,

> is reserved for a small and highly selected group. . . . It is exceptionally expensive. . . . [And] education confers benefits which reveal themselves in the form of higher earnings. A graduate tax would enable the community to recover the value of the resources devoted to higher education from those who have themselves derived such substantial benefit from it.

Despite their very different starting points, the ability-to-pay approach in the latter quote and the benefit principle implicit in the Friedman quote lead to identical policy prescriptions.[4]

Given the UK objective of expansion, a second key aspect of policy design is that the source of borrowing, to the extent possible, should be the private sector. In theoretical terms the source of funds should not matter. Suppose it is efficient to expand higher education, and that students borrow from public funds. If additional public borrowing crowds out private investment, it will only be less efficient private investment which is crowded out – a result which is itself efficient. That conclusion, however, rests on stringent assumptions, in particular that government and taxpayers must be rational and well-informed. Neither is true. Public funding requires that taxation is higher than would otherwise be the case, with possible disincentive effects; and higher public spending may affect financial and foreign-exchange markets. If students borrow from private funds no issue

---

4 Robbins (1980, p. 35) was eventually converted to this policy.

of taxation arises, and adverse incentives are minimised. Separately, it can be argued that diversifying the sources of funding contributes to the independence of higher education.[5]

III Alternative policy packages

Table 7.1 sets out a simple framework for analysing funding sources. The columns show different sources of support. The three major beneficiaries of higher education, are students, their employers and 'society', the last represented by government. The first three columns therefore refer to Students (taken to include parents, acting on behalf of their children), the Private sector (notably employers) and the Taxpayer (including, for example, the Funding Councils and Research Councils in the United Kingdom and the National Science Foundation in the United States). The fourth column contains other sources of student support, in particular the educational institutions themselves and other private donors (e.g. the Ford Foundation), which can act as surrogates for agents in the first three columns. The different types of income, shown in the left-hand column, fall into three categories: Transfers; Current earnings; and Loans, which are repaid out of future earnings.

Funding institutions

The major source of transfers to institutions are block recurrent grants (e.g. funding from the former UGC in the United Kingdom), capital grants, and tax expenditures (e.g. universities' charitable status). The major sources of earnings are tuition fees, which can be paid by students, by sponsoring firms, by government (e.g. the Higher Education Funding Councils in the United Kingdom), or by other outside bodies; from research contracts from industry or government, or from abroad; and from other commercial activities (e.g. the use of university property for conferences). A third, though typically smaller, source of income is through loans.

   In policy terms, institutions can be funded in either or both of two generic ways: directly (e.g. via a block grant); or through students and other demanders of higher education services, e.g. via fees and user charges.

Model 1: Direct funding of institutions

This is the common model in mainland Europe, where resources, by and large, are channelled to institutions in the form of transfers (line 1), usually tax funded (column C), with low or no fees for students. In Britain also, until recently, tax funding with low fees for home students was the norm.

5 For further discussion of loan regimes, see Barr (1989, 1991) and Barden, Barr and Higginson (1991).

Model 2: Funding institutions via students and other demanders of higher education services

With substantial private funding, as with private universities in the United States, universities receive much of their income from fees, research grants and contracts, and commercial activities, i.e. line 2, columns A and B.

A variant of model 2 is the vouchers model, the utility of which depends on the extent to which student choices are regarded as superior to those

Table 7.1 Sources and types of higher education funding

	Sources			
Mechanisms	*(A) Student* *(i) Him/herself* *(ii) Parent*	*(B) Private* *sector*	*(C) Taxpayer*	*(D) Other* *(i) University* *(ii) Philanthropy*

Funding for institutions
1   Transfers
   (a)   Block recurrent grant
   (b)   Capital grant
   (c)   Tax expenditure
2   Current earnings
   (a)   Tuition fees
   (b)   Research contracts
   (c)   Commercial activities
   (d)   Other
3   Loans
   (a)   Commercial
   (b)   Subsidised

Funding for students
4   Transfers
   Cash
      (a)   Grant
      (b)   Scholarship
      (c)   Tax expenditure
   Subsidies
      (d)   Subsidised tuition fees
      (e)   Subsidised accommodation
      (f)   Subsidised food
5   Current earnings
      (a)   From university
      (b)   From other sources
6   Loans
   Commercial
      (a)   Mortgage
      (b)   Income-related
   Subsidised
      (c)   Mortgage
      (d)   Income-related

of planners. In the simplest model, the state gives students tax-funded vouchers which they spend at the institution of their choice, thus combining taxpayer support (column C) with funding mainly through institutional earnings (line 2), hence without the need for the apparatus of central planning. The model is very flexible. It is both possible and desirable to give larger vouchers to students from poorer backgrounds. If it is thought that some subjects (classics, perhaps) are less suitable to competitive behaviour by institutions than others (economics, accounting) it is possible to issue vouchers tied to subjects (or institutions) which one wishes to protect. Vouchers can also be issued by private firms, for instance tenable at a local institution. With vouchers, in short, the system can be given any desired redistributive tilt; and appropriately designed constraints can make the degree of competition a policy variable which, moreover; can be varied by subject and by region (Barnes and Barr (1988, ch. 6); Glennerster (1991); Le Grand (1989)).

Funding students

The lower part of Table 7.1 discusses the funding of students, again through the generic methods of transfers, current earnings and loans. Transfers can come from the student's family (true in all countries), from industry (e.g. sponsorship), from taxpayer grants (as in the United Kingdom) or from higher education institutions themselves (more common in the United States). A second type of transfer is scholarships, i.e. a transfer related to the student's academic performance (to oversimplify, grants are normally income-related, scholarships performance-related). Students may also receive transfers which are not specific to the educational system, e.g. cash benefits for which students and non-students are eligible. Finally, students may receive transfers in the form of tax expenditures, e.g. tax relief on certain types of educational spending.

There are also various forms of in-kind transfer. Assistance with living expenses includes subsidised accommodation, food or transport. Accommodation can be subsidised by the student's family (if he/she is living at home), by the taxpayer or by the university. Second, and highly important, are subsidised tuition fees, which are the major tax-funded transfer to students in mainland Europe. Student income also derives from current earnings whilst a student, a common source in the United States, and increasingly common in Britain.

With unsubsidised loans the source of student support is the student him/herself, i.e. the student is redistributing from himself in later life to himself during student days. Subsidised loans are a mixture of loan and implicit grant; the source of support is in part the student himself and in part the taxpayer (if it is the state which pays the subsidy). As a practical matter loans in most countries are subsidised, in some cases substantially (for arguments against such subsidies, see Barr, 1991, pp. 161–2).

Historically loans in most countries have had mortgage repayments, and the United Kingdom introduced such a scheme in 1990. As discussed shortly, however, Australia and Sweden have recently introduced loans with income-contingent repayments.

The world, of course, does not always conform neatly with the simple categorisation in Table 7.1. There are sources of support other than the beneficiaries, e.g. a named endowment, whose purpose is to perpetuate the name of the benefactor. But the categorisation gives a framework for simplifying complex institutional data; and it facilitates discussion of which packages offer the most efficient and equitable forms of funding.

IV Policy in the OECD

The United Kingdom: a botched reform

Abstracting from a mass of detail (see Cave and Weale (1992) for further discussion), policy is threefold.

(1) *A move towards a more market-oriented system* of higher education (see UK Department of Education and Science, 1991) implies *inter alia* that institutional funding will come less from transfers and more from current earnings in the form of fees and, separately, research grants and contracts (i.e. a move from line 1 in Table 7.1, to line 2). As argued earlier (though the matter is controversial) such a move could increase the efficiency of higher education by giving students and other consumers a greater role on the demand side, and by allowing competition between institutions to facilitate the supply-side response. In reality, the centralising tendency of recent years has, if anything, been exaggerated.

(2) *A stated desire for expansion without any significant increase in public spending* implies a move from tax-funding towards funding from students and other private-sector sources (i.e. a move from column C to columns A and B). In the late 1980s, only about 15 per cent of the relevant age range went on to higher education, a smaller fraction than in any advanced industrialised country (UK Department of Education and Science, 1988, Chart F). A central inconsistency in government policy is the introduction of competitive pressures to expansion without either a significant increase in public spending or policies to facilitate private expenditure. Policy has therefore failed completely to grasp the dilemma posed at the end of Section I.

(3) *The recent introduction of student loans* (UK Department of Education and Science, 1988) illustrates this failure precisely. Students borrow taxpayer money, with mortgage repayments. Since the scheme introduces no private funds, there is no public expenditure saving in the short or medium term (on the Government's own figures (*Hansard,*

WA, 24 July 1989, col. 441) the scheme produces no cumulative net saving for at least 25 years).[6] Thus the scheme simultaneously harms access and yields no savings, and hence frees no resources for expansion. The introduction of private funds is central to the expansion of student numbers. A loan scheme which combines private funding with income-contingent repayments is proposed in Barr (1989).

The United States: the finger-in-the-dyke approach

The funding of institutions is decentralised. Alongside a large range of private institutions, funded mainly by student fees and other forms of earnings, is a range of state colleges and universities funded in part by transfers and in part by student fees. The age-participation rate is about 40 per cent. The major concern of US policy-makers is not expansion or access, but the quality of the system and its contribution to economic growth. As discussed at the start of the paper, these problems are the result of a system with limited public funding, coupled with no supply-side constraints.

Student funding derives largely from transfers from their families, from current earnings and from various forms of loan. The problems of student loans in the United States are well known (see Reischauer, 1989, pp. 34–42). First, it is unduly kind to talk about a loan 'system': '[t]he complex range of grants and loans from federal, state and campus sources is a major administrative problem for most institutions. Students seldom understand all that is available' (UK Department of Education and Science, 1989, para. 123). Mortgage repayments are the rule. Interest subsidies are pervasive and default rates high. The combined effect of interest subsidies and defaults is that the system is costly and of only questionable benefit in encouraging participation from lower-income groups (Bosworth, Carron and Rhyne, 1987, ch. 6).

Reischauer (1989) proposes a system with income-contingent repayments piggy-backed onto the federal social security system. To date there has been no action.

Sweden: the evolutionary approach

In Sweden, as in most of the rest of mainland Europe, institutions receive substantial tax funding, with only a limited role for fees. Student support in the 1960s was mainly in the form of a tax-funded grant plus parental support. A loan scheme with interest subsidies and mortgage repayments was introduced in the mid-1960s, which over time took on an increasing fraction of student support. Worries about student indebtedness led to major reform in 1989 including an increase in tax-funded student support,

6 Even that figure is an under-estimate, in that it omits any interest charge on the cumulative deficit over the 25 years.

the abolition of mandatory parental contributions, a reduction in interest subsidies and the introduction of income-contingent repayments. Sweden, in short, introduced loans early, learned from its mistakes and, through a process of evolution, moved towards an increasingly well-designed system (for details, see Morris, 1989).

Australia: the revolutionary approach

Until 1989, institutions were mainly tax funded. Expansion and improved access entered the policy agenda in the mid 1980s, and the recommendations of the Wran Report (AGPS, Australia, 1988), as amended, took effect in January 1989. The core of the reform package was a Higher Education Contribution Scheme, whereby students became liable to a contribution intended to be about one fifth of the average tuition fee (i.e. the contribution does not vary across subjects). Students have the option of paying the contribution on enrolment at a 15 per cent discount. Otherwise the contribution is paid out of a loan at a zero real interest rate. Repayment is suspended for individuals with annual earnings below the national average. Thereafter, repayment is 1 per cent of taxable income, rising to 2 per cent and, at the highest incomes, to 3 per cent, collected through the tax system.

Though often represented as a tax, the scheme is properly thought of as a loan: it is voluntary, since the fee charge can be paid upon enrolment; and the additional contribution is 'switched off' once the charge has been paid. Several points are noteworthy: the revenue from the scheme will finance expansion of higher education; and repayments are income-contingent explicitly to avoid compromising access (see Hope and Miller, 1988). In the latter aim, research findings strongly suggest, the scheme has been successful (Chapman, 1992, ch. 12).

V Conclusion

Overall conclusions are twofold. First, higher education funding should be designed as a coherent strategy, not as a patchwork of *ad hoc* policies. Second, funding should not rely excessively on any one source. This is not a very dramatic conclusion, but non-economists seem to have a strong (and usually inappropriate) attraction to corner solutions.

The high public-sector cost per student, through Treasury control of public expenditure, kept the higher-education sector in the United Kingdom small. In contrast, higher education in the United States is substantially funded from the private sector and faces much less constraint. This is the dilemma posed earlier: the greater the public-sector subsidy to higher education the greater the pressure on the system not to grow. There are two possible solutions. One is to keep expenditure constant, but admit more students, i.e. to trade off quality against increased enrolment. The second is to set up mechanisms which allow a greater role for private-sector funds.

As a response to the tradeoff between size, quality and public expenditure, countries like Britain and Australia, with substantially tax-funded systems, are seeking to introduce more private funding. Countries like Sweden, whose reliance on loans in the past was excessive, are moving in the opposite direction. Any move away from tax funding, however, must rest on a loan scheme which (a) does not deter access and (b) brings in private funds. Loans, from both an efficiency and an equity perspective, are thus the key to reform.

References

AGPS, Australia (1988). *Report of the Committee on Higher Education Funding* (the Wran Report). Canberra: AGPS.

Ahamad, Bashir (1973). 'Teachers in England and Wales.' In *The Practice of Manpower Forecasting: A Collection of Case Studies* (eds B. Ahamad and M. Blaug), pp. 261–84. London: Elsevier.

Akerlof, George (1970). 'The market for "Lemons": qualitative uncertainty and the market mechanism.' *Quarterly Journal of Economics,* vol. 840, pp. 488–500.

Albrecht, Douglas and Ziderman, Adrian (1992). 'Student loans and their alternatives: improving the performance of deferred payment programmes.' *Higher Education,* vol. 23, No. 4.

Barden, Laing, Barr, Nicholas and Higginson, Gordon (1992). *An Analysis of Student Loan Options.* CVCP/CDP Occasional Paper, London: Committee of Vice-Chancellors and Principals and Committee of Directors of Polytechnics.

Barnes, John and Barr, Nicholas (1988). *Strategies for Higher Education: The Alternative White Paper.* Aberdeen University Press.

Barr, Nicholas (1989). *Student Loans: The Next Steps.* Aberdeen University Press.

Barr, Nicholas (1991). 'Income-contingent student loans: an idea whose time has come.' In *Economics, Culture and Education. Essays in Honour of Mark Blaug* (ed. G. K. Shaw). Aldershot, Hants: Edward Elgar [this volume, Ch. 6].

Bennett, Robert, Glennerster, Howard and Nevinson, Douglas (1992). 'Investing in skill: to stay on or not to stay on?' *Oxford Review of Economic Policy,* vol. 8, pp. 130–45.

Blaug, Mark (1976). 'The empirical status of human capital theory: a slightly jaundiced survey.' *Journal of Economic Literature,* September, pp. 827–56, reprinted in Blaug (1987, pp. 100–28).

Blaug, Mark (1985). 'Where are we now in the economics of education?' *Economics of Education Review,* vol. 4, pp. 17–28, reprinted in Blaug (1987, pp. 129–40).

Blaug, Mark (1987) *The Economics of Education and the Education of an Economist.* Aldershot, Hants: Edward Elgar.

Bosworth, Barry, Carron, Andrew and Rhyne, Elisabeth (1987). *The Economics of Federal Credit Programs.* Washington, DC: The Brookings Institution.

Cave, Martin, Dodsworth, Ruth and Thompson, David (1992). 'Regulatory reform in higher education in the UK: incentives for efficiency and product quality.' *Oxford Review of Economic Policy,* vol. 8, pp. 79–102.

Cave, Martin and Weale, Martin (1992). 'The assessment: higher education: the state of play.' *Oxford Review of Economic Policy*, vol. 8, pp. 1–18.

Chapman, Bruce (1992). *Austudy: Towards a More Flexible Approach*. Canberra: AGPS.

Friedman, Milton (1962). *Capitalism and Freedom*. University of Chicago Press.

Gannicott, Kenneth and Blaug, Mark (1973). 'Scientists and engineers in Britain.' In *The Practice of Manpower Forecasting: A Collection of Case Studies* (eds B. Ahamad and M. Blaug), pp. 240–60. London: Elsevier.

Glennerster, Howard (1991). 'Quasi-markets for education?' *Economic Journal*, vol. 10, pp. 1268–76.

Glennerster, Howard, Merrett, Stephen and Wilson, Gail (1968). 'A graduate tax.' *Higher Education Review*, vol. 1, no. 1.

Hope, Julie and Miller, Paul (1988). 'Financing tertiary education: an examination of the issues.' *Australian Economic Review*, vol. 4, pp. 37–57.

Johnes, Geraint (1992). 'Performance indicators in higher education: a survey of recent work.' *Oxford Review of Economic Policy*, vol. 8, pp. 19–34.

Le Grand, Julian (89). 'Markets, welfare and equality.' In *Market Socialism* (eds J. Le Grand and S. Estrin), pp. 193–211. Oxford: Clarendon Press.

Morris, Martin (1989). 'Student aid in Sweden: recent experience and reforms.' In *Financial Support for Students: Grants, Loans or Graduate Tax?* (ed. M. Woodhall). London: Kogan Page.

Psacharopoulos, George and Woodhall, Maureen (1985). *Education for Development: An Analysis of Investment Choices*. Oxford University Press.

Reischauer, Robert (1989). 'HELP: a student loan program for the twenty-first century.' In *Radical Reform or Incremental Change? Student Loan Policies for the Federal Government* (ed. L. E. Gladieux). New York: College Entrance Examination Board.

Robbins, Lionel (1980). *Higher Education Revisited*. London: Macmillan.

UK Department of Education and Science (1988). *Top-Up Loans for Students*, Cmd 520. London: HMSO.

UK Department of Education and Science (1989). *Aspects of Higher Education in the United States of America: A Commentary by Her Majesty's Inspectorate*. London: HMSO.

UK Department of Education and Science (1991). *Higher Education: A New Framework*, Cmd 1541. London: HMSO.

World Bank (1986). *Financing Education in Developing Countries: An Exploration of Policy Options*. Washington, DC: The World Bank.

Iain Crawford and Nicholas Barr, 'Baker's Time Bomb Defused', *The Times Higher Education Supplement*, No. 1176, 19 May 1995, pp. 14–15.

Baker's time bomb defused

Iain Crawford and Nicholas Barr

Kenneth Baker, the former education minister, started the clock on what, in his memoirs, he genially referred to as his time bomb for the Treasury in his Lancaster speech in January 1989. In that speech he set the goal of doubling the participation rate of school-leavers entering universities on undergraduate degree courses.

His reference to time bombs refers to his recognition that he was proposing to double the undergraduate system with no mention of additional resources. We are all familiar with the resulting overcrowding and related ills.

It is true that an undergraduate student loan system was introduced, but any savings that this scheme may eventually produce will arrive long after the bomb has exploded. Mr Baker's time bomb was obvious back in 1989. There is some evidence that the Education Department recognised it, and a number of us from the London School of Economics had lengthy discussions with ministers and officials; but the Treasury was not ready to recognise the danger, nor was it as committed as Mr Baker to expansion.

What was less obvious was that Mr Baker left behind not one bomb, but two. The doubling of undergraduate numbers, as people are starting to realise, triggered off an increase in demand also for postgraduate – in particular masters-degree – places, not least because the best students need a way to signal their ability to prospective employers.

The point is not just academic. About as many young people are getting degrees today as got A levels at the time of the Robbins expansion of the mid-1960s. Those who used to mark themselves out by getting a degree now increasingly seek to do so through a higher degree to meet employers' demands for a better and better educated workforce.

Both of these time bombs can be defused through more resources. There is now a consensus that these additional resources will not be provided by the taxpayer. Not even the National Union of Students is arguing for that any more. We have been arguing since 1989 that there is a simple and effective solution, which is to bring private-sector capital into higher education. Probably the only way to do so on any scale, and in a way which is both efficient and equitable, is for students to repay their loans as an additional penny in the pound collected alongside their National Insurance Contributions (NICs).

This is automatically fully related to the graduate's subsequent income and is administratively cheap. It is also very secure, because NICs have a very low default rate. Thus it is possible for students to spread repayments over a much longer time period, making repayment easier and fairer. This, together with the security of the loan, is what makes it possible to attract private sources of finance. The result is a loan, for which repayment ceases once the individual's debt has been repaid.

This is a genuine loan scheme. It is not, repeat 'not', a new tax. The body administering the loan (there is no reason why it should not be the existing Student Loan Company (SLC) under its new management) would bring in private finance by selling the debt to the private sector. This technique, known as securitisation, is widely used, for example by credit card companies.

Suppose the SLC wishes to sell £1 billion of student debt. If it thought that 10 per cent of total student borrowing will not be repaid (because of low earning, emigration, premature death, etc.), the private market would be prepared to pay about £900 million for the debt. The Treasury would pay only the remaining £100 million rather than the whole of student borrowing, as at present. The new owners of the debt would be entitled to the loan repayments of the students.

Figure 7.1 Barr and Crawford: bomb disposal

Thus no Treasury guarantee is needed; the financial market bears the risk of loan repayments falling short of £900 million. That is what financial markets are for.

But who might buy such debt? Since degrees are a long-term asset, it is efficient if students are allowed to spread repayment over an extended period. Thus the resulting long-term, secure, low-interest asset will be attractive to longer-term fund managers, for instance pension funds.

The asset opens up the (far from fanciful) prospect of the National Union of Mineworkers pension fund owning a stake in the long-term prospects of graduates; retired miners would be living off the sweat of young graduate financial analysts. This is the scheme which, we argue, would have solved the problem of resourcing the expansion at undergraduate level. By shifting the responsibility for student maintenance away from the taxpayer, public resources can be concentrated on teaching and research.

Postgraduate students, however, have never enjoyed the generous taxpayer support that has been available to undergraduates. Our loan arrangements solve this problem. There are good reasons for dealing with postgraduates first. The problem is urgent since most United Kingdom graduate students have no systematic source of support.

Many top universities are increasingly concerned at the declining proportion of UK students in graduate schools. Given that masters students are both fewer in number and study for fewer years than undergraduates, they are an ideal group for a pilot, scheme. If there are any remaining doubts about the attractiveness of such student debt to financial markets, this group, given the quality of their earnings profiles, is the ideal place to start.

It will be attractive for a minister to announce in Parliament a pilot scheme that addresses the next problem and channels resources to a group which currently has none. The fact that we are suggesting a pilot scheme for masters students does not, however, disguise the urgency with which Mr Baker's original time bomb – that of funding undergraduates – must be addressed. This need not be the political nightmare which has hitherto inhibited politicians. The political advantages are enormous.

- Government will be able to offer undergraduates the opportunity to take out a larger loan, thus making it possible to abolish the parental contribution;
- There would be no need for further county court summonses for defaulters (the SLC currently projects up to 490,000 defaulters by the end of the decade);
- Students would benefit, because they would no longer be forced into dependence on their parents – a dependence made all the more cruel because of the number of parents who do not pay their contribution;
- Parents would benefit, because they would no longer be compelled to offer support (though they could of course continue to do so if they

and their children so wished). Parental guilt trips would be greatly reduced. There are nearly two million parents of current students, to say nothing of the parents of the increasing numbers of future students. Parents, in general, are voters;

- The providers of higher education would benefit. The expansion in student numbers of recent years, with no parallel increase in funding, has eroded quality. Restoration of quality requires more resources for teachers, for researchers, for libraries and for computer networks.

The proposal fulfils the Conservative public-private finance initiative by suggesting a 'public' sector collection mechanism as an enabler of 'private' finance. It puts flesh on the bones of Labour's learning bank idea. There are no losers and, unusually in politics, it is hard to see where opposition arguments could come from.

Iain Crawford and Nicholas Barr, 'A Loan Source of University Income', *The Times Higher Education Supplement*, No. 1259, 20 December 1996, p. 11.

A loan source of university income

Iain Crawford and Nicholas Barr

Adequate public funding of higher education is not possible for a mass system. The only way British universities will get more resources is from the private sector. What is needed is a loan system that allows students to borrow private money.

To achieve this, student loan repayments should take the form of an add-on to borrowers' national insurance contributions and student debt should be securitised, that is, sold to the private sector. Repayments would depend on income levels after graduation so they do not affect access. This and a securitised debt bring immediate cash into higher education.

There are advantages if the Student Loans Company is private, not least because of Treasury rules about what is and what is not private spending. It is an open secret that the Government is about to sell the SLC. The worry is that a commercial owner would load loan terms in favour of the lender.

But there is a solution, The proper owners of the SLC are the 104 universities. They are uniquely placed to own the SLC because they alone face a double market test. Students are their main business and therefore universities' priority is to get them the best deal. They also face a financial market test; since the price at which student debt can be privatised is higher the more credible the repayment mechanism. The use of national insurance contributions is crucial in this context.

If universities own the SLC, they are less subject to political interference, thus protecting academic freedom and assisting rational financial planning. Any profits on SLC operations return to the universities. One source of profits is the SLC's list of graduates. The benefits from the list should accrue to the university system through better loan terms.

Would universities bear any of the financial risk? The answer is no. The mechanism for bringing in private funds is to sell student debt to the private sector through a technique known as securitisation. Suppose the SLC wishes to sell £1 billion of student debt. Simulation studies suggest that in the long run 15–20 per cent of borrowing will not be repaid because of low earnings, emigration, premature death, etc. If loans pay a satisfactory interest rate, the private market would buy £1 billion of student debt for about £800 million. The Treasury pays only the remaining £200 million, rather than total student borrowing as at present. The financial market bears the risk of loan repayments falling short of £800 million.

How would administration work? Universities already own the Universities and Colleges Admissions System. There could be efficiency gains from integrating some aspects of the administration of UCAS and SLC. There is also the potential for cost recovery. Banks would pass administrative costs on to the borrower. The SLC would use the proceeds from the list of graduates to offer borrowers a better deal.

How would the universities manage the SLC? The universities would be the shareholders. They would elect a board of directors that would include some vice chancellors, but could (and should) include directors who are not vice chancellors, and possibly student representation. Given Treasury involvement, the board of directors would include a Government Treasury nominee. Vice chancellors do not necessarily have the skills to manage what is in important respects a bank. But the SLC management team does, and that capacity could be expanded.

Finally, how would universities find the money to buy the SLC? The only real value of the company is its stock of accumulated debt, currently around £2 billion, which would be sold to the market. The remaining value (computers, software, etc.) is at most £2 million. Thus the universities could buy the SLC for about £20,000 each.

This may sound as though universities would become heavily involved in higher education finance. They would and should. There will be tough negotiations between Government and financial markets. If universities own the SLC they become central participants instead of powerless spectators in talks about their future.

Universities need to move fast. The Government is likely to sell the SLC and its debt book soon. Meanwhile, universities are grappling with the dilemma addressed by the London School of Economics court of governors last week, namely the worry that fees risk access but the lack of fees harms access – most particularly for UK students – and reduces quality. The objective is to promote access and restore quality. Both are possible with the right loan scheme administered the right way. In a world of mass higher education and plural funding sources, it is essential that universities have the capacity to be active financial as well as academic participants.

Chapter 8

1995 Education and the life cycle

Howard Glennerster, Jane Falkingham and Nicholas Barr (1995), 'Education Funding, Equity and the Life Cycle', in Jane Falkingham and John Hills (eds), *The Dynamic of Welfare: The Welfare State and the Life Cycle*, Prentice-Hall/Harvester Wheatsheaf, 1995, Ch. 8, pp. 150–66.

Until recently higher education for undergraduates was provided free of charge but access to it was limited. This has resulted in perverse distributional effects with those who benefit from education receiving higher lifetime incomes, yet the cost of this education being spread across the total population. It has also resulted in perverse, but not necessarily irrational, private decisions with those who might be expected to face the highest private rates of return to tertiary education also being the least likely to participate in it. This chapter discusses the benefits received from education and training and examines various options for the funding of higher education – options which result both in a more equitable distributional outcome and which would allow the release of additional resources necessary for the expansion of tertiary education.

1 Education as investment

Education and training have a number of characteristics that make them unusual. Though partly enjoyed for its own sake education is, to a large extent, undertaken because it increases an individual's future earning capacity. It has all the characteristics of a personal investment (Becker, 1964; Schultz, 1963). The asset is, however, the individual's own human capital, her knowledge and capacity. This cannot, outside a slave society, be used as collateral for a loan. Rich parents *can* act as lenders, relying on their own stock of assets or credit worthiness, but to rely on this alone would lead both to under-investment in human capital and to inequity between potentially equally able people.

Employers also have an interest in a trained and educated labour force but the market fails here too. Any employer who educates an employee or gives her a general training is likely to find that person competed away by an employer who has no training scheme. Big employers who have other long term claims on their staff may think the risk worthwhile but most firms will aim to free-ride on others. The result is that the costs of general training are either borne by the young employee or not under-taken at all (Becker, 1964; Bennett, Glennerster and Nevison, 1992a). The market will again produce too little training and training that is not open to those from lower income families.

Education and training are very costly in relation to income. The costs are of two kinds:

- Learning takes time. Some learning can be done on the job but many skills need to be acquired before a person is worth employing and others can only be learned by devoting exclusive time to the task. Something has to be given up to do this, either paid work and thus earnings or leisure which individuals value. Carers must pay for substitute care. All three kinds of *opportunity cost* may be incurred by a woman returning to education after the birth of a child.
- Formal education is expensive, people-intensive and difficult to auto-mate, especially for young children. In higher education top quality learning best takes place in an environment where those doing the teaching are also researching – an environment of discovery and ques-tioning. Teachers must devote much of their time to that activity as well as instruction.

Taken together, the opportunity cost and the formal tuition costs of staying on beyond 16 to reach a first degree, for example, amounted to about £40,000 in 1985 prices, in our average LIFEMOD case. That is a scale of investment equivalent to the average family buying a house. If the family were trying to invest this sum in two children, let alone improving the education of the husband or wife, education would become by far the most expensive investment decision of its life cycle.

Households' different capacities to move income through time to pur-chase education have important efficiency and equity effects. The result of leaving educational finances entirely to households would be both inefficient for the wider society as well as inequitable. The state therefore has a critically important role in making widespread educational investment possible and the cost equitably spread.

2 The case for a different kind of intervention

The state has, in the past century, stepped in to remedy some of the market failures outlined above, but in the process it has created other inefficiencies and inequities. The possible means the state could adopt to finance education include:

- Free provision of state schools and universities paid for out of taxes levied on all people during periods of work.
- Provision of vouchers, financed out of general taxation, to enable parents and students to buy education at any level.
- State guarantees for private loans for educational purposes taken out from a bank or other lender.
- Provision of loans to individuals free of security but backed by the state's capacity to tax that individual later in life. The individual has to repay, whatever her future income, a mortgage type scheme.
- Provision of loans but with repayments linked to the individual's capacity to pay – an income-contingent loan which the individual ceases to repay when the debt is paid off (Blaug, 1966).
- Provision of free education beyond the statutory school-leaving age that carries with it an obligation to pay a higher rate of income tax in perpetuity – a graduate tax addition (Glennerster *et al.*, 1968).
- A subvention on employers to pay for the higher human capital content of their labour force.

In practice, until very recently, the state in the UK has relied on the first of these mechanisms to the exclusion of the rest. Other countries have been more adventurous (Woodhall, 1989; Chapman, 1992; Chapman and Harding, 1993). More recently, much interest has been shown in a variety of schemes to diversify the income of higher education institutions (Barden, Barr and Higginson, 1991; Barnes and Barr, 1988; Barr, 1991, 1993; Russell, 1993). The results of relying on the present form of tax-based lifetime redistribution of education costs can be illustrated by looking at the experience of the LIFEMOD cohort. A number of features stand out.

The distribution of education benefits

Spending on education is heavily front-loaded (see Figure 8.1). Like physical assets, human capital depreciates, becomes obsolete, during a lifetime. This is now occurring with greater rapidity than ever before. The opportunity cost of taking time out to restore a person's human capital, however, rises the older the person and the higher her normal earnings. As a result, little educational expenditure in the UK is incident on individuals above the age of 25. In many other European countries employers are required to give their older employees time off to enhance their training and some countries put a levy on employers which is used to finance older workers' education and training (Glennerster, 1982).

The benefits of education are perversely redistributional. [. . .] Those located in the highest lifetime income group in LIFEMOD receive on average 50 per cent more in benefits in kind from education than those individuals in the bottom group. The vast majority of this is due to differences in receipt of post-16 education. Figure 8.2 shows that the value of higher education benefits derived by the lifetime richest fifth of the model population is worth more than five times that derived by the poorest fifth. Barriers still exist for those from less fortunate homes, cultural and financial. The most favoured leap those barriers and then gain the much higher in-kind benefits available to those receiving higher education.

The benefits of education are still substantially restricted. Although education is compulsory from the ages of 5–16 in the UK, pre-school education is very limited in access compared to other European countries and so is participation in higher education.

There are two reasons for this low participation. First, higher education has been very expensive for the reasons outlined above. The resource cost of undergraduate university courses has probably been the highest in the world. Pupil-teacher ratios have been low, research treated as an

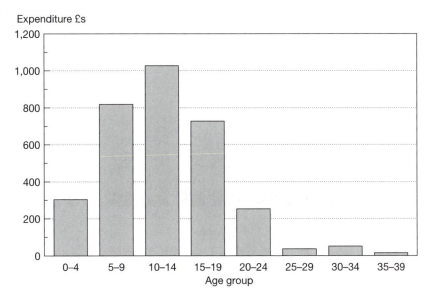

Figure 8.1 Average per capita education expenditure by age group

integral part of all university activity, and the Government has paid students' living expenses. This was a uniquely generous settlement on the post-war generation of students. It was, however, incompatible with mass higher education. The generality of taxpayers have not been willing to pay the taxes required to finance such generosity to the younger generation. This has restricted the *supply* of places in higher education.

Second, UK employers have traditionally not rewarded those who stay on to gain qualifications as much as employers in other countries. This has been especially true for lower level further education and training (Bennett, Glennerster and Nevison, 1992a). This has restricted the demand for higher and further education from individual young people who see it may not be in their best interests to forego wages in return for little extra later.

The private investment decision

Despite the fact that the state has provided free instruction for all undergraduates in the UK since the early 1960s, and substantial subsidies on other forms of post-school instruction, the decision to stay on at school or continue with further education is not costless. A young person foregoes the earnings that they could have gained if they had entered the labour market directly. Young people therefore weigh up the immediate loss they

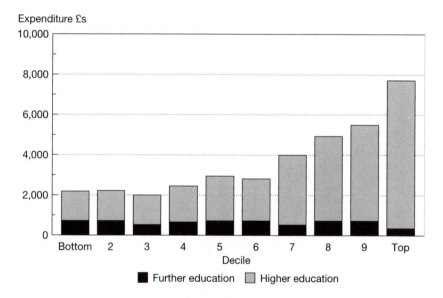

Figure 8.2 Expenditure on further and higher education by decile group of annualised lifetime net income

suffer by deciding to continue with their education against the benefits. Large amongst those benefits will be the expectation of higher future earnings but it also matters to young people when those higher earnings will come. Some may prefer to earn quickly and place a relatively low valuation on high earnings late in their career and thus apply a high discount rate to their future earnings stream. They may also see the investment as a risky one or they may lack personal or family experience of the rewards of higher education or training and be suspicious of them. Low demand to stay on at school may therefore result from entirely rational calculations by young people about their life cycle.

Bennett, Glennerster and Nevison (1992a, b) show that, on average, young people might expect a private rate of return on their investment in A levels of 6 per cent for men and 10 per cent for women. For those who stay on into higher education there was an expected additional return of 6 per cent for women and 7 per cent for men (see Table 8.1). However, the rates of return middle-class young people might deduce they could earn by staying on were lower than those for working-class children. Boys from professional homes would expect a private rate of return of only 4 per cent compared with 7 per cent for all boys. Children from middle-class homes will be more acceptable to employers, have better contacts in the labour market and hence be likely to land a good job anyway. Hence, a university course may not increase their opportunities as strikingly as for someone from a working class home.

But although children from working-class homes might expect to gain a higher private rate of return for staying on into higher education, evidence from cross-sectional studies shows that they are still less likely to do so than their working-class contemporaries (figures from General Household Survey (GHS), 1992). Two plausible explanations can be put forward. One is that those from working-class families have different time preferences. If they apply plausibly higher discount rates to their future income streams the decisions we observe at 16 become consistent and rational. The other hypothesis is that the costs of borrowing are higher for children from poorer homes, their access to the capital market is more restricted.

We can, therefore, see how intertwined are the issues of lifetime and 'Robin Hood' income distribution in the case of education. If the state makes it possible for individuals, and the economy, to benefit by helping to finance an individual's investment in education or training but only some members of the population make use of that opportunity, for reasons of taste or ignorance, the benefits will accrue unevenly. They may fall most beneficially on those who are already in the highest social or income groups.

Where the state decides to finance education beyond the compulsory school leaving age questions of equity as well as efficiency arise. If only some choose to use this lifetime redistribution facility, should all taxpayers contribute to it? In so far as higher education contributes to all our

Table 8.1 Expected private real rates of return

Father's socio-economic group					
	Professional employer manager	*Intermediate junior non-manual*	*Skilled, semi-skilled, manual*	*Unskilled manual*	*Overall (at sample mean)*
Males					
A levels	10.41	-0.25	5.78	-0.90	6.04
Higher education	4.00	7.95	6.10	25.10	7.08
Females					
A levels	4.85	15.32	10.59	13.49	9.80
Higher education	6.28	5.15	5.33	8.42	5.84

Source: Bennett, Glennerster and Nevison, 1992b, Table 2, p. 136.

well-being the answer may be yes, but, in so far as the benefits are captured by those who earn the higher incomes *as a direct result of their fellow citizens' investment* in them the answer is no.

Both efficiency and equity arguments therefore suggest that part of education expenditure that is used to finance individuals' chosen investment in education should be recovered in the form of income-related payments. In the next section we discuss the various means by which this might be done. Because LIFEMOD simulates complete life histories, it is possible to estimate how much of any loan will be repaid and how quickly. Thus both the tempo and the quantum of repayments under alternative loan regimes can be estimated.

3 Principles for reform

Any reform of higher education should, we argue, have the following characteristics (Barr and Falkingham, 1993; Barr, Falkingham and Glennerster, 1994):

- For reasons of efficiency and equity, costs of extended education should be shared between the general taxpayer, who gains from the side-effects of a highly educated workforce, and the individual student who benefits from enhanced earning potential.
- Any scheme should minimise any deterrent effect on poorer potential students.
- Students should not be asked to repay more than the cost of their own loan. Any redistribution or subsidy to poorer students should be organised explicitly through direct grants, the cost of which should be borne by taxpayers generally.
- Repayment should be made in such a way as to minimise default both on grounds of equity for those who do pay and to maximise revenue.

- Repayment should be spread over an extended period. First, it eases the burden of repayment, reducing the deterrent effect for students with a high discount rate and high earnings late in life. The early repayments of mortgage-type loans like the current Government scheme fall most heavily and riskily upon those with little parental support. Second, since human capital is a lifetime asset, it is efficient if repayments are spread over a longer period.
- Any scheme should maximise access to post-school education. One of the main restrictions on university and other further education expansion has been the cost to the exchequer. Therefore, loans should be organised in such a way that they do not count towards public expenditure, otherwise the public expenditure saving will be lost. The scheme should be capable of being privatised even if part of the risk is guaranteed by the state. If the state takes on the collection role as part of the tax system, that risk should be minimal.

These basic principles lead on to a second set of derived principles of administration:

- Repayments must be income-related or income-contingent in the jargon of student loans. This reduces the potential barrier for those who may not believe they will earn enough to repay. Income-contingent loans in other countries have not reduced access from poorer social groups. Fully income-related schemes also enable them to tax back contributions from those with lower incomes. Schemes like the present UK student loan scheme are only partially income-related (Department of Education and Science (DES), 1988, 1993). They ask nothing of those below an earnings limit and full repayment above that figure. This proves inefficient in terms of recovery, as we shall see.
- The repayment system best adapted to achieving low default, at present in the UK, is the National Insurance system. A student wishing to take out a loan to help pay for higher education would have an addition made to her National Insurance number and for the rest of working life, up to the point when the debt was repaid, a 1 per cent addition, for example, could be made on the NI contribution. In Australia the general income tax system is used for this purpose and such a mechanism would be perfectly practicable in any reformed tax-benefit system in the UK.

In what follows we test such a scheme on our LIFEMOD population. We also compare it to the present UK Government's student loan scheme and to a full 'graduate tax' as well as an employer user charge.

4 Alternative schemes investigated

Loans

We look at loans for full-time and part-time students in higher education and advanced further education on the assumption that each borrows £1,000 (in 1985 prices) for each year of her studies.[1] The sum borrowed could be used for maintenance, for tuition fees (as in Australia), or for both. Two schemes are investigated.

Scheme 1 is the current UK Government scheme for higher education. Students borrow £1,000 which they repay in ten equal annual instalments at a zero real interest rate,[2] except that repayment is suspended in any year in which the individual's earnings fall below 85 per cent of the national average for full-time male employees.

Scheme 2 is an income-contingent loan (ICL) in which students borrow £1,000, with repayment in the form of an additional 1 per cent on their National Insurance contributions (NICs).[3] Repayment stops once the loan, plus any interest, has been repaid. The income-contingent scheme would be operated alongside National Insurance contributions, with repayments withheld at source in parallel with the main NIC.

The two schemes are investigated under different assumptions. Four ICL repayment regimes are considered: where loans pay a zero real interest rate (like the Government scheme), and where they pay a real interest rate of 1, 2 or 3 per cent. The results are estimated assuming that graduate earnings (i) do not grow at all in real terms, (ii) grow annually at 1½ per cent or (iii) grow annually at 3 per cent.[4] This growth is in addition to the endogenous 'seniority earnings pattern' implicit in LIFEMOD. We assume that all full-time students and 50 per cent of part-time students take out a loan.

No loan scheme will have 100 per cent compliance. NICs have a default rate of 1 to 1½ per cent. The rate is low partly because most NICs are deducted at source by employers. In addition, there is little *incentive* to evade contributions, since evasion generally has a cost in present or future benefit, in particular pensions. Furthermore, the administrative cost of such

---

1 This figure was chosen because it is easy to rescale. Note, however, that £1,000 was somewhat over 10 per cent of average earnings in 1985. Thus a three-year undergraduate leaves with debts of about 30 per cent of average male earnings, in today's (1994) terms an amount just over £4,500.

2 The real interest rate is the excess of the rate of interest over the rate of inflation. With a zero interest rate, the loan is indexed to changes in the price level, but no interest is charged (an equivalent formulation is that the interest rate is equal to the inflation rate).

3 The repayment is 1 per cent of income below the upper earnings limit for National Insurance contributions, for individuals whose earnings exceed the lower earnings limit.

4 The government costings presented in the White Paper on student loans (Department of Education and Science, 1988) assumed 3 per cent real earnings growth.

repayments will be small because collection is 'piggy-backed' onto an existing, well-functioning system. Mortgage loans have none of the desirable built-in incentives of NICs. In the USA the default rate on the Federal Government loan scheme is about 13 per cent (DES, 1988, para. 94; Reischauer, 1989). In addition, and separately, mortgage loans have high administrative costs, especially when (as in the UK) the administration of student loans is on a stand-alone basis. The estimates below assume a default rate of 1½ per cent for the income-contingent scheme and 10 per cent for the Government scheme. We use the latter figure because that is the assumption underlying the calculations in the student loans White Paper (DES, 1988). Although it is too early for quantitative analysis, early outcomes give grounds for believing that this estimate is distinctly optimistic.

Graduate tax

The income contingent loan scheme just described should be clearly distinguished from a graduate tax. With a loan, repayment is 'switched off' once the loan plus interest has been repaid, so that no one repays more than she has borrowed. With a graduate tax, in contrast, repayment continues until some specified time, e.g. the age of retirement, with the result that high-earning graduates repay more than they have borrowed. Here we investigate a graduate tax of 1 per cent of taxable income below the National Insurance upper earnings limit for all persons who have attended at least two years of post-18 education. The default rate, once more, is assumed to be 1½ per cent.

Employer user charges

Students are one set of beneficiaries of education and training. Employers are another. One way of increasing industry's contribution and avoiding the incentive to free-ride (referred to above) is through a user charge on employers of trained men and women, the resources thereby derived being channelled back into the education/training of the next generation of young people. Under such an arrangement, employers would not contribute to the costs of training their competitors' workforces; they would pay only for those workers whom they deemed it worthwhile to employ, and only for as long as they employed them. Such user charges get round the disincentive to provide training.

The specific scheme investigated here is a user charge of 1 per cent added to the employer NIC for all employees with at least two years of post-18 education. Unlike the graduate tax it is payable on *all* gross income, i.e. it is not limited to earnings below the NIC upper earnings limit. A default rate of 1½ per cent is assumed.

5 How the different schemes performed[5]

The results for the different loan schemes are shown in Tables 8.2 and 8.3 for men and women respectively, for full- and part-time students in advanced further and higher education. The tables show the amount of loan repaid by individuals in the LIFEMOD cohort, (i) for different loan schemes, (ii) for different assumptions about the interest rate paid on student loans and (iii) for different assumptions about the rate with which graduates' earnings will grow.

Four performance indicators are considered. The first column shows the proportion of *debtors* who repay in full by retirement (at which stage any outstanding loan is assumed to be written off); likewise the Government absorbs the outstanding loan of people who die before statutory pensionable age. Thus, with zero earnings growth, 83.9 per cent of male borrowers repay in full under the Government scheme, 73.1 per cent under the comparable income contingent scheme.

The second column shows the proportion of the total *debt* the cohort as a whole repays; thus with zero earnings growth, 87.2 per cent of total

Table 8.2 Loans: advanced further and higher education, full-time and part-time: men

	Proportion of borrowers who repay in full	Proportion of loan repaid	Mean repayment period (years)	Repayment as percent of annual earnings
Zero earnings growth				
Government scheme	83.9	87.2	16.0	1.90
Income-contingent scheme	73.1	91.5	25.7	0.88
Income-contingent scheme (1%i)[a]	57.4	85.8	27.1	0.88
Income-contingent scheme (2%i)	39.7	74.6	27.3	0.88
Income-contingent scheme (3%i)	22.6	58.1	23.4	0.88
1½ percent earnings growth				
Government scheme	83.9	87.1	16.0	1.64
Income-contingent scheme	78.9	94.0	22.3	0.88
Income-contingent scheme (1%i)	75.3	91.3	24.3	0.88
Income-contingent scheme (2%i)	65.9	86.6	26.5	0.88
Income-contingent scheme (3%i)	49.1	76.5	27.5	0.88
3 per cent earnings growth				
Government scheme	83.9	87.1	16.0	1.44
Income-contingent scheme	82.9	95.3	19.8	0.88
Income-contingent scheme (1%i)	80.5	93.7	21.4	0.88
Income-contingent scheme (2%i)	76.9	91.0	23.3	0.88
Income-contingent scheme (3%i)	73.1	86.7	26.0	0.88

Source: LIFEMOD.

Note: a This line shows repayments if the real interest rate on student loans is 1%, and analogously for subsequent lines.

5 These results are drawn from Barr and Falkingham (1993), which also contains results for loans and employer user charges for the 16–19 age group.

Table 8.3 Loans: advanced further and higher education, full-time and part-time: women

	Proportion of borrowers who repay in full	Proportion of loan repaid	Mean repayment period (years)	Repayment as percent of annual earnings
Zero earnings growth				
Government scheme	44.9	64.3	22.2	2.20
Income-contingent scheme	27.2	67.3	24.8	0.96
Income-contingent scheme (1%i)	18.5	53.4	23.6	0.96
Income-contingent scheme (2%i)	13.6	39.5	22.5	0.96
Income-contingent scheme (3%i)	10.6	27.8	23.4	0.96
1 1/2 per cent earnings growth				
Government scheme	45.1	63.7	22.2	1.80
Income-contingent scheme	45.5	77.4	25.8	0.96
Income-contingent scheme (1%i)	34.3	66.1	25.9	0.96
Income-contingent scheme (2%i)	22.3	51.9	24.0	0.96
Income-contingent scheme (3%i)	15.3	36.0	22.5	0.96
3 per cent earnings growth				
Government scheme	45.1	63.0	22.2	1.50
Income-contingent scheme	61.9	83.9	25.1	0.96
Income-contingent scheme (1%i)	51.7	76.2	25.8	0.96
Income-contingent scheme (2%i)	39.8	65.0	25.9	0.96
Income-contingent scheme (3%i)	27.0	51.1	24.7	0.96

Source: LIFEMOD.

lending is repaid under the Government scheme, 91.5 per cent under the comparable income-contingent scheme. The third column shows the average repayment period for individuals who repay in full whilst the fourth column gives the burden of loan repayments as a percentage of the graduate's subsequent earnings.

Zero earnings growth

With zero real earnings growth, more men repay in full under the Government scheme, 84 per cent, compared with 73 per cent under the income-contingent scheme. The picture is reversed, however, if we look at the fraction of total borrowing which is repaid – 87 per cent under the Government scheme and over 91 per cent under the income-contingent scheme. Thus under the income-contingent scheme, men would be seen by lenders as good risks. A 10 per cent guarantee would cover the short-fall, if the world continued as assumed by LIFEMOD.

This result merits explanation. Under the Government scheme, repay-ment is zero for people with incomes below 85 per cent of the national average; otherwise it is 10 per cent of the loan. In contrast, the income-contingent loan, precisely because it *is* income-contingent, makes it possible to impose some repayment on people on lower incomes. Thus it is possible to collect repayments (albeit often small) on earnings above the lower earnings limit for NICs (currently about £54 per week), whereas the Government scheme collects only from people whose earnings exceed 85 per cent of the national average (currently about £200 per week). Thus two effects are operating: (i) repayments under the income-contingent scheme are often smaller than those under the Government scheme, but (ii) at least some repayment is possible in the £54–£200 range, where repayment under the Government scheme is zero. As a practical matter, the effect of (ii) is stronger than (i), and therefore the income-contingent scheme ends up collecting more than the Government scheme.

The average repayment period for men who *do* repay is sixteen years for the Government scheme, given the provision that repayment is suspended for people earning less than 85 per cent of the national average. Under the income-contingent scheme it takes about twenty-six years to repay. As suggested earlier, the longer repayment duration under the income-contingent scheme is a point in its *favour*. It is efficient if repayment of a loan can be spread over the life of the asset. Thus repayment should be spread over three years for a new car; for a university degree they should be distributed over the entire duration of labour market activity.

Because the Government scheme is spread over a shorter period, repayments constitute a much higher proportion of income than under the income-contingent scheme (1.9 per cent compared with 0.9 per cent). Like any conventional mortgage loan, the scheme involves 'front-loading' of repayments, i.e. requiring high repayments at a time when income is lower than in future.

Differences between men and women are significant. About 45 per cent of women repay in full under the Government scheme, but only 27 per cent under the income-contingent scheme. Looking at the fraction of borrowing repaid, however, we find again that women's total repayments are slightly more under the income-contingent scheme (67 per cent) than under the Government scheme (64 per cent). As discussed shortly, the picture for women improves considerably with a positive real earnings growth.

The effect of earnings growth

The effect of earnings growth depends on which scheme is examined. Repayments under a mortgage-type scheme depend little, if at all, on earnings. Thus repayments are higher and/or faster under the government scheme only to the extent that more people creep over the 85 per cent threshold. In contrast, repayments under the income-contingent scheme depend very directly on earnings, and so earnings growth considerably improves repayment prospects.

Figure 8.3 illustrates the effect of real earnings growth on repayment patterns, showing the fraction of *total borrowing* which is repaid. For men the Government scheme performs better in the early years but in later years repayments under the income-contingent scheme catch up and eventually overtake the Government scheme. With real earnings growth of 1½ per cent, men's repayments under the income-contingent scheme increase to 94 per cent of total loans, compared with 87 per cent for the Government scheme, and the proportion of men who repay in full rises from 73 per cent to 79 per cent. Given the high proportion of men who repay fully, the effect of earnings growth is more to speed up repayment than to increase the number of men repaying. For women, in contrast, the introduction of real earnings growth substantially increases the proportion who can repay their income-contingent loan in full (from 27 per cent to 46 per cent); and women repay a larger share of total borrowing under the income-contingent scheme (77½ per cent of total lending is repaid) than under the Government scheme (64 per cent).

With 3 per cent real earnings growth the income-contingent scheme repays 95 per cent of lending for men, significantly more than the Government scheme. In principle, the income-contingent scheme for men and women combined, would require only a 10 per cent guarantee. Such loans could pay a real interest rate of 2 per cent and still yield slightly more repayments than the Government scheme (which charges no real interest).

Graduate taxes and employer user charges

We have analysed loans in order to compare income-contingent arrangements with the existing scheme. We now briefly discuss two additional, but separate, options. Graduate taxes could be used *instead* of a loan scheme; employer user charges could be used in *addition* to either a loan scheme or a graduate tax.

The yield of such alternatives is substantial. Table 8.4 shows that a *graduate tax* of 1 per cent would repay 132.5 per cent of total borrowing compared with around 80 per cent if repayment ceased once the loan was repaid. Thus with a graduate tax, assuming zero earnings growth, richer graduates repay 50 per cent more than they would under a loan. The yield increases to over 180 per cent of the cohort's borrowing with earnings growth of 1½ per cent, and to nearly 2½ times total lending with 3 per cent earnings growth. *Employer user charges*, in the case of full-time and part-time students, yield over 1½ times as much as an equivalent loan at zero earnings growth, rising to 3 times total lending if real earnings grow at 3 per cent. A possible implication is a user charge at a lower rate, say ½ per cent.

Although a graduate tax appears to hold out the possibility of raising more revenue than an ICL it is less attractive on equity grounds. In contrast with an ICL a graduate tax repayment continues after the loan has been repaid in full, with the result that high-earning graduates repay more than

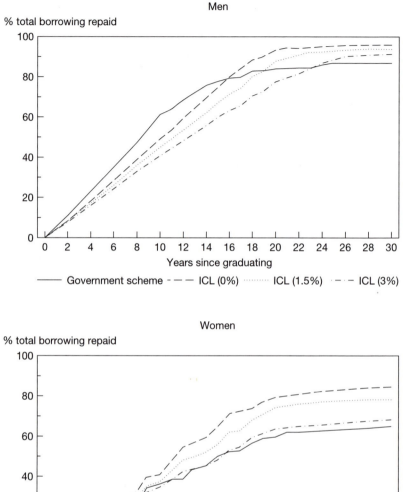

Men

% total borrowing repaid

Years since graduating

—— Government scheme - – – ICL (0%) ········· ICL (1.5%) ·– ·– ICL (3%)

Women

% total borrowing repaid

Years since graduating

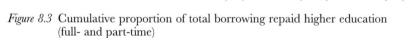

—— Government scheme - – – ICL (0%) ········· ICL (1.5%) ·– ·– ICL (3%)

Figure 8.3 Cumulative proportion of total borrowing repaid higher education (full- and part-time)

Note: Three variants of Income-Contingent Loans (ICL) are shown. Figures in brackets give assumed real earnings growth.

Table 8.4 Graduate tax and employer user charge as per cent of total loan liability: advanced further and higher education: full-time and part-time

	Yield of graduate tax	*Yield of employer user charge*
Men and women		
Zero earnings growth	132.5	156.4
1½ per cent earnings growth	181.4	215.4
3 per cent earnings growth	253.3	302.0
Men		
Zero earnings growth	167.1	204.0
1½ per cent earnings growth	231.2	283.7
3 per cent earnings growth	326.4	401.7
Women		
Zero earnings growth	87.3	94.5
1½ percent earnings growth	116.1	125.9
3 per cent earnings growth	157.0	170.7

Source: LIFEMOD.

they have borrowed. They contribute to the cost of educating poorer graduates. We do not see the justice in that. If there is a case for helping poorer graduates, the cost should fall upon taxpayers generally, like any other redistributive measure. In the case of employer user charges, we wish merely to point out the possibility that they might be used further to increase the resources available for higher education; alternatively, they might be used as a funding mechanism for other parts of the education and training system.

6 Conclusion

We have suggested that the current loan scheme for higher education should be reformed (i) by collecting repayments alongside National Insurance contributions, and (ii) by largely privatising student loans. This makes it possible to improve quality and increase equity at minimal cost in public expenditure. Bennett, Glennerster and Nevison (1992a, b) suggested that the average rate of return to education for middle-class children has been fairly low. Is it desirable in those circumstances to follow the policies suggested in this chapter? There are several reasons why the present policies are not in conflict with the earlier findings. First, Bennett, Glennerster and Nevison (1992b) found that the rate of return is higher for children from non-professional backgrounds, i.e. the very people for whom access is most important. Second, we know that if entry gates are narrow, middle-class applicants 'crowd out' other students; supply-side expansion widens the gates, to the particular benefit of applicants from poorer backgrounds. Third, figures for the later 1980s suggest an upward trend in rates of return to at least some types of education and training.

The point, however, highlights the need to design policy with considerable care, precisely to avoid deterring both potential applicants and their subsequent employers. The main conclusion is the effectiveness of the income-contingent mechanism in achieving this, through (a) its high repayment yield, despite (b) the low burden it places on individuals. The mechanism makes it possible to achieve a number of desirable objectives simultaneously.

- It raises substantial additional resources for education and training without major reliance on additional tax funding (a desirable result if only because major public expenditure increases on education and training are clearly not on offer).
- The cost would fall on those who benefit most from the expenditure.
- It minimises the deterrent to young people to pursue education or training. Moreover, the introduction of loans raises resources which can be used inter alia to give the greatest help to those who need it most, e.g. by giving 100 per cent vouchers to groups whom one wants particularly to help.
- Even if all the savings were used to reduce government borrowing, there would still be significant gains: the tax burden of financing higher education would be fairer; it would be possible to raise the ceiling on student borrowing, thereby increasing the amount students have to live on; it would be possible to make loans available to students returning to higher education whose grant entitlement has been exhausted; and it would be possible to extend the loans available to graduate students.

References

Barden, Laing, Barr, Nicholas and Higginson, Gordon (1991), *Options for Student Loans*, Committee of Vice-Chancellors and Principals and Committee of Directors of Polytechnics.

Barnes, John and Barr, Nicholas (1988), *Strategies for Higher Education: The Alternative White Paper*, Aberdeen University Press for the David Hume Institute and the Suntory-Toyota International Centre for Economics and Related Disciplines, London School of Economics and Political Science.

Barr, Nicholas (1991), 'Income-Contingent Student Loans: An Idea Whose Time Has Come', in Shaw, G.K. (ed.), *Economics, Culture and Education: Essays in Honour of Mark Blaug*, (Edward Elgar, 1991), pp. 155–70 [this volume, Ch. 6].

Barr, Nicholas (1993), 'Alternative Funding Resources for Higher Education', *Economic Journal*, Vol. 103, No. 418 (May), pp. 718–28 [this volume, Ch. 7].

Barr, Nicholas and Falkingham, Jane (1993), 'Paying for Learning', Welfare State Programme Discussion Paper No. WSP/94, Suntory-Toyota International Centre for Economics and Related Disciplines, London School of Economics.

Barr, Nicholas, Falkingham, Jane and Glennerster, Howard (1994), *Funding Higher Education*, London School of Economics and Political Science, and British Petroleum Educational Service.

Becker, Gary (1964), *Human Capital*, New York: NBER Columbia University Press.

Bennett, Robert, Glennerster, Howard and Nevison, Douglas (1992a), 'Investing in Skill: To Stay On or Not To Stay On?', Welfare State Programme Discussion Paper No. WSP/83, Suntory-Toyota International Centre for Economics and Related Disciplines, London School of Economics.

Bennett, Robert, Glennerster, Howard, and Nevison, Douglas (1992b), *Learning Should Pay*, London: British Petroleum Education Services.

Blaug, Mark (1966), 'Loans for Students', *New Society*, 6 October, pp. 538–9.

Chapman, Bruce (1992), 'Austudy: Towards a More Flexible Approach', mimeo, Canberra: Australian National University.

Chapman, Bruce, and Harding, Ann (1993), 'Australian Student Loans', mimeo, Canberra: Australian National University.

Department of Education and Science (DES) (1988), *Top-Up Loans for Students*, Cm 520, London: HMSO.

Department of Education and Science (DES) (1993), *DES Expenditure Plans 1993–4 to 1995–6*, Cmnd 2210, London: HMSO.

Glennerster, Howard (1982), 'The Role of the State in Financing Recurrent Education', *Public Choice*, 36, pp. 551–71.

Glennerster, Howard, Merrett, Stephen and Wilson, Gail (1968), 'A Graduate Tax', *Higher Education Review*, Vol. 1, No. 1, pp. 26–38, reprinted in *Higher Education Review*, Vol. 35, No. 2 (Spring), pp. 25–40.

Reischauer, Robert (1989), 'HELP: A Student Loan Program for the Twenty-First Century', in Gladieux, Lawrence E. (ed.), *Radical Reform or Incremental Change? Student Loan Policies for the Federal Government*, New York: College Entrance Examination Board.

Russell, C. (1993), *Academic Freedom*, London: Routledge.

Schultz, T.W. (1963), *The Economic Value of Education*, New York: Columbia University Press.

Woodhall, Maureen (1989), *Financial Support for Students: Grants, Loans or Graduate Tax?*, London: Kogan Page.

Chapter 9

1997 Evidence to the Dearing Committee: funding higher education in an age of expansion

Nicholas Barr and Iain Crawford (1998), 'Funding Higher Education in an Age of Expansion', *Education Economics*, Vol. 6, No. 1, pp. 45–70.

Rapid, inadequately funded expansion of British higher education between 1990 and 1996, superimposed on an extended period of financial stringency, led to a funding crisis. As a response, the government established a National Committee of Inquiry into Higher Education (the Dearing Committee) (1997a,b) to report by summer 1997. This paper, a slightly updated version of our first submission to the Dearing Committee, is the first part of a trilogy. It seeks to establish a coherent strategy for reform involving (a) a wide-ranging system of student loans, (b) flexibility to allow universities to charge variable fees and (c) a move away from central planning of higher education. This paper discusses the design and implementation of a student loan system with income-contingent repayments collected by the tax or national insurance authorities; considers how to arrange the scheme so that a significant fraction of student borrowing derives from private sources; and reports on a simulation exercise suggesting the likely repayment performance of the proposed scheme. The second part of the trilogy (Barr, 1997) discusses the treatment of student loans in the public accounts, while the third (Barr and Crawford, 1998) offers a critique of the Dearing Report's funding recommendations and the government's response, based on our evidence to the Parliamentary Select Committee on Education and Employment.

The strategy

The central fact of British higher education is the increase in the participation rate from an élite 5% in the early 1960s to a mass 30% by the
mid-1990s. So far as funding is concerned, this expansion has three
principal implications:

- the need for a wide-ranging system of student loans;
- flexibility to allow universities to charge fees which reflect their differential costs;
- a move away from central planning of higher education.

This paper explains why – in the absence of a return to an élite system
– these implications are inexorable, and offers practical solutions for dealing
with them. It is taken as common ground that higher education is important – important for economic growth, important for the transmission of
cultural values and important in sustaining individual freedom. The policies
discussed here are all instrumental, in the sense that they are concerned
mainly with the 'how' of higher education finance.

Implication 1: The need for a wide-ranging loan system

Until 1990, UK students at a UK university paid no tuition fees and
received a tax-funded maintenance grant to cover living costs. The maintenance grant was income tested on parental or spouse income: students
from poorer backgrounds received a full grant; for students receiving
less than the full grant, it was assumed that their parents or spouse would
make up the difference. In 1990, a loan scheme was introduced to
cover half of student maintenance, the other half coming from grant and
parental/spouse contributions.

Such reliance on public funding of a high-quality system is viable –
albeit regressive – for a 5% system but it is not viable for a mass system.
A mass system, therefore, requires public funding to be supplemented on
a significant scale by private funding.

Private funds can derive from four potential sources: the student's family;
student earnings while a student; employers; and students' future earnings.
The first three are only partial answers. Although family resources will
always be part of the picture, it is well known (Barr and Low, 1988) that
the system of parental contributions works badly; it is, in addition, grossly
inequitable to rely on family resources as a major source of finance. Paid
work while a student is widespread, but offers only partial support; in any
case, such activities have to compete with study time and leisure activities.
Employer contributions, although worth reassessment, cannot be pushed
too far without becoming a tax on graduate employment.

It follows that in a mass system, the only potential funding source which
is (a) large and (b) not grossly inequitable is a system of loans that allows

students to borrow against their future earnings. The source of private funds is student repayments. These will accrue slowly if students borrow from the government (since, in the early years, the government will be lending large amounts but receiving only a small flow of repayments). If students borrow from the private sector, however, the injection of private funds into higher education is immediate and substantial.

What is needed, therefore, is a system of loans which fulfils the following core objectives:

- Promoting access, both for equity reasons and for efficiency, to minimize the waste of talent in an increasingly competitive global market. Access has at least two major dimensions: student loans should not deter applicants; and students should have an adequate standard of living while students.
- Restoring quality, which has been eroded by particularly sharp expansion (from 14% to 30% participation) since 1989 with little increase in total resources going to universities.[1] Additional resources for universities are an essential component in restoring quality. Another is the development of a system which allows universities to respond to student and employer demand.
- Containing taxpayer cost. This is an objective for several reasons. The taxpayer cannot shoulder the major burden of financing a mass system. It is not realistic to expect significant increases in public spending on higher education, not least because of other educational demands, for example, pre-school education (see National Education Commission, 1993), further education (Further Education Funding Council, 1997) and action to increase staying-on rates at school.
- Liberating private funds immediately. Given the previous objective, the issue is not just to bring in private funding through students' eventual repayments, but to bring it in quickly by devising a mechanism which allows students to borrow from the private sector.

As far as funding is concerned, therefore, the central consequence of the move to a mass system is the inescapable need to draw in private funding which, in practice, means a system of student loans.

Implication 2: Price differentiation

With an élite system, it was possible, at least as a polite myth, to assume that all universities were of equal quality, that degrees were worth the same whichever university conferred them and hence that universities could, broadly, be funded equally. With a mass system, this myth is no longer sustainable. The characteristics, the quality and the costs of different degrees at different institutions will vary much more widely than in the past. To illustrate the argument, assume that there is a strong, positive correlation between quality and cost. Assume further, for simplicity, that there are three types of institution: internationally competitive institutions with high costs (not least because of the need to pay internationally competitive salaries); average institutions with average costs; and institutions with low costs (not least because staff costs do not cover time spent on research). The problems, if all universities receive broadly equal funding, are as follows:

- If all institutions are funded at the level of the internationally competitive universities, the resulting allocation of resources is inefficient, wasteful, unaffordable and politically unsustainable.
- If all institutions are funded equally at an average level, the quality of the internationally competitive institutions cannot be sustained. Lower quality institutions, in contrast, are overfunded which is both wasteful and gives them no incentive to improve.
- If all institutions are funded equally at a low level, the best universities, a fortiori, are disadvantaged and the average quality also suffers.

In theory, differential costs could be accommodated by differential allocations by an all-knowing central planner. In practice, the task is far too complex. Given the increasing diversity (much of it desirable) in what institutions offer, loans therefore need to be compatible with a funding régime in which institutions can charge differential prices to reflect their differential costs.

Implication 3: Central planning of higher education is no longer feasible or desirable

Although many people – including us – mourn the loss of many aspects of the 1960s, the past is no longer on offer. Forty years ago, universities in England and Wales offered a fairly standard package of 3-year, full-time degrees in a fairly limited range of subjects for 18–21-year-olds. This model, it can be argued, was appropriate for a more static and less technological era. Today, in contrast, technology requires more people to receive more education and training, and the labour market requires learning to be a lifelong experience. Thus, there are many more students, the training they require is much more diverse and it is changing and will continue to change. The task has become vastly too complex for central planning to be possible any longer.

Neither is central planning desirable (Barnes and Barr, 1988; for the underlying theory, see Barr, 1998, Chapters 4 and 13). Market forces work best when consumers are well informed. It is our firm view that students are more than capable of making the necessary choices (which they make already) and will, in future, be capable of making more complex choices provided they have the necessary information. There has been considerable improvement in the provision of information about what each university offers, particularly in the broadsheet press and, more recently, over the Internet.

If students in future pay a significant fraction of the costs of their higher education, their behaviour will change and that, in turn, will create demands for greater variation in what universities provide. Some students will demand more time-efficient courses, e.g. if the content of a 3-year degree is taught over a 2-year period without lengthy vacations, students have to finance only 2 years of living costs and can enter the labour market a year earlier. Others will demand more flexible part-time options which can be combined with continuing labour market activity. Both effects will be accentuated by people's knowledge that they will almost certainly have to return for additional training at a later stage in their career. Such strong changes in demand will require universities to respond in ways which are wholly impossible within a centrally planned funding mechanism. Universities have to be free to decide the prices they charge, the types of courses and the number of places. Quantity, quality and price would result from the interactions of universities, students and employers within an appropriate regulatory framework. Student demand will be more attuned to continually evolving employer demand than central planning ever could. If the government wishes to influence outcomes (e.g. to encourage more students to study engineering), they would do so by providing financial incentives for relevant courses.

The rest of the paper focuses mainly on implication 1, the need for an effective system of student loans, with less discussion of implications 2 and 3. Many equally important issues are not discussed, including different ways of organizing degrees, action to restore quality and the maintenance of academic freedom in a market environment.

The next section discusses the design of a loan system intended to achieve the objectives set out earlier. The third section looks at how that design might be implemented, including discussion of the mechanics of administration and of how to ensure that student debt is largely privately financed. The fourth and fifth sections examine, in turn, macro-economic outcomes (the overall effectiveness of the proposed arrangements and the broad magnitude of the resulting saving in public expenditure) and micro-economic effects (repayments from a student perspective, plus a brief discussion of the possible impact on the incomes of universities). The final section looks at the way ahead, in terms of further work and political aspects of implementation.

A new design for student loans

The starting point is to ask why a new student loan scheme is necessary. The present scheme was introduced in 1990. Loans are disbursed by the Student Loans Company (SLC), which also collects repayments. Loans carry a zero real interest rate, i.e. the loan incorporates an interest subsidy.

People who have borrowed while a student (henceforth, for short, graduates) normally repay in 60 equal monthly instalments, i.e. repayments are organized like a mortgage or a bank overdraft. Repayment can be deferred for 12 months at a time if the graduate's income is below 85% of national average earnings. The source of funds is the Treasury, i.e. the taxpayer.

The argument against this scheme is simple. It fails totally to achieve any of the objectives set out earlier.

* Its mortgage-type repayments harm access. For a person with the maximum loan, earning just over the 85% threshold, the annual loan repayment (20% of the total loan) absorbs 10% of total income. Further expansion would put graduates at a disadvantage in buying a house.
* It provides no additional resources for universities and, hence, does nothing to restore quality.
* It is hugely and unnecessarily costly in public expenditure terms: students borrow public money; loans carry an interest subsidy; deferments slow the repayment flow; and administrative costs are unnecessarily high.
* It mobilizes no private funding at all.

All this was both predictable and predicted (Barr, 1989, Chapter 4; 1993).

Collecting repayments

Whatever the controversy about other elements of higher education policy (e.g. tuition fees), there is virtual unanimity (including the Committee of Vice-Chancellors and Principals and the National Union of Students) that policy for financing higher education should include student loans with two characteristics: repayments should be fully income contingent (i.e. should take the form of x% of the borrower's subsequent earnings, collected weekly or monthly from pay packets); and, to the maximum extent possible, loans should derive from non-budgetary sources.

Earlier work (Barr, 1989, Chapter 6; Barr and Crawford, 1996) explains how to put into place both legs of the strategy.

* Income-contingent repayments should be implemented by piggybacking student loan repayments onto national insurance contributions (NICs).[2] Repayments should be calculated using the national insurance tax base, and collected by the Inland Revenue or Contributions Agency, whichever computer can more cost effectively talk to the SLC computer. This approach automatically gives full income contingency, is administratively cheap and is secure.
* Because repayments are collected at source, they are secure; thus they can be spread over an extended period; thus weekly repayments are

low; and thus students can afford to pay a positive real interest rate. The combination of a positive real return plus security makes such loans interesting to the private sector.

A number of characteristics of the scheme should be stressed.

- It is a loan, not a graduate tax. Nobody who has borrowed while a student repays more than he/she has borrowed, plus interest (a possible exception is discussed below). This is deliberate. A central problem with a graduate tax (i.e. an additional tax for life or until retirement) is that it releases no additional resources to restore quality, except in the longer term.
- Because the scheme is fully income contingent, it is possible for low earners to make repayments. Specifically, repayment starts at the lower earnings limit for NICs (£62 per week in 1997–1998). At that level of income, a graduate whose loan repayment takes the form of an add-on to his/her NIC of 3 pence in the pound would have repayments of under £2 per week.
- Because repayment is spread over an extended period, weekly repayments are low, so that students can afford to pay a market interest rate. Thus, the scheme contains no interest subsidy (as discussed below, the scheme could accommodate a targeted interest subsidy, e.g. for people looking after young children).
- Graduates have the option at any time to accelerate repayments including repayment in full, e.g. on receipt of an inheritance or a 'golden hello'. Since there is no interest subsidy, graduates face no artificial incentive to prolong loan duration.

Bringing in private funds

Student loans will bring in private resources, but only in the medium term, once the loan scheme is mature. However, higher education needs additional resources now. There are two broad ways forward: bringing in private resources or continuing to lend taxpayer resources to students, but organizing the public accounts so as to exclude from public spending that fraction of lending which will be repaid. Both approaches are discussed in detail in Barr (1997).

There are two ways of bringing in private funds: either students can borrow directly from private lenders; or students can continue to borrow from the SLC, which then sells the student debt to the private sector. Work on the first approach is still in its early stages. In this paper, we discuss only the second – debt sales. Suppose the SLC wishes to sell £1 billion of student debt. A simulation study by Barr and Falkingham (1993), discussed in more detail later, suggests that, in the long run, between 15 and 20% of total student borrowing will not be repaid because of low earnings, emigration, premature death, etc. Thus, provided the loans pay a satisfactory interest rate, the private market would buy £1 billion of student debt for about £800 million. Throughout, this paper deliberately uses this conservative estimate to illustrate the argument. The Treasury pays only the remaining £200 million, rather than the totality of student borrowing, as at present. The new owners of the debt are entitled to the loan repayments of the graduates. The financial market bears the risk of loan repayments falling short of £800 million.

Advantages

The income-contingent (IC) scheme described in the foregoing, in sharpest contrast with the current scheme, achieves the objectives described earlier: (a) promoting access; (b) restoring quality; (c) containing taxpayer cost; and (d) liberating private funds immediately.

First, the arrangements assist access, as Australian experience confirms (Chapman, 1997). The tax/national insurance system offers a user-friendly form of repayment, which most graduates would actively prefer to mortgage-type arrangements. In contrast with the loan scheme introduced in 1990, repayments are fully income contingent and, hence, automatically affordable. The threshold at which repayment starts is the lower earnings limit for NICs, a figure which – in contrast with the 85% threshold of the current scheme – takes account of incentives and poverty traps. The repayment period varies with the student's ability to repay, becoming shorter as his/her earnings increase. All this happens automatically, without any application from the student and without the need for complex enquiries and frequent reviews by the SLC. In addition, there is a ceiling on repayments, since there is an upper earnings limit for NICs. This eliminates any major disincentives for higher earners.

Any other repayment mechanism inevitably harms access. The SLC, as permitted by current regulations, goes to great lengths to avoid students appearing on credit blacklists. Despite the SLC's best endeavours, however, credit agencies blacklist any student against whom a summons is issued. Undoing the damage is difficult, even when the student was guilty of nothing worse than inefficient paperwork: credit agencies look at each other's lists and a name, once entered on one list, tends to be perpetuated on others, blighting applications for credit cards, to say nothing of mortgages. Current regulations allow the SLC to sell its debt to private debt collection agencies, but impose no constraint on the methods used by such agencies. The publicity surrounding private debt collection activities would simultaneously deter access and create political embarrassment for ministers (it is easy to imagine a mistaken midnight raid on two young women students the night before an important examination).[3]

For these and other reasons, the consensus – that living costs should be financed by loans rather than grants – depends critically on loans being fully income contingent. Any other approach would immediately destroy the consensus.

The proposed arrangements also contribute to the second core objective: in sharpest contrast with current arrangements, they release resources which make it possible to restore quality. The IC scheme allows larger loans and brings in private funding, contributing to quality in either or both of two ways: with less public spending on maintenance, there could be more public spending on the universities themselves; and/or part of the loan could be used to pay fees.

So far as reducing taxpayer costs (the third core objective) is concerned, savings arise for several reasons. First, there is an accelerated repayment stream in comparison with the current system. The IC scheme performs better than other loan schemes for two separate reasons. Unlike current arrangements in Britain and the US, repayments are not organized like a mortgage but are tied into general tax enforcement and, hence, have a low default rate. In addition, because repayments are income contingent, they can start at a much lower level of income, thus collecting repayments from a much denser part of the income distribution. Specifically, graduates start to repay as soon as their income exceeds the lower earnings limit for NICs. The current scheme, in contrast, collects no repayments from anyone whose income is below a threshold of 85% of national average earnings (about £315 per week in 1997/98). By collecting at least some repayment from people earnings between £62 and £315 per week, the IC scheme has a faster repayment stream (Barr and Falkingham, 1993, Figure 1; Harding, 1993, provides similar findings – for similar reasons – in the Australian system). This point is important: currently, nearly half of all graduates defer repayment;[4] when repayment is organized as an add-on to NICs, deferment is (a) automatic below the lower earnings limit and (b) applies to vastly fewer graduates.

There are other reasons why the repayment stream is faster. Because NICs operate on a weekly basis, it is possible to collect repayments from the graduate's first pay cheque onwards. Under current regulations, in contrast, a student graduating in July, in effect, has an automatic deferment until the start of the new tax year the following April. In addition, recovery through NICs captures earnings from all work, for both employed and self-employed graduates, and for however short the period, irrespective of the number of concurrent or consecutive employers involved. Furthermore, NICs more easily capture income from work abroad for UK employers – important in the EU context.

A second major source of saving to the taxpayer arises because there is no interest subsidy. Since repayments are fully income contingent, it is possible to charge students a positive real interest rate. Because the IC mechanism is secure, students could borrow at only a fraction above base rate.

Further savings to the taxpayer arise because the default rate for NICs is low, at around 1.5%, and through potential savings in SLC administrative costs (discussed in detail by Barr and Crawford, 1996, Appendix 1 and Table A1). Despite early criticisms, the SLC is now well on top of its administrative task. Discussion in our earlier paper relates to criticisms, not of the SLC, but of the task. The great advantage of the IC scheme is that repayments automatically adjust to fluctuations in weekly/monthly income, in contrast with the current scheme, which requires manual calculations and adjustments and only responds to annual income.[5]

The fourth core objective is to liberate private funds rapidly. The IC arrangements do this. The taxpayer savings listed in the previous paragraphs are those which arise if loans do not derive from private sources. It is precisely those advantages (strong repayment stream, no interest subsidy, a low default rate and low administrative cost) which attract the private sector.

If student loans derive from private resources, the savings to the taxpayer are larger and occur sooner. If loans cover all maintenance, the SLC, with current student numbers, would lend about £2 billion per year. The estimates discussed here suggest that this debt could be sold for around £1.5 billion, producing immediate savings in public spending of that amount per year. This 'pot of gold' could be used to restore quality and promote access.

Further expansion is possible and desirable. Loans should be available to cover all living costs, hence abolishing 'compulsory' parental contributions.[6] In addition, loans should be increased to improve student living standards. Finally, loans should be available to cover fees.

In summary, these arrangements allow large loans, an extended repayment period and market interest rates. They bring in private funds. They also have major political benefits: student support would no longer be means tested; the 'compulsory' parental/spouse contribution could be abolished; and graduates would rarely be involved in court cases, would not appear on credit blacklists and would not be pursued by private debt collectors. The scheme is also flexible in that, as discussed later, it can be readily expanded to postgraduate students, part-time students and students in further education and vocational training.

Implementation: the mechanics of the scheme

Sequencing

Implementing policy in the right order – sequencing – is critical but frequently overlooked. First, loans must precede additional fees. Loans can be introduced whether or not students are charged an additional fee. Additional fees, however, cannot be effective unless they are supported by a wide-ranging loan system. Fees without loans would be a policy with as few redeeming features as the current student loan scheme:[7]

- They would be inequitable, socially divisive and inimical to access.
- Without an effective loan scheme, such fees could not be very high. Thus, they would bring in relatively little extra income to universities.
- Fees without loans would also require universities to run an extensive system of fee remissions. The high administrative costs involved would further reduce the resulting net income to universities.

A second aspect of sequencing is that income-contingent repayment through the tax or national insurance system should precede the quest for private resources. Bringing in private funds cannot take place at any sensible price until collection of repayments at source has been put into place. It is precisely the security of the tax/national insurance system which makes it possible to sell student debt for around 80% of its face value rather than, say, 50%. A critical (and novel) feature of the IC scheme is its use of a public repayment mechanism to liberate private funds. Attempts to bring in private funds without collection of repayments at source would fetch a low price, at large and continuing waste of public expenditure.

Administering repayments

It is useful to divide administration into five logical functions: (a) disbursing loans; (b) keeping records; (c) administering the collection of repayments; (d) administering deferments; and (e) finalizing recovery (for more detailed discussion, see Barr and Crawford, 1996, Appendices 1 and 2).

At the disbursement stage, the SLC would set up an account for each new borrower and pay out loan payments broadly as at present. In addition, it would transmit the borrower's name and national insurance number to the Contributions Agency so that a revised national insurance number could be issued, most simply by adding a suffix 'E' to his/her national insurance number for the duration of the loan.[8] The purpose of the suffix would be to inform employers of the need to withhold the add-on to NICs.

The SLC needs to maintain two sorts of record: about the borrower, and about the loan. The key information about the borrower is the graduate's name and national insurance number. The SLC would also need the graduate's address to send annual statements of loan balances, as required by the Consumer Credit Act, and, in most cases, to send a final refund when the loan had been repaid. This task of record keeping, however, is smaller and easier than at present. First, under the present scheme, a missing address can mean a missing repayment; with the IC scheme it merely means that the graduate will not receive his/her annual statement. Thus, the repayment stream is independent of SLC knowledge of addresses. Second, the graduate has an incentive, rather than a disincentive, to keep in touch with the SLC in order to receive statements and his/her final refund. Third, if necessary, addresses are generally available from the social security or income tax database. Thus, the IC scheme has a double advantage: it is not necessary to have a current address in order to collect repayments; but if an address is needed, it is generally available from social security or tax records.

Recording the progress of the loan requires the SLC to set up and maintain graduates' repayment records, ascertaining when the debt was repaid and then closing the account. For most graduates, recording debt and repayment would be done by electronic communication between the tax or national insurance authorities, on the one hand, and the SLC on the other. Record keeping would be cheaper than under the current system (a) because it would be smaller (less detailed records on borrowers) and (b) because the recording of debt and repayment would be streamlined, computerized and would exploit administrative economies of scale.

Administering the collection of repayments, the third core administrative function, remains the responsibility of the SLC. Under the present scheme, the SLC devotes considerable resources to administering graduates' entitlement to defer repayments. Under the IC scheme this time-consuming and costly function almost disappears totally. For the great bulk of graduates, compliance is through enforcement by the tax/national insurance authorities. Employers would implement enhanced national insurance deductions automatically through payroll computer deductions or deduction tables. Under current arrangements, employers transfer withholdings of income tax and NICs to the Inland Revenue, which strips out the income tax and passes the NICs on to the Contributions Agency. The only change is that either the Inland Revenue or the Contributions Agency would transfer loan repayments electronically to the SLC on a monthly basis, a cheap operation from the SLC's perspective, since repayments for the great bulk of graduates would come mostly through this single channel. Development work is needed for this last task. Note, however, that this is a once-and-for-all cost.

The fourth aspect of administration is administering deferments. Under present arrangements, the SLC (a) informs students that they are entitled to defer repayments if their income is below 85% of national average earnings, (b) seeks evidence, for example from pay slips, which confirms the graduate's earnings and (c) follows up on graduates who have neither made a repayment nor applied for deferment. This involves a large, sophisticated computer/telephone operation. Under the IC scheme, this function would almost entirely disappear, leaving a much smaller service function to respond to student queries.

Finalizing recovery is simple. Once a loan was fully repaid, the SLC would ask the Contributions Agency to remove the suffix E from the graduate's national insurance number. It would also be necessary to refund any overpayment. Small overpayments would be frequent, since the Contributions Agency remits repayments to the SLC monthly, but transmits information about individuals only at the end of the tax year.

These arrangements are feasible and create no precedent. No major new administrative task is involved. The national insurance system already collects repayment at different rates for different people. In the past, married women could choose to restrict their contribution to industrial injury insurance, and there are still some remaining claimants of this option. In addition, anyone who continues to work after pensionable age pays a zero employee contribution. Existing software is designed to cope with these differential contribution rates.

No precedent is broken either. There is no issue of principle in using the NIC system to collect private debt, since the national insurance system already does so. Under present arrangements, people can (a) belong to the state earnings-related pension scheme (SERPS), paying NICs at the full rate, (b) contract out and belong to an occupational scheme, paying NICs at the (lower) contracted out rate or (c) contribute to a personal pension. In the case of (c), people pay NICs at the full rate. The personal pension component is stripped out once a year by the Contributions Agency and passed on to the personal pension scheme to which the person belongs. This is an example of public collection on behalf of a private firm. Many of the private pension schemes would not exist if they did not have the guarantee of the income through the national insurance system.

These administrative arrangements are not only feasible; if properly implemented, they could have a number of significant advantages for current and future students. First, a list of the names and addresses of UK graduates of any generation is very valuable. The SLC could include appropriate advertising with each graduate's annual statement. The money thereby raised would, wholly or in part, offset administrative costs, thus lowering the charge to students. It is important that the list of graduates remains under the control of the SLC to ensure a continuing benefit to student borrowers.

Second, the standard loan agreement should include a requirement that the student would complete a series of questionnaires after graduation. Such questionnaires (which would probably be organized on a sample basis), would provide universities, employers and future students with labour market information. By focusing on outcome rather than input, this would assist well-informed choices by subsequent students of their course and institution. Information is vital to informed consumer choice; it also creates pressures to maintain quality.

The central point is that the administration of loan repayments through an add-on to NICs is feasible, will be more effective than current arrangements and raises no issue of principle or precedent.

Bringing in private funds

One mechanism for bringing in private funds rapidly is to sell student debt. There are two broad approaches to putting the idea into practice. Under the first, the Treasury gives no guarantee whatever to private lenders. The scheme would work as follows:

- The SLC decides it needs £1 billion to finance the next tranche of student loans, and offers £1 billion of debt for sale.[9] Private buyers pay, say, £800 million to buy the future repayment stream and the Treasury pays the SLC the shortfall of £200 million. Thus, the SLC has £1 billion to lend to students.
- The total amount of debt being sold would be offered in small chunks, say of £10 million, deliberately relatively small to make it easier for smaller financial institutions to participate, hence making the process more competitive.
- The scheme would go well beyond the commercial banks. Bidders would also include merchant banks, life insurance companies and, importantly, pension funds.
- Such offers would be made periodically (i.e. once or twice a year) as the SLC needed to replenish its coffers.
- Bidding would be through sealed bids or by auction. Each bid would specify two things: the number of units being bid for, say, 10 units (£100 million), and the offer price per unit.
- Each bidder could make more than one bid, e.g. five units at £9 million each, 10 units at £8 million each, etc.
- The units would be sold to the highest bidders. The bidder offering the highest price would get as many units as it had bid for and, similarly, for the next highest until all the units had been sold.

This approach costs the taxpayer a one-time payment of £200 million. That payment would be current public spending in the year in question. There would be no guarantee to private markets and, hence, no contingent liability. The private sector faces the entire risk that repayments will fall below the £800 million it paid for the debt.

An alternative approach, which privatizes matters even further, involves a limited guarantee. The approach differs from that above in two main ways. First, the Treasury would not make a cash payment but would instead offer a guarantee on the first £200 million of losses incurred in the portfolio.[10] With such a guarantee, the market would buy the debt for around £1 billion. In this way, the government never has to pay more than £200 million, but may benefit if losses are below the expected 20%. This may have advantages in meeting the Treasury's value-for-money criteria.

Second, the SLC does not sell debt directly to a range of financial institutions, but to a single institution. It has been suggested by financial market practitioners that government involvement of this type would make it attractive for one underwriter to buy the entire issue. The underwriter then sells bonds to individual institutional investors who have the option of buying in larger or smaller amounts, possibly as small as £10,000. In effect, the SLC does not act as a retailer of debt but sells the debt wholesale.

From the perspective of financial markets, a £1 billion transaction launched with government sponsorship rather than a cash discount, and with a 100% credit wrap by a AAA-rated institution, would be very well received. The view of the market is critical; the more favourable, the lower the interest rate necessary to sell the debt for its face value of £1 billion.

As mentioned earlier, debt sales are one way to bring in private resources the other – as yet not fully worked out – is for students to borrow directly from private lenders, with repayments collected by the tax or national insurance authorities. Any attempt to bring in private resources will require detailed work, not least to make sure that it does not fall foul of international statistical criteria concerning the dividing line between public and private spending (for a fuller discussion, see Barr, 1997).

Outcomes 1: The aggregate performance of the scheme

A central issue in earlier discussion was the fraction of total student borrowing which would be repaid. This question was investigated using the LSE Welfare State Programme's LIFEMOD, which contains synthetic life cycles for 4,000 individuals, based on 1985 data, including 1985 probabilities of marriage and its breakdown, of having one, two, three, etc. children and of entry into and exit from unemployment or ill health.[11] Barr and Falkingham (1993) investigated in some detail a loan of £1,000 (1985 prices) for each year of a 3-year degree, i.e. a total loan of £3,000, repaid by an add-on to NICs of 1 penny in the pound, under various assumptions about (a) the real rate of growth of graduates' earnings and (b) the real interest rate paid by graduates on their loans. Barr and Falkingham (1996) tested the sensitivity of the earlier simulations for add-ons between 1 and 2.5 pence.

The two papers investigated four variables: the percentage of individuals who repay their loans in full; the percentage of total lending which is repaid; the average duration of repayment; and loan repayments as a proportion of gross earnings. This section looks mainly at the results for the second variable – the fraction of total lending which is repaid – shown in Table 9.1, although, where relevant, it also refers to the other variables (for the full results see Barr and Falkingham, 1993, Tables 1A, 1B and 1C).

Repayment performance

In Table 9.1, students are assumed to make loan repayments as an add-on to NICs of 1 penny in the pound for each £3,000 (1985 prices) they have borrowed.

The benchmark case (zero earnings growth, zero real interest rate) shows the very different repayment dynamics of mortgage repayments and income-contingent repayments. Taking men and women together, the

Table 9.1 Proportion of lending repaid: current loan scheme and income-contingent scheme with a repayment rate of 1 penny per pound of earnings[a]

	Proportion of loan repaid		
Earnings growth and real interest rate on loan	*Men/women*	*Men*	*Women*
Zero real earnings growth			
Current scheme	78.8	87.1	68.2
IC[b] scheme			
0% real interest	79.1	90.3	64.8
1% real interest	69.3	85.0	50.9
2% real interest	56.3	74.2	37.1
3% real interest	41.7	57.4	25.6
1.5% real earnings growth			
Current scheme	78.6	87.1	67.6
IC scheme			
0% real interest	84.8	92.6	74.9
1% real interest	77.9	89.9	63.6
2% real interest	68.2	85.4	49,7
3% real interest	55.7	76.0	35.8
3% real earnings growth			
Current scheme	78.4	87.2	67.0
IC scheme			
0% real interest	88.6	94.0	81.5
1% real interest	83.7	92.2	73.5
2% real interest	76.4	89.3	62.4
3% real interest	66.8	85.1	49.0

Notes:
a Simulations are for full-time students in advanced further and higher education.
b IC = scheme in which loan repayments take the form of an add-on to borrowers' NICs.

Source: Extracted from Barr and Falkingham (1993, Tables 1A, 113 and IC).

fraction of borrowers who repay in full (not shown in the table) is seven out of ten under the current scheme, but only five out of ten under the IC scheme. In sharp contrast, as shown in the upper part of Table 9.1, there is virtually no difference in the fraction of total lending which is repaid under the two schemes, each repaying about 79%.

This result merits explanation. Under the current scheme, repayment is zero for people with incomes below 85% of the national average (around £315 per week); otherwise, it is 10% of the loan. In contrast, the income-contingent loan, precisely because it is income contingent, allows people above the lower earnings limit for NICs (£62 per week) to make at least small repayments. Because repayments are lower, more people do not repay in full. But, because the IC scheme collects repayments on earnings between £62 and £315 per week, total repayments match those of the current scheme. Under the assumptions of Table 9.1 (in particular, zero real earnings growth), both schemes could operate with a government contribution of slightly over 20% of total lending to students.

The average repayment period (not shown) is 17 years for the current scheme and 28 years under the IC scheme. The longer repayment duration under the IC scheme is, in many ways, a point in its favour. In efficiency terms, it should be possible to spread repayment over the life of the asset. Thus, repayment should last 3 years for a new car while, for a university degree or similar long-lasting qualification, the option of a longer repayment duration is efficient.

Earnings growth of 1.5 and 3% is investigated in the middle and lower parts of Table 9.1. With mortgage-type schemes, repayment depends little, if at all, on earnings; thus, repayments are higher and/or faster under the government scheme only to the extent that more people creep over the 85% threshold. In contrast, earnings growth has a dramatic effect on the performance of income-contingent schemes. With a zero real interest rate, the combined repayments of men and women rise to 85% of total lending with 1.5% earnings growth and to nearly 90% with 3% earnings growth, compared, in both cases, with about 79% for the government scheme. It should be noted that real earnings growth of 3% is not implausible: individual earnings rise over time, both because the overall structure of earnings increases and because of life-cycle effects, as individuals move up their pay ladder. The Government Actuary's estimate of long-term overall annual earnings growth is 1.5%, entirely compatible with 3% growth in individual earnings.

The second and third columns of Table 9.1 show the very different repayment patterns of men and women. Even with zero real earnings growth, men repay 90% of total borrowing under the IC scheme at a zero real interest rate. With 3% earnings growth and a zero real interest rate, men repay 94% of their total borrowing. Given the high proportion of men who repay in full, the effect of earnings growth is more to speed repayment than to increase the number of men repaying; the average loan duration falls from 28 years with no earnings growth to 21 years with 3% growth.

With men, the effect of earnings growth was mainly to speed repayment. With women, in contrast, earnings growth dramatically increases total repayments (column 3). At a zero interest rate, women's repayment rises from about 65% of total borrowing with zero earnings growth to over 80% with 3% earnings growth, compared with 67% under the government scheme.

Income-contingent loans are also highly effective for students in further education (Barr and Falkingham, 1993, Tables 5A, 5B and 5C, Figure 4). Although such students have more heterogeneous earnings profiles than graduates, they study for shorter periods and, hence, take out smaller loans. In the benchmark case, men repay nearly 96% of their total borrowing, women 78%, and men and women together over 85%. Earnings growth

Table 9.2 Proportion of lending repaid with different repayment rates[a]

Earnings growth and real interest rate on loan	Proportion of loan repaid with repayment rates of			
	1 penny	1.5 pence	2 pence	2.5 pence
Zero real earnings growth				
0% real interest	79.1	89.2	92.9	94.6
1% real interest	69.3	83.2	89.1	92.1
2% real interest	56.3	74.2	82.8	87.7
3% real interest	41.7	62.7	73.7	80.8
1.5% real earnings growth				
0% real interest	84.8	92.0	94.2	95.3
1% real interest	77.9	88.1	91.8	93.5
2% real interest	68.2	81.8	87.8	90.8
3% real interest	55.7	72.6	81.2	86.2
3% real earnings growth				
0% real interest	88.6	93.3	94.9	95.7
1% real interest	83.7	90.8	93.1	94.2
2% real interest	76.4	86.8	90.3	92.0
3% real interest	66.8	80.2	86.2	90.0

Note: a Simulations are for men and women full-time students in advanced further and higher education.

Source: Barr and Falkingham (1996, Table 2A).

leads to further improvement: with 3% earnings growth, men could pay a real interest rate of 3% and still repay 92% of total borrowing. There are two reasons for this excellent performance: students in further education generally spend longer in the labour force than graduates; and income-contingent arrangements are able to collect at least some repayments from relatively low earners.

Sensitivity analysis

The fraction of total lending which is repaid is the variable of greatest interest for funding purposes. Table 9.1 investigated the repayment performance of an add-on to NICs of 1 penny in the pound per £3,000 borrowed. Table 9.2 repeats the simulations in the first column of Table 9.1 for add-ons of 1.5, 2 and 2.5 pence per £3,000 borrowed (more detailed results are given in Barr and Falkingham, 1996, Tables 2A, 2B and 2C).

In principle, raising repayment rates has two effects: it speeds up repayment and it may increase the fraction of total borrowing which is repaid. The relative importance of the two effects is an empirical matter. A higher repayment rate will always speed up repayment; it does not necessarily increase the fraction of total borrowing which is repaid. To illustrate, assume that there are two sorts of graduate: those who go straight into high-earning, stable employment and those who never find a job of any sort. If that is the case, higher repayment rates do nothing to increase total repayments; they merely lead to a faster repayment stream.

Starting with the benchmark case (zero earnings growth and zero real interest rate), increasing the repayment rate has a dramatic effect on the fraction of student borrowing which is repaid. The first line of Table 9.2 shows the benchmark case for men and women together. An add-on of 1 penny in the pound to NICs leads to repayment of 79% of total borrowing. This rises to 89% at 1.5 pence, to 93% at 2 pence and to nearly 95% at 2.5 pence.

Looking at men and women separately (Barr and Falkingham, 1996, Tables 2B and 2C), the fraction of total lending repaid by men in the benchmark case increases significantly, from 90% with a 1 penny add-on, to 95% at 1.5 pence, to 97% at 2.5 pence. Higher repayment rates for women have an even more dramatic effect, increasing the fraction of total lending which is repaid from 65% for a repayment rate of 1 penny, to 81% at 1.5 pence, to 91% at 2.5 pence.

Earnings growth, as expected, sharply improves results. With 1.5% earnings growth and a 2% real interest rate, the fraction of total lending repaid by men and women together (the middle section of Table 9.2) rises from 68% at 1 penny, to 82% at 1.5 pence, to over 90% at 2.5 pence. Similarly, with 3% earnings growth, where graduates pay a 3% real interest rate on their loans, 67% of total borrowing is repaid with a 1 penny repayment rate, rising to 80% at 1.5 pence, to 86% at 2 pence and to 90% at 2.5 pence.

The different pattern of results for men and women, although not shown in Table 9.2 (see Barr and Falkingham, 1996, Tables 2B and 2C), is revealing. Looking at the example in the previous paragraph of 3% real earnings growth and a 3% real interest rate, the fraction of total lending repaid by men increases from 85% of total lending for a 1 penny add-on to 92% at 1.5 pence. With positive earnings growth, increasing repayment rates above 1.5 pence speeds repayment but, in the case of men, does not greatly increase the fraction of total borrowing which is repaid. For women, in contrast, the fraction of total lending which is repaid rises steadily with the repayment rate, from 49% with 3% earnings growth, a 3% real interest rate and a repayment rate of 1 penny, to 68% with a repayment rate of 1.5 pence, to 78% at 2 pence and to 83% with a repayment rate of 2.5 pence.

Interpreting the results

What fraction of total borrowing will be repaid? Higher add-ons bring in more repayments more quickly. However, they also increase the risk of work disincentives. The discussion which follows is therefore based on two assumptions: that the repayment rate is 1.5 pence per unit of borrowing; and that the government, as in other areas, rightly insists that men and women are treated as a single pool.

Thus, the relevant figures are those in the second column of Table 2: if the real earnings of graduates rise by 3% per year and students pay a 3% real interest rate, an add-on to NICs of 1.5 pence will generate a repayment stream which ends up repaying 80% of total lending to students, i.e. £1 billion of student debt could be sold for £800 million. Repayment would be similar with an increase in real earnings of only 1.5% and a real interest rate of 2%.

These results, although fairly robust, should not be invested with spurious precision. As described at the start of the section, LIFEMOD, from which the numbers derive, is based on 1985 data. Although marriage and fertility patterns have not changed significantly since then, labour market conditions have. Thus, the results just described do not automatically apply today. Detailed, up-to-date estimates of repayment rates are needed.[12]

The intuition of income-contingent repayments requires discussion because it differs significantly from that of mortgage-type loans. In 1985 terms, a 1.5 pence add-on repays a total loan of £3,000. Anticipating later discussion, translation into today's terms means that an add-on of 2.3 pence can repay a loan of £10,000 at 1995 prices. At first sight, this repayment rate appears too low to repay a loan of this size. Consider a new graduate earning £16,000 per year (broadly the national average) and paying an interest rate of 6% (3% superimposed on an inflation rate of 3%). The first year's interest charge is 6% of £10,000, i.e. £600; but the loan repayment, 2.3% of £16,000, is only £368. Thus, her repayment does not cover the interest liability, and the nominal debt increases.

This result is entirely characteristic of income-contingent repayments. With mortgage-type loans, the annual repayment is fixed. As earnings rise, repayments therefore fall as a fraction of earnings – mortgage repayments are front loaded. With income-contingent loans, in contrast, what is fixed is not the amount of annual repayment, but the fraction of income which is repaid. As real earnings rise so, therefore, do repayments. Income-contingent repayments are end loaded, with heavy repayments in later years. A typical pattern, therefore, is for nominal debt to rise in the early years of repayment, then to start to fall and to fall very rapidly in the final years of the loan.

Figure 9.1 illustrates the time path of the two methods of repayment, assuming an initial loan of £1,000, income-contingent repayments of 0.23 pence per pound of earnings, a starting salary of £16,000, inflation of 3% per year and real earnings growth of 3%. In the early years of the loan, income-contingent repayments (dotted line) fail to cover interest charges and nominal debt rises. As real earnings rise, however, so do real repayments; the steep slope of the dotted line shows the speed with which the loan is extinguished in the later years of repayment. The loan is repaid in year 28. For comparison, the darker line shows the time path of mortgage repayments designed to repay the same loan over the same period.

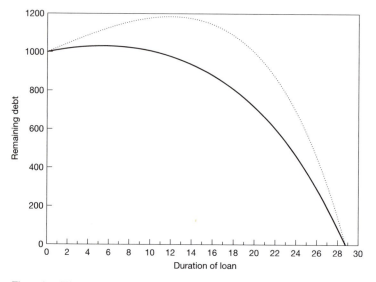

Figure 9.1 The trajectory of loan repayments; income-contingent (- - -) and
         mortgage-type loans (——)

Being front loaded, repayments are larger in the early years and smaller
in the later years.

More radical options

The heavy repayments in later years under income-contingent arrangements opens up the possibility of more radical options for pushing
repayment rates closer to 100%.

First, one way to increase total repayments is to 'switch off' repayments
with a lag of, say, 3 years. Since income-contingent loans have an end-
loaded repayment trajectory, additional years of repayment significantly
increase the total amount paid (Barr, 1989, Appendix 2). This arrangement need not violate the integrity of the scheme as a genuine loan. A
person who borrows to buy a house repays only what they borrowed;
many lenders, however, make mortgage protection insurance obligatory.
Student loans, similarly, could have a repayment component and an
insurance component.

An even simpler way to cover a 20% shortfall is for each student
borrower to agree to repay 125% of what they had borrowed. The cohort
of students would thus mutually insure each other.

Another way to improve the performance of the loan scheme is through
targeted interest subsidies. A case can be made for using general revenues
to make real interest repayments (although not repayment of principal)
on behalf of people caring for young children and for people who are
unemployed, thus 'stopping the clock' on the real value of the debt.

Abolishing the upper earnings limit for NICs, at least for loan repayments, is another way to speed repayment. It would also (although the matter is empirical) probably increase the fraction of total borrowing repaid.

The impact on public spending

Under present arrangements, the maintenance grant and loan are both entirely publicly funded, expenditure currently running at around £2 billion per year. The scheme set out above would reduce this figure very substantially.

If loans covered the entire maintenance package and the debt was sold for 80% of its face value, there would be an instant saving of over £1.5 billion per year.

The SLC currently has an accumulated stock of about £3 billion of loans made under the current system. If these were sold, there would be an additional – albeit once-and-for-all – saving of about £2.4 billion (i.e. 80% of £3 billion). Saving on this scale, however, depends on graduates transferring to the new repayment mechanism. This is plausible. Most graduates would actively prefer to repay through the tax/national insurance system, so holders of loans issued under the current system could readily be persuaded to switch to this type of repayment. If incentives are needed, there are good ways of persuading holders of old loans to transfer: there could be a small rebate to those who converted; there could be an amnesty to defaulters who agreed to repay their old loan through the IC mechanism; and, in the case of students with an old loan who become students again, a condition for a new loan could be to convert the old loan to the new repayment mechanism.

The scale of debt sale could be higher. If all maintenance grants plus parental contributions were replaced by loans (i.e. if students were allowed to borrow an amount equal to grant plus parental contribution plus loan), expenditure on student support would rise from £2 billion to over £2.5 billion. Some £2 billion of this could come from private sources. Thus, the parental/spouse contribution could be abolished, and there would still be a large annual saving in public spending.

The real value of the grant fell by about 25% between the early 1960s and the mid-1980s. If the student support package was increased to allow students to borrow an amount whose real value approximated the early 1960s grant plus parental contributions, the total package would increase from £2.5 billion to around £3.1 billion. If the debt was sold at 80% of its value, the Treasury share would be around £625 million. Students could, if they wished, increase their living standards to those of students in the 1960s without resorting to compulsory parental contributions, at a saving in public spending, compared with present arrangements, of over £1 billion per year.

Table 9.3 Repayment rates for loans of different sizes

Borrowing		Repayment add-on to NICs per pound of earnings[a]	
Loan per year	Total loan	1 penny regime	1.5 pence regime
Undergraduate degrees			
1 £2000	£6000	0.92	1.38
2 £4000	£12000	1.84	2.76
3 £5000	£15000	2.30	3.45
4 £6000	£18000	2.76	4.14
5 £9000	£27000	4.14	6.21
1-year Master's degree			
6 £12000	£12000	1.84	2.76

Note: a In comparison with an add-on of 1 penny per pound of earnings, an add-on of 1.5 pence has the dual effect of accelerating repayments and increasing the fraction of total borrowing which is repaid. See the discussion on pp. 155–6.

Alongside more generous loans, it would be desirable to extend loans to larger numbers of borrowers – to part-time students, postgraduate students and students undergoing vocational training, or to cover any further increase in student numbers. Further expansion would be possible to cover innovative educational ideas.

Outcomes 2: The impact on students and universities

Repayments from the perspective of students

Earlier discussion used a benchmark loan in 1985 of £1,000 per year of study (roughly half of the 1985 grant), repaid by an add-on to NICs of 1 penny in the pound. Table 9.3 translates these figures into 1995 terms. Since repayments are directly related to a person's earnings, the relevant adjustment factor is the increase in nominal earnings. The earnings index for non-manual workers rose from 100 to 217.3 between 1985 and 1995. Thus, in 1995 terms, a loan of £2183 per year, or just over £6500 for a 3-year degree, could be repaid by:

- an add-on to NICs of 1 penny in the pound using the data in Table 9.1; in this case, each £1,000 (in today's prices) borrowed could be repaid by an add-on of just over 0.15 pence in the pound;
- an add-on of 1.5 pence using the data in the second column of Table 9.2; in this case, each £1,000 borrowed could be repaid by an add-on of just below 0.23 pence in the pound.

Starting with undergraduate degrees, Table 9.3 gives some examples, based on the latter figure. Thus, students repay their loan with an add-on of 0.23 pence per £1,000 of borrowing.

- A loan of £2,000 per year (roughly half the current London mainten-ance grant), hence £6,000 over 3 years, paying a 3% real interest rate, can be repaid through an add-on to NICs of about 1.4 pence in the pound (line 1).[13]
- A loan of £4,000, roughly the full London maintenance grant, leading to a total loan of £12,000, could be repaid through an add-on of 2.75 pence in the pound (line 2).
- If the support package were increased by 25% to restore the erosion since the early 1960s, students would have about £5,000 per year to live on, repaid by an add-on of about 3.5 pence (line 3).
- If, in addition, students paid fees of £1,000 per year, leading to an annual loan of £6,000, the add-on would be just over 4 pence (line 4).
- A student doing a 4-year degree outside London, borrowing £4,000 per year for maintenance and £500 per year for fees, would take out a total loan of £18,000, repaid by an add-on of just over 4 pence (line 4).
- A student doing a 3-year degree at an internationally competitive insti-tution in London might borrow £5,000 per year for maintenance plus £4,000 per year for fees. The total loan of £27,000 could be repaid by an add-on of 6.2 pence (line 5).

Loans could be made available on the same terms to graduate students.

- If students doing a 1-year Master's degree paid fees of £7,000 and bor-rowed £5,000 for maintenance, the add-on would be 2.75 pence (line 6).
- A student doing a 3-year degree outside London, borrowing £4,000 per year for maintenance, and then doing a 1-year Master's degree would borrow a total of £24,000, repaid by an add-on of 5.5 pence (lines 2 + 6).
- An identical student, doing a degree in London and paying under-graduate fees of £1,000 per year and then proceeding to a Master's degree, could repay with an add-on of 6.9 pence (lines 4 + 6).

Thus, an add-on to NICs of 4 pence in the pound would cover all but the most expensive undergraduate degrees. Those borrowing less would repay faster. To allow flexibility, an alternative approach is through an add-on of 3 pence in the pound for students whose total borrowing was below, say, £12,000 and 6 pence in the pound where total borrowing was between £12,000 and £24,000 with, possibly, a 7.5 pence add-on for larger loans. Since loans pay a market interest rate and repayments cease once the loan has been repaid, the larger add-on has no major equity implications. This is not a trivial point. If interest rates are subsidized, any change which speeds repayment is equivalent to reducing the subsidy, raising potential equity issues and political problems. Unsubsidized interest rates avoid both problems. They also give graduates no artificial incentive to defer repayments.

The figures in Table 9.3 can be applied to other options. It has been suggested, for example, that all students would receive 2 years of free tuition (i.e. there should be no additional fees for the first 2 years), but that thereafter they should receive no additional public support.

Consider a student outside London, who takes out a loan to cover maintenance of £4,000 per year for 3 years plus an additional £5,000 to cover fees in the third year. The total loan of £17,000 could be repaid by an add-on of 3.9 pence.[14]

An identical student doing a degree in London would take out a loan of £5,000 per year for 3 years plus an additional, say, £7,000 to study at an internationally competitive institution, borrowing a total of £22,000, which could be repaid by an add-on of just over 5 pence.

Potential effects on university income: the great unknown

The basic arithmetic is simple. If there are 1 million students, an average additional fee of £1,000 per student per year generates a gross increase in university income of £1 billion.

Simplicity, however, ends there, since increases in fee income from students may, to a greater or lesser extent, be offset by reductions in public funding for universities. At its worst, taxpayer support could be reduced by £1 million for each £1 million in fee income. Thus, the effect on university income of introducing student fees is unknown and unknowable.

What can be said, however, is that many, if not all, universities have no choice. Public funding will never cover the costs of the internationally competitive institutions. Realistically, it is unlikely that it will cover the costs of universities with above-average quality and above-average costs. These institutions, if no others, will be compelled – eventually, if not immediately – to charge additional fees.

More generally, the price of not charging fees is to continue to be under-funded, with no possibility of restoring quality. British universities would become like many continental universities. The realistic choice is not between adequate public funding and the uncertainties of the market-place. With a mass system, the only choice is between inadequate public funding, on the one hand, and a chance to supplement public funding with private earnings on the other.

The way ahead

Areas for more detailed work

Although the policy design is fairly complete, a number of details need to be established, for example the maximum amount a student is allowed to borrow (a) in any one year and (b) in total.

The discussion of mechanics – much of it based on contact with administrative and financial practitioners – was intended to establish the administrative and financial feasibility of the scheme. The next step is detailed work in both areas.

On the administrative side, the SLC, which has already given thought to future possibilities, and the tax and national insurance authorities need to discuss the most cost-effective way of administering the scheme, basing cost estimates on the marginal cost of additional activities.[15]

Making the scheme operational on the financial side involves the right steps in the right order. If resources are to come from the private sector, financial institutions must be involved in discussion of all relevant aspects of the scheme prior to legislation.[16]

- It is necessary, first, to establish the criteria required by international statistical conventions on the divide between public and private expenditure. For that reason, the Office for National Statistics and, also, the Treasury must be involved.
- The detailed mechanics of the way in which students borrow from private lenders or in which student debt is sold require discussion by all interested parties.
- Work is needed on the level of the interest rate paid by students, and on whether it would be fixed in nominal terms (like government bonds), fixed in real terms (like indexed gifts) or variable (like mortgages).
- The details of targeted interest subsidies need to be worked out.
- Additional estimates are needed for the fraction of total student borrowing which is likely to be repaid.

Priorities and sequencing

Now that Dearing has reported and the government responded (for a critique, see Barr and Crawford, 1997, 1998), the desired sequencing of events is clear.

Two elements of the Dearing Report (National Committee of Inquiry into Higher Education, 1997a,b) are central. The government has accepted Recommendation 78, endorsing full income contingency; having argued for this for 10 years, we welcome the decision most warmly. Recommendation 80 argues forcibly that the treatment of student loans in the public accounts needs to be modernized. Action on this recommendation is imperative and should be immediate.

On fees (recommendation 79), Dearing is more circumspect, suggesting as the Committee's preferred option, a flat-rate fee of £1,000 per student per year. The government has announced that the fee will be income tested so that students from poorer backgrounds do not pay.

Flat fees may be correct as an interim measure. In the medium term, we are convinced, a large and diverse system of higher education will inevitably require fee differentials across universities. If the government can find adequate resources, however, variable fees can be postponed for a few years. This would be desirable. In an ideal world, differential fees should be introduced after the new income-contingent loan scheme has been properly run in and is fully understood. Change can thus be incremental – much better than forcing universities to introduce top-up fees as an emergency measure.

Political aspects

One of the reasons why the Dearing Committee was established was the political sensitivity of higher education finance. Yet, if the nettle is grasped, the politics of student loans need not be the source of political terror they have become. If loans are properly structured, there will be few people who experience loss but no gain. Four groups are particularly relevant: students, parents, the taxpayer and universities.

Starting with students, there is only one group of unambiguous losers: those students who would have found a place at university even in the old, élite days. Instead of receiving a generous tax-funded grant, they now have to take out loans. For other students, the balance of gains and losses under the IC scheme proposed above is more complex.

- They lose relative to perceptions of a long-gone grant system.
- They also lose in that they, generally, have to take out a larger loan than under the post-1990 arrangements. There are, however, offsetting factors: repayment is exactly tailored to the individual graduate's earnings; repayment is spread over more years than under the 1990 scheme; and even the highest-earning graduates receive protection, since the upper earnings limit for NICs imposes a ceiling on annual repayments.
- The great bulk of students gain because they can obtain a place at university in the first place. Under the old system, although, in principle, eligible for generous grants, they would mostly not have found a university place. If we were to return to the participation rates of the early 1960s, nearly five-sixths of current university students would have to be asked to leave.
- Students also benefit because they gain access to their future earnings and are therefore no longer compelled, via the parental contribution, to depend on family support. Parents who wish to help their children can do so; and children who are prepared to accept parental assistance can take out a smaller loan. The same is true for spouse contributions.
- Students also gain, if the scheme is properly structured, because they can have a higher living standard than they do currently.
- Those who gain also include students just above the 85% threshold, whose payments, being exactly related to their income, are lower under the IC scheme than under present arrangements.

Parents gain unambiguously. They are no longer subject to a means test; and the abolition of parental contributions, coupled with a non-penal loan system, leaves a neutral choice for families about whether, how much and in what form, parents assist their children. They retain the freedom to do so as much as at present, but are no longer under moral pressure to do so, greatly reducing parental guilt trips.

The taxpayer benefits, provided student debt can, at least partly, be derived from private sources. Taxes can be cut or the savings used for other purposes, for example, addressing critical problems elsewhere in the education sector.

A central part of the politics of universities is the pent-up demand for pay increases, estimated by the Committee of Vice-Chancellors and Principals to be £1.2 billion in 1995/96. Alongside the need for internationally competitive institutions to pay internationally competitive salaries, is the more general need to maintain overall quality in the university sector. A co-equal source of discontent is the concern of university staff about protecting and enhancing the quality of higher education. Reform of the type described is the only way to free the resources to deal with these problems.

In short, most students benefit, parents benefit, taxpayers benefit and universities benefit.

Concluding thoughts

In principle, there are three avenues for higher education:

* to return to an élite system;
* to continue to be underfunded, becoming more and more like continental universities;
* to introduce an effective system of loans, which allows universities to move towards a régime with variable fees.

In practice, however, there is no choice, because the first two options are not viable. By 1989, higher education funding in Britain was already stretched with a 14% participation rate – the lowest in the developed world. Global competition requires an increasing fraction of the labour force to be increasingly well trained in broad, flexible skills. Labour market trends increasingly show the bleak employment prospects of those with little education. A return to an élite system is both unthinkable economically and impossible politically.

Continued underfunding of a mass system, similarly, puts national competitiveness at risk. Furthermore, with the large number of overseas students studying in Britain, higher education is one of the country's most successful export industries. Underfunding undermines both the direct exports and the subsequent, more wide-ranging exports which result indirectly.

The Asian 'tigers', it should be noted, do not aspire to the Continental model and, not least because of their geographical proximity, the Australians were among the first to recognize the need to put more resources into their system of higher education.

The third option is the only one remaining. There really is no choice.

Acknowledgements

Financial support from the Nuffield Foundation is gratefully acknowledged. This paper draws heavily on joint work with Jane Falkingham. The original idea of using national insurance contributions as a springboard for the organization of student loans came from Mervyn King. Many London School of Economics colleagues have contributed to this work over the past 10 years, including John Barnes, Meghnad Desai, Howard Glennerster, Richard Jackman, David Webb and Gail Wilson. Others who have helped include Gill Barr, Mark Blaug and Jeremy Green. Alan Thomson, formerly of the Department of Social Security, provided helpful comments on factual matters, as did Cohn Ward and his team at the Student Loans Company. The views expressed, and remaining errors and infelicities, are our responsibility.

Notes

1 Real funding per student fell by nearly 30% between 1990 and 1995 (CVCP, 1996, p. 4).
2 The employee NIC is zero for earnings below the lower earnings limit (£62 per week in 1997/98); for earnings above £62, the contribution is £1.24 (i.e. 2% of £62) plus 10% of earnings between £62 and the upper earnings limit (£465 per week in 1997/98).
3 The point is critical. Two objectives of any well-designed loan scheme are (a) to maintain access while (b) producing a high repayment stream. If (b) is enforced through a deterrent such as debt collectors arriving at midnight, or frequent, highly publicized court cases, there is a direct conflict with (a). The only way to square the circle is through a scheme with a repayment mechanism sufficiently watertight so as not to require a deterrent. The tax/national insurance mechanism does exactly that.
4 According to the most recent figures, 62% of graduates defer in the first year in which repayment is due. The figures for all graduates is 47% (see Student Loans Company, 1996).
5 The resulting savings in SLC administrative costs include the fact that there will be no annual requests for deferment (since it is automatic); no need for the student to declare income to the SLC; no follow up action on graduates working but failing to make payments; and no need to consider any write-off – the debt will remain until the student retires.
6 The arguments against compulsory reliance on parental and spouse contributions are set out in Barr and Crawford (1997, Appendix 3).
7 That, nevertheless, is what the government has done in its response to the report of the Dearing Committee. For a detailed critique of the Dearing recommendations and governments' response, see Barr and Crawford (1997, 1998).

8 All current national insurance numbers have a suffix A, B, C or D. Although no longer used for their original purpose (to stagger the issuing of new national insurance cards across the four quarters of the year), they have been retained. The suffix E (for education) would distinguish graduates with outstanding loans from other payers of NICs. If more than one additional rate of withholding were needed, suffixes E, F and G could be used.

9 For technical reasons, the SLC might not sell the debt itself, but could enter into a contract to sell the loan agreements to a special purpose vehicle established for the sole purpose of raising the finance. The SLC would transfer to the special purpose vehicle the loans and the entitlement to collect repayments.

10 As an alternative to a straight government guarantee, the SLC could be established as a government agency. The SLC could then guarantee the first 20% in its own capacity, but with the benefit of a Crown covenant. This route has been followed very successfully in the US.

11 LIFEMOD is a policy simulation model which makes it possible to test social policy options and look at their financial consequences over the life cycle. The model comprises 4,000 imaginary people for whom complete life histories have been simulated. The likelihood of any event occurring to an individual at any given age – such as their education choices, labour market activity, patterns of family formation and dissolution – is based on the actual probabilities, taking account of age, sex and other distinguishing characteristics, for the population in 1985. This gives a dynamic but compliant population who can be run endlessly through the computer, taxing them, paying them benefits and looking at the lifetime effects of this. It is not yet possible to look at second-order behavioural changes, e.g. of taxation on work behaviour. For further details, see Falkingham and Lessof (1991, 1992) and Glennerster *et al.* (1995).

12 Unfortunately, updating LIFEMOD is not a short-term option because of the amount of work which would be involved (the original model took 4 person-years to build).

13 Since each £1,000 can be repaid by an add-on of 0.23 pence, £6,000 is repaid by an add-on of 6 × 0.23 pence, i.e. 1.38 pence.

14 Since the graduate can repay £1,000 with an add-on of 0.23 pence, a loan of £17,000 can be repaid by an add-on of 17 × 0.23 pence = 3.91 pence.

15 In the past, the civil service convention for costing activities has been to cost them as a freestanding activity (i.e. to base estimates on total cost) rather than in terms of marginal cost. The cost to the Inland Revenue or Contributions Agency of the proposals here is the extra cost of additional activities given that they are already collecting income tax or NICs.

16 The several failures of past governments to reach agreement with financial institutions about student loans prior to major policy announcements are object lessons about how not to proceed.

References

Barnes, J. and N. Barr (1988) *Strategies for Higher Education: The Alternative White Paper* (Edinburgh, Aberdeen University Press for the David Hume Institute, and London, Suntory-Toyota International Centre for Economics and Related Disciplines, London School of Economics).

Barr, N. (1989) *Student Loans: The Next Steps* (Edinburgh, Aberdeen University Press for the David Hume Institute, and London, Suntory-Toyota International Centre for Economics and Related Disciplines, London School of Economics).

Barr, N. (1993) Alternative funding resources for higher education, *Economic Journal*, 103, pp. 718–728 [this volume, Ch. 7].

Barr, N. (1997) Student loans: towards a new public/private mix, *Public Money and Managementt*, 17, pp. 31–40.

Barr, N. (1998) *The Economics of the Welfare State*, 3rd Edn (Oxford, Oxford University Press, and Stanford, Stanford University Press).

Barr, N. and Crawford, I. (1996) Student loans: where are we now?, Welfare State Programme, *Discussion Paper WSP/127* (London, London School of Economics).

Barr, N. and Crawford, I. (1997) 'The Dearing Report, the Government's response and a view ahead', in *Third Report: The Dearing Report: Some Funding Issues*, vol. II, Minutes of Evidence and Appendices, House of Commons Education and Employment Committee, session 1977–8, HC241-II (TSO, 1997), pp. 88–103.

Barr, N. and Crawford, I. (1998) 'The Dearing Report and government response: a critique', *Political Quarterly*, 69, pp. 72–84 [this volume, Ch. 10].

Barr, N. and Falkingham, J. (1993) Paying for learning, Welfare State Programme, *Discussion Paper WSP/94* (London, London School of Economics).

Barr, N. and Falkingham, J. (1996) Repayment rates for student loans: some sensitivity tests, Welfare State Programme, *Discussion Paper WSP/127* (London, London School of Economics).

Barr, N. and Low, W. (1988) Student grants and student poverty, Welfare State Programme, *Discussion Paper No. WSP/28* (London, London School of Economics).

Chapman, B. (1997) Conceptual issues and the Australian experience with income-contingent charges for higher education, *Economic Journal*, 107, pp. 738–751.

CVCP (1996) *Our Universities, Our Future: Part 4: The Case for a New Funding System – Special Report*, The CVCP's evidence to the National Committee of Inquiry into Higher Education (London, Committee of Vice-Chancellors and Principals).

Falkingham, J. and Lessof, C. (1991) LIFEMOD – the formative years, Welfare State Programme, *Research Note No. 24* (London, London School of Economics).

Falkingham, J. and Lessof, C. (1992) 'Playing God – the construction of a dynamic microsimulation model', in: Hancock, R. and Sutherland, H. (Eds) *Microsimulation Models for Public Policy Analysis: New Frontiers* (London, London School of Economics).

Further Education Funding Council (1997) *Learning Works: Widening Participation in Further Education* (the Kennedy Report) (Coventry, Further Education Funding Council).

Glennerster, H., Falkingham, J. and Barr, N. (1995) Education funding, equity and the life cycle, in: Falkingham, J. and Hills, J. (Eds) *The Dynamic of Welfare: The Welfare Stare and the Life Cycle*, pp. 137–149 (Hemel Hempstead, Prentice-Hall /Harvester Wheatsheaf).

Harding, A. (1993) Lifetime repayment patterns for HECS and Austudy loans, *Discussion Paper No. 1* (Canberra, National Centre for Social and Economic Modelling, University of Canberra).

National Committee of Inquiry into Higher Education (the Dearing Committee) (1997a) *Higher Education in the Learning Society: Summary Report* (London, HMSO) (also available at http://www.leeds.ac.uk/educol/ncihe).

National Committee of Inquiry into Higher Education (the Dearing Committee) (1997b) *Higher Education in the Learning Society: Report of the National Committee* (London, HMSO) (also available at http://www.leeds.ac.uk/educol/ncihe).

National Education Commission (1993) *Learning to Succeed*, Paul Hamlyn Foundation National Commission on Education (London, Heinemann).

Student Loans Company (1996) *Annual Report 1996* (Glasgow, Student Loans Company).

Chapter 10

1998 The Dearing Report and the Government's response: a critique

Nicholas Barr and Iain Crawford (1998), 'The Dearing Report and the Government's Response: A Critique', *Political Quarterly*, Vol. 69, No. 1, January–March 1998, pp. 72–84.

The central fact of British higher education is the increase in the participation rate from an elite 5 per cent in the early 1960s to a mass 30 per cent by the mid-1990s. Recent expansion has been particularly sharp – from 14 per cent in 1990 – but has occurred without any parallel increase in funding, leading to problems which are both economic and political.

There are three sets of economic problems. First, universities are poor. Student numbers in Britain almost doubled between 1990 and 1996. Real funding per student fell by nearly 30 per cent.[1]

Second, students are poor. There is widespread agreement that students need about 20 per cent more to cover their living costs than is available from the current mix of grant, parental contribution and loan. To make, matters worse, many students do not receive even that inadequate amount. Studies show that in the early 1980s about half the students entitled to a parental contribution received less than the assessed amount, and the shortfall was substantial; on average, those students whose parents gave them less than the grant system supposed received only £53 of every £100 of assessed parental contribution.[2]

Third, the top-up loan scheme introduced in 1990 has major design deficiencies which were predictable, predicted[3] and wholly accepted by Sir Ron Dearing. Its central problems are twofold: it organises repayments like a mortgage, rather than making them contingent on income (whereby a person pays x per cent of income until he or she has paid off the loan); and it saves the taxpayer little, if anything.

The political problems are in many ways a consequence of the economic problems. The major debate is over whether students should pay fees. There is an emerging international consensus that they should, but *only* if any such fee contributions are supported by income-contingent loans: that is, there should be no up-front charges. Even more contentious is whether different universities should be able to charge different fees. The issue has a major economic dimension (discussed below), but it is also political and cultural.

In the face of these problems, a National Committee of Inquiry into Higher Education (the Dearing Committee) was established in 1996 with a broad remit and instructions to report in summer 1997, thus ensuring that higher education finance was off the election agenda.

Notwithstanding its breadth, the key parts of the report concerned funding, and it is on these parts that this article concentrates. It is funding which is at the core of the current crisis; and it is the funding regime which establishes the foundation on which higher education will grow and adapt. The next section of the article reviews the objectives of higher education funding. The two sections which follow describe and assess the key Dearing recommendations on funding and the government's initial response. The concluding section sketches out a way ahead.

Objectives

Expansion of higher education on the scale noted above has major (and obvious) implications. Public funding of a high-quality system is possible for a 5 per cent system; it is not possible for a mass system. Thus a mass system requires public funding to be supplemented on a significant scale by private funding.

Private funds can derive from four potential sources: family resources, student earnings while a student, employers and students' future earnings. The first three provide only partial answers. Excessive reliance on family resources is inequitable;[4] and earning activities while a student compete with study time and leisure. Employer contributions, though worth reassessment, cannot be pushed too far without becoming a tax on graduate employment. In a mass system, therefore, the only source of funding which is large and not grossly inequitable is an arrangement which allows students to borrow against their future earnings.

Two core objectives follow directly. What is needed is a financing mechanism which:

- *Improves access* – an objective about which Dearing is passionate. It is well known that this means a loan system which does not deter applicants; but also – and less explicitly recognised – it means that students should have an adequate standard of living while students.
- *Makes more resources available,* so as to restore quality and continue expansion, and to finance the actions necessary to improve access. Since these resources cannot be public, they must be private.

Both the Dearing Report and the Government's response should be judged by the extent to which they achieve these objectives.

Dearing's key recommendations

The report contains a summary and a main report,[5] a report of the Scottish Committee, five appendices and fourteen supplementary reports, also available on a website (http://www.leeds.ac.uk/educol/ncihe) and on CD-ROM. Coverage includes higher education systems in other countries (appendix 5); widening participation by ethnic minorities, women and alternative students (report 5), and by students from lower social classes and students with disabilities (report 6); a DfEE [Department for Education and Employment] submission on real rates of return to higher education (report 7); externalities and higher education, a review of the new growth literature (report 8); the development of a framework of qualifications in relation to continental Europe (report 11); modelling funding options (report 12); and individual learning accounts and a learning bank (report 13).

The report's ninety-three recommendations (listed in the summary report, pp. 42–54, and main report, pp. 370–82) are commensurately wide-ranging. It can, however, be argued that three elements were central: quality, access and funding.

A whole series of recommendations concerned the quality of teaching and facilities. Recommendation 14 states that 'the representative bodies . . . should immediately establish a professional Institute for Learning and Teaching in Higher Education'. Recommendations 23–6 strengthen the powers and broaden the remit of the Quality Assurance Agency.

The emphasis on access is shown by the three reports (5, 6 and 13) which concern the issue. Specific recommendations include 'pilot projects allocating additional funds to institutions which enrol students from particularly disadvantaged backgrounds' (recommendation 4). As discussed below, the committee also advocated retaining the maintenance grant explicitly for reasons of access.

We shall be critical both of the Dearing recommendations on funding and of the Secretary of State's response. However, both sets of recommendations are shaped by a binding assumption that there will be few, if any, extra resources for higher education in the short run. As discussed below, a key constraint is the way the Treasury classifies student debt in the national accounts (the subject of recommendation 80). We assume that, in compiling the report, the Dearing Committee felt it would be unsafe to expect an immediate change in public accounting practice, not least because resolution of that problem lies outside the power of the committee's sponsoring department. We firmly believe that if the committee had felt able to relax that assumption, the shape of its recommendations would have been significantly different.

Most of the rest of this article is about funding. In view of this focus, it is worth emphasising here the breadth of the issues addressed by the report, as reflected in the following recommendations:

- A series of recommendations (54–60) relate to the governance of institutions.
- On the births and deaths of universities, recommendation 64 establishes powers for 'the removal of degree-awarding powers where the Quality Assurance Agency demonstrates that the power to award degrees has been seriously abused', and recommendation 66 calls for 'greater clarity about where responsibility lies for decisions about the establishment of new universities'.
- Recommendation 67 seeks the integration of further and higher education into a seamless whole.
- Recommendation 88 suggests another review of higher education in five years' time, and ten-yearly reviews thereafter.

The rest of this section discusses in turn (a) those recommendations which are emphatically right, and (b) those which are potentially problematical. In the first category, two of Dearing's recommendations – 78 and 80 – are utterly essential and stand out as by far the most important in the report. The former asserts the central role of income contingency, stating: 'We recommend to the Government that it introduces, by 1998/99, income contingent terms for the payment of any contribution towards living costs or tuition costs sought from graduates in work.' This recommendation represents an essential reform of the present mortgage-type loan scheme. Full income contingency means that people make repayments of (say) 3 per cent of their weekly or monthly income. Income contingency is central to achieving the access objective, as Australian experience amply demonstrates.[6] It does so because it is rooted in ability to pay: it tailors repayments week by week to what people can afford, thus protecting individuals from risk. It means that those who can afford to repay do so, and those who cannot are protected from debt.[7]

The second critical issue is the classification problem. The Treasury currently takes the view that *all* student loans count as public expenditure just as if they were grants, taking no account of the fact that a large fraction of the sum disbursed will be repaid. Thus student loans bring in little extra money until the system is mature.[8] The report rightly stresses that it is vital to solve this problem-and does so in remarkably strong language: 'We have noted that the UK adopts a broader definition of PSBR [Public Sector Borrowing Requirement] than a number of other countries and a broader one than it is required to adopt under the Maastricht criteria' (para. 20.89); 'We see no merit in the present practice of treating loans in the same way as grants. It misleads rather than informs' (para. 20.90).

The Treasury takes this view even if student debt is sold to the private sector. Here, the report argues (para. 20.97) that 'to classify loans as public expenditure because the repayments are collected on an agency basis through the Inland Revenue, even though much of the risk of non-payment is borne by the private sector owners of the repayment rights, seems to be at variance with the substance of the matter' (para. 20.97). Thus recommendation 80 states: 'We recommend to the Government that it looks urgently at alternative and internationally accepted approaches to national accounting which do not treat the repayable part of loans in the same way as grants to students.'

Any change must satisfy a range of IMF and EU criteria. There are two potential ways forward:

- Continue with publicly funded loans, but adjust the way in which they enter the public accounts. This approach can be implemented rapidly and in ways compatible with international statistical criteria. Australia has just such an adjustment.[9]
- Sell student debt to the private sector so as to bring in private funding.

The report is spot-on in saying that this problem needs to be fixed, and fixed fast. If not resolved, it is terminal. It is true that loans will bring in additional resources from around 2020 – but you cannot revive a corpse. Resolution, in contrast, will release a 'pot of gold' of over £1 billion, *immediately* and *every year*.[10]

Turning to the more problematical recommendations, the report's preferred funding option (Option B in Table 2.2 of the report; see also Table 10.1 below) has three elements:

(a) 50 per cent of student living costs from an income-contingent loan;
(b) 50 per cent of living costs from a mixture of grant and parental contribution;
(c) a tuition contribution of 25 per cent of average tuition costs.

Of these, (a) has already been widely welcomed; (b) and (c) require discussion.

The Dearing Report argued for the retention of the grant because it is targeted on the poorest students. There are several counterarguments.

First, retaining grants wastes a ready-made political consensus. The principle of income-contingent loans to cover all living costs was endorsed in submissions to Dearing by the CVCP (the suppliers), the NUS (the consumers) and others, including ourselves.[11]

Second, keeping grants wastes the chance to abolish parental contributions, which create problems more serious than is generally appreciated: they aggravate student poverty, reduce student freedom and have a pernicious gender bias, particularly for certain ethnic groups.[12]

Third, grants become unnecessary with universally available income-contingent loans. Resources are scarce, and it is necessary to target them on those who need help most. One way of doing so is through an income test. The right income to test is the student's future income, not her parent's or husband's current income. That is exactly what income-contingent repayments do: by basing repayments on where people end up rather than on where they start, they get the income test right, and hence increase the progressivity of the system in comparison with means-tested grants.

Finally, grants waste resources which could do more to facilitate access if used differently. If, after due consideration, the Treasury accepts recommendation 80, the replacement of maintenance grants by loans will release significant resources in the short as well as the long run. These resources can do more to improve access if used in other ways, of which examples are given in the concluding section of this article.

A second problematical area is recommendation 79, which states: 'On a balance of considerations, we recommend to the Government that it introduces arrangements for graduates in work to make a flat-rate contribution of around 25 per cent of the average cost of higher education tuition, through an income contingent mechanism . . . The contributions made by graduates in work in this way should be reserved for meeting the needs of higher education.' In practice, the recommendation is to impose on students a flat fee of about £1,000 per student per year, irrespective of subject studied or university attended – broadly along the lines of reform introduced in Australia in 1989. The report rightly argues that students should make a contribution to the costs of their tuition. It is also right to argue (report 8) that there are broader benefits to society from higher education, so that the state should continue to make a significant contribution to its funding.

There exist widely divergent views about the rightness, or otherwise, of charging fees to students.

View 1 is that it is wrong – there should be no fees at all. The counter-arguments can be expressed simply. First, free tuition is quite simply unaffordable in the mass system of higher education which we now have. Second, graduates generally earn more than non-graduates. In 1996/7 the gross weekly earnings of the average graduate were £457 per week; the comparable figure for non-graduates was £237. Thus it is both efficient and fair that graduates make a contribution. Third, charges are levied for most education and training after school leaving age. It is thus unfair that only full-time undergraduate students – in many ways tomorrow's best-off citizens – are completely exempt from payment. Fourth, it is unnecessary to offer free tuition if universal income-contingent loans are available. Finally, free tuition, like maintenance grants, wastes resources which could do more for access if used differently.

View 2 is that recommendation 79 is an important stepping stone. It can be argued that the flat-fee approach worked well in Australia, and is a model from which we can learn. It is also argued that Dearing has made an important advance by establishing the principle of a student contribution to fees. A move from no fees to variable fees is too big a jump, according to this view, and establishing flat fees is therefore an important stepping stone towards an eventual system of differentiated charges.

View 3 is that, on the contrary, recommendation 79 is unhelpful to the long-run inevitability of variable fees. This depends on the nature of the Government's response, and is therefore taken up below.

Dearing was well aware of the arguments about variable fees and the replacement of grants by loans. Why, then, did the report recommend retaining the grant and introducing flat-rate fees? The answer is simple: the classification problem discussed earlier left the committee with nowhere else to go. If loans count as public spending, then making them more generous – for example by extending loans to replace parental contributions – and making them available to larger numbers of students adds to public spending, as does intervention to encourage staying on in school. Thus there was no way to give students more money. Yet there is a funding crisis: not only students, but also universities, need money. The only way to get money for universities was to impose a fee and hope that the Treasury would not claw it back, at least not immediately.

The Government's response

Given the potentially unpopular and controversial nature of some of the main recommendations of the Dearing Committee, the Secretary of State clearly felt that there were advantages in outlining at an early stage the direction of the Government's thinking. His response (*Hansard* [Commons], 23 July 1997, cols 949–51) had five key elements, discussed here-in turn.

The first three elements were:

- *Endorsement of the principle of income contingency.* This announcement has been welcomed by virtually everybody in higher education (having argued for this since 1988, we warmly endorse the decision).
- *A flat-rate means-tested fee of up to £1,000 towards the cost of tuition.* Though not much detail was announced, some features were immediately apparent. The most glaring is that the fee will be paid out of the parental contribution, i.e. it will be payable up-front and not supported by a loan entitlement.
- *Replacement of the grant by an income-tested loan entitlement.* The grant will be abolished, and replaced by a loan entitlement minus any remaining parental contribution.

These arrangements are complex, so that a simplified numerical example is helpful. Suppose that a student is deemed to need £4,000 to cover living costs, made up, under present arrangements (line 1 in Table 10.1) of a loan entitlement of £2,000 and grant/parental contribution of £2,000. Thus the maximum parental contribution (for a student not eligible for any grant) is £2,000. Under Dearing's preferred Option B, a student receives £2,000 in grant/parental contribution and a £3,000 income-contingent loan to cover the remaining £2,000 of living costs plus the £1,000 tuition fee. Under the Government's proposals, a 'poor' student is eligible for an income-contingent loan of £4,000 to cover living expenses, and does not have to pay a tuition fee; a 'rich' student receives £2,000 in parental contribution, £1,000 to cover the tuition fee and £1,000 towards living costs, and is eligible for an income-contingent loan of £3,000 to cover remaining living costs.

The fourth key element of the Government response was a lack of *enthusiasm for top-up fees*. If not immediately, then certainly in the medium term, this is problematical. A system of mass higher education is too complex for central price control to be compatible with quality and diversity. One of the desirable features of a mass system should be greater diversity of activities and hence greater diversity of costs. In theory, differential costs could be accommodated by an all-knowing central planner. In practice, that task is too complex to be feasible. It is not yet clear whether the Government will move legislation to prohibit differential pricing.

The fifth key element was the *timetable*, with the Secretary of State announcing his intention to bring in the fee contribution for all students entering university at the start of the 1998/9 academic year.

The Government's proposals raise four sets of serious problems: (a) they produce no more resources for students or universities; (b) they put access at risk; (c) they create inequities in other ways; and (d) they cannot be implemented within the proposed timeframe.

Table 10.1 The current system, Dearing's preferred option and the government's initial response

	Living expenses	*Tuition*
Current system	50% mortgage-type loan; 50% grant/parental contribution	Free
Dearing, Option B	50% income contingent loan; 50% grant/parental contribution	£1,000 flat-fee from income-contingent contributions
Government proposal		
'Poor' student	100% income contingent loan	Free
'Rich' student	Parental contribution of 50% of living costs minus £1,000; Income contingent loan, the rest	

On the lack of resources, the logic is distressingly compelling. Public spending on higher education will not go up (the budget said so); parental contributions (i.e. private spending) will not go up (the Secretary of State said so); and loans to students (the other potential source of private spending) count in their entirety as public spending. If public spending is unchanged and there is no extra private spending, there is nothing extra for higher education. Both Dearing and the Government propose a genuine and brave solution of long-run funding problems but, as things stand, do not produce a brass farthing in the short run.

Two potential counterarguments do not stand up. First, it is argued that loans will bring in private resources. This is true, but in only the medium term at the earliest. Official figures (*Hansard*, 24 July 1989, WA col. 441) show that the current scheme will make no cumulative saving until 2015 (i.e. twenty-five years after its introduction). On more realistic assumptions, the scheme will not make a net saving to the taxpayer for 100 years. The new scheme will be better designed; but any scheme which lends to large numbers of students and allows extended repayment periods (both of which are desirable to facilitate access) will disburse large amounts from day one, but will begin to receive its first trickle of repayments only in the fifth year.

Second, it can be argued that the Government will raise resources through its planned sale of the existing stock of student debt. This, again, is true; but those revenues are already included in the higher education budget. Moreover, as the Dearing Report points out (para. 20.97), the proposed debt sale fails to meet the Treasury's value for money criteria. The arrangement has been described as a firesale and – after allowing for the cost of guarantees and continuing interest subsidies to the buyers – is unlikely to yield more than 50 per cent of the face value of the debt.

The Government's proposals might, indeed, make things worse by *increasing* public spending. If students have to cover tuition fees as well as maintenance, the take-up of loans will increase. Currently about 63 per cent of students take up their loan entitlement, borrowing a total of £879 million in 1996/7. If take-up increases to 90 per cent, total lending will increase by about £375 million. This outcome is plausible for two reasons: with no grant and a charge for fees, students will *need* to borrow more; and income-contingent repayments reduce the inhibition against borrowing – which is indeed the whole point of income contingency, given its critical role in protecting access.

There is one partial offsetting factor. Suppose a parent voluntarily pays more than the assessed parental contribution and, in consequence, the student takes out a smaller loan. This substitutes parental contributions (private funding) for loans (public funding), on the face of it improving matters. These private resources, however, are unquantifiable in advance, and hence cannot be allocated to the higher education budget; so they will probably revert to the Treasury.

None of this precludes a small increase in resources from administrative or other savings, for example the additional resources announced in September 1997. But given the Government's spending commitments and stated priorities in other areas, the scale of any such additions cannot begin to approach the needs of the current financial crisis.

In short, as the current proposals produce no additional resources, they can do nothing to restore quality, to finance continued expansion, or to improve access. Students remain poor; universities remain poor.

The second strategic worry about the Government's proposals is that they will have precisely the opposite effect on access to that so passionately desired by Sir Ron and the Secretary of State. The fee proposals pursue an equity objective through a *price* subsidy (i.e. reduced fees for poorer students) rather than an income subsidy (through income-contingent loans).[13] The problem with this approach – which is rather Old Labour – is that it can frequently hurt the very people it is intended to help, as for example with excessive rent subsidies, which have led over the years to waiting lists and labour immobility. It is therefore not surprising that the proposed arrangements, notwithstanding the Government's strong commitment to improve access, are profoundly unhelpful.

Access is harmed, first, because the proposed loans are too small to give students adequate living standards. Even if a student receives all assessed parental contributions or, in the case of a poor student, a loan to cover all living costs, the level of payment is 20 per cent too low.

A second problem is strengthened reliance on parental contributions, which are profoundly regressive social policy.[14] It is wrong in principle to force young adults to depend on their parents; and it is at least as wrong to force people to depend on their spouses. In practice, many parents do not pay in full, contributing to student poverty, and others do so only on the basis of conditions about choice of subject or university.

A third difficulty is the source of fee payments. Under the Government's proposals, the fee contribution is deemed to be paid through the parental contribution. It is therefore an up-front fee (which is what parental contributions amount to). No government committed to facilitating access should contemplate such a policy. Though the Government has said that parental contributions will not increase, the effect of a fee charge unsupported by loans does just that – not by increasing the total parental contribution but by increasing the proportion of the costs to be paid up-front. It is already the case that many bills (e.g. hall fees) have to be paid on day one, at a time when students have not yet received their loans. It is thus often the case that a parent has to make up to half of the annual parental contribution up-front. From 1998, the bill on day one will also include fees.

Parental contributions and up-front fees are regressive with respect to gender. Women students are more likely to be hard hit by poverty. They are also likely to suffer greater curtailment of freedom, since parents are more prone to impose conditions on daughters than on sons, and husbands are more likely to put pressure on wives than *vice versa*. Such disempowerment is likely to be particularly acute for women from ethnic backgrounds with weaker traditions of educating daughters.

A further impediment to access is the incentive to discriminate against British students. A flat fee will continue the erosion of quality at the best universities, which face the biggest shortfalls in funding. British students could suffer in one of two ways. The quality of the best institutions might fall; though British students could still get places, the quality of the degree would be less. Alternatively, the best institutions will largely stop teaching British undergraduates (for whom they receive on average £4,000 per year) and will use the fees from foreign undergraduates (around £8,000 per year) to preserve their excellence. The Government is considering trying to prevent British universities from charging additional fees to UK/EU students. Again, this is done for equity reasons; again, it ends up harming the very people it is aimed at helping.

In short, *no* student is any better off than currently; many are worse off; and women are likely particularly to be affected.

Impediments to access are one source of inequity. There are other ways in which the proposals are inherently unfair. In the first place, the proposals focus on starting point rather than outcome. Lucky the shopworker's son who becomes a successful barrister, who pays no fees; unlucky the managing director's daughter who becomes a social worker. What matters is not where people start from but where they end up. The Secretary of State has said (*The Times*, 24 July 1997, p. 20): 'Our solution reflects the graduate's earnings of the future, not the circumstances of today's student.' Alas, the Government's proposal, by retaining an income test on parental/spousal income, does exactly the opposite.

Second, price does not vary with quality. It is unfair (and will soon be seen to be unfair and hence politically unpopular) to expect parents to pay the same flat fee for a degree at Oxford as for a degree at Balls Pond Road Technical College, since the degree from Oxford is worth so much more – a fact of which employers are already well aware.

The final strategic problem concerns the proposed timetable. Even if the policy were ideal, it cannot be put in place effectively by 1998/9. Such dramatic changes as are being suggested require detailed planning. It is essential that administrative arrangements work smoothly and do not create unnecessary resistance. Excessive haste can cause, and has caused, problems. Ministers had to move quickly in August 1997 to defuse public worries about the gap year. A further consequence of the Secretary of State's announcement, at a time when the details of income-contingent repayments had not yet been worked out, was to focus the attention of the press, and hence of prospective students and their parents, on the *stock* of debt (£12,000 over a three-year degree course), rather than the *flow* of repayments (an extra 3p in the pound once the student starts earning). People generally think more naturally in terms of flow prices than in terms of stock – we all know roughly how much the weekly grocery bill is, but most of us would be horrified if we knew how much we will spend on food (or drink) over the next twenty-five years. A much better way of presenting matters is to say to students (and their parents): 'You go to university; you have enough to live on; it is all free at the time; you get your degree and then you go out and start earning. Only when your earnings are high enough will you pay an extra few pence per pound of earnings, which helps to pay for the education of the next generation.'

There are serious doubts about whether the many detailed changes necessary can be effectively implemented by October 1998. Who, for example, will collect fees from students? If universities, what will be the implications for administrative costs if they are asked to accept fees on a monthly basis? What will universities do in cases where students or their parents cannot or will not pay? It is easy to imagine a situation where nonpayment of fees will absorb far more than the additional hardship money proposed of £250 million per year; and how absurd it would be to be forced to use scarce hardship resources to support the sons and daughters of middle-class parents who refuse to help their own children.

These are not merely administrative matters: they have major implications for the political acceptability of reform. Administrative mishaps erode ministerial credibility and public confidence, costing ministers the chance to lead on the front foot and putting the new Government's credibility at risk.

Over the next year or so, a series of political rows is almost inevitable, for example over the withdrawal of grants and introduction of fees. If reform is to be successful, it is imperative to avoid rows where they are not necessary. A realistic timetable for implementation is a critical ingredient in pursuit of that end.

The Government's objectives are entirely right. But current policy does nothing to achieve those objectives in the short run: they bring in no more resources; they do not help access, and are unfair; and their unrealistic timetable puts the entire reform enterprise at risk.

A view ahead

If the Government's present policies and current proposals are pursued unchanged – in particular if the expenditure classification issue is not resolved – the crystal ball reveals a clear but disturbing picture:

- With few or no extra resources going into the system, the funding crisis will continue, resulting in declining quality of degree courses and rising student poverty.
- Access, at best, will not diminish, but there will be no increase in university attendance by students from poorer backgrounds.
- There will be increased problems with unpaid parental and spousal contributions, putting at risk participation by groups who depend on

such contributions. In parallel, if the task of collecting fees falls on universities, they will face a large and expensive new administrative burden pursuing bad debts.

- There will be increasing resentment by parents who have to pay the £1,000 fee for a child at their local technical college, but see their neighbour paying the same fee for a son or daughter at Oxford or Cambridge.

- If the proposed timetable is not extended, there will be a long and inevitable series of implementation gaffes, with consequent – and entirely unnecessary – ill-feeling and hostility from the public. Ministers will spend a lot of time in television studios explaining administrative hiccoughs such as the gap year problem, rather than actively promoting the benefits of new policy.

Most of these problems are avoidable. Many policy directions are clear and imperative.

First, income-contingent repayments should be based on the graduate's weekly or monthly income and collected by the tax or national insurance authorities.[15]

Second, the expenditure classification issue should be addressed. Government should have two instruments for financial lending to students:

(a) the capacity to classify publicly funded student debt in the public accounts in a sensible way;
(b) the capacity to involve private finance.

The respective weight of (a) and (b) would be a matter for government choice in the light of prevailing economic circumstances.[16] Australia, New Zealand and (closer to home in the EU) The Netherlands have all solved this problem, so that most lending to students is outside the budget.

More broadly, there are important lessons to be learned from the way in which other governments have approached this issue. For example, the Australian method of classifying debt was the result of dialogue between the departments concerned, including the Australian Bureau of Statistics, in which all participants understood the objectives and cooperated in devising a solution which achieved them. This contrasts with the UK model, in which the Office for National Statistics is portrayed as a quasi-judicial authority rather than as an active participant in policy design. There are a number of policy areas – housing, transport, urban regeneration – which could be dramatically affected by a more transparent approach to this issue. It is a problem which should be addressed urgently by a government committed to reform. The wind of change must be felt in Whitehall as well as Westminster.

These two policies – income-contingent loans, and extra-budgetary resources – are essential, the first to protect access and bring in private resources, the second to make resources available now rather than a long time in the future. The classification problem, as stated repeatedly, is a straitjacket which has bound Sir Ron and the Secretary of State; if it is not removed, there is no escape from the ill-effects described above. Resolution of the problem, in contrast, opens up a whole range of options for enhancing access and improving quality.

The third way forward is promoting access. Expanding loan entitlement is essential in this context. This should include:

•   increasing the size of loans to 120 per cent of the current main-tenance package, available without a test of parental/spouse income; [. . .]
•   extending loans to part-time and postgraduate students whose current entitlement is negligible.

Active policies to promote access are also necessary. They include:

•   targeted scholarships at university level;
•   policies directed at 16–18-year-olds.

The last point bears amplification. If policy-makers are serious about improving-access, the real push has to come earlier in the system. The Dearing Report shows that only 16 per cent of 18-year olds from the low-est socioeconomic groups qualify for university entrance by gaining two 'A' levels or equivalent; of that total, however, nearly half go on to higher education. The implication is clear: if a student from a poor background can get two 'A' levels, she has a very good chance of going to university – the trick is to help her to get those 'A' levels. Thus there is a significant role for targeted interventions to encourage young people from poorer back-grounds to stay at school or further education until age 18.

Looking somewhat into the future, policy towards fees should move towards a regime with two core elements:

•   a £1,000 tuition contribution for all students, covered by a loan avail-able without income test;
•   variations about this fee level, determined by individual universities, subject to a regulatory regime, with income-contingent loans to cover such fees.

Other issues for the medium term include a new inquiry (Son of Dearing) in five years' time (recommendation 88). Its remit should include the finance of higher education in the light of the inevitable change in patterns of demand which will result from students bearing a greater fraction of the costs themselves. For example, there will be increasing demand for part-time courses and, at the other end of the spectrum, for accelerated full-time degrees. For such purposes, university funding should not be calculated per year of full-time study, but per course unit. The follow-up report will also need to evaluate improvements in access and, particularly, impediments to access resulting from any changes made. This is more necessary the greater the extent of continued parental/spousal contributions.

Another issue for the medium term is the likely need for a further Scottish report (McDearing), since it is highly probable that the proposed Scottish parliament will wish to consider matters in the context of Scottish specifics.

Acknowledgement

Financial support from the Nuffield Foundation is gratefully acknowledged. This article is a shortened version of evidence to the House of Commons Education Selection Committee (Nicholas Barr and Iain Crawford, 'The Dearing Report, the Government's Response and a View Ahead' in *Third Report: The Dearing Report: Some Funding Issues*, volume II, Minutes of Evidence and Appendices, House of Commons Education and Employment Committee, Session 1997–98, HC241-II (TSO, 1997), pp. 88–103).

Notes

1 *Our Universities, Our Future*, Part 4: *The Case for a New Funding System – Special Report*, the CVCP's evidence to the National Committee of Inquiry into Higher Education, London, Committee of Vice-Chancellors and Principals, 1996, p. 4.

2 Nicholas Barr and William Low, *Student Grants and Student Poverty*, Welfare State Programme, Discussion Paper No. WSP/28, London: London School of Economics, 1988, pp. 31–4; Nicholas Barr, *Student Loans: The Next Steps*, Aberdeen University Press for the David Hume Institute, Edinburgh, and the Suntory-Toyota International Centre for Economics and Related Disciplines, London School of Economics, 1989, pp. 17–18.

3 Barr, *Student Loans: The Next Steps*, ch. 4.

4 Barr and Low, *Student Grants and Student Poverty*.

5 UK National Committee of Inquiry into Higher Education (the Dearing Committee), *Higher Education in the Learning Society: Summary Report*, London, HMSO, 1997 (also available at http://www.leeds.ac.uk/educol/ncihe); UK National Committee of Inquiry into Higher Education (the Dearing Committee), *Higher Education in the Learning Society: Report of the National Committee*, London, HMSO, 1997 (also available at http://www.leeds.ac.uk/educol/ncihe).

6 Bruce Chapman, 'Conceptual Issues and the Australian Experience with Income-Contingent Charges for Higher Education', *Economic Journal*, 1997, pp. 738–51.

7 For fuller discussion, see Nicholas Barr and Iain Crawford, 'The Dearing Report, the Government's Response and a View Ahead', in *Third Report: The Dearing Report: Some Funding Issues*, volume II, Minutes of Evidence and Appendices, House of Commons Education and Employment Committee, Session 1997–98, HC241-II (TSO, 1997), pp. 88–103.

8 For fuller discussion and a range of solutions, see Nicholas Barr, 'Student Loans: Towards a New Public/Private Mix', *Public Money and Management*, July–September 1997, pp. 31–40.

9 See Barr and Crawford, 'The Dearing Report', Appendix 2.

10 Barr, 'Student Loans: Towards a New Public/Private Mix'.

11 Nicholas Barr and Iain Crawford, 'Funding Higher Education in an Age of Expansion: Submission to the National Committee of Inquiry into Higher Education', *Education Economics*, 1998 [this volume, Ch. 9].

12 For fuller discussion, see Barr and Crawford, 'The Dearing Report', Appendix 3.

13 For the analytics, see Nicholas Barr, *The Economics of the Welfare State*, 2nd edn, Oxford, Oxford University Press, 1993, ch. 4).

14 For fuller discussion, see Barr and Crawford, 'The Dearing Report', Appendix 3.

15 For details, see Barr, 'Student Loans: Towards a New Pubic/Private Mix'.

16 The two approaches are discussed in more detail in Barr, 'Student Loans: Towards a New Public/Private Mix'.

Nicholas Barr and Iain Crawford, 'Opportunity Lost', *Guardian Education*, 2 September 1997, p. v.

Opportunity lost

Nicholas Barr and Iain Crawford

As the summer vacation comes to an end we must face the post-Dearing reality. It comes in two parts. The good news is that we now have a mass higher education system in place of the exclusive system that we have been running, educated in and brought up to expect. The bad news is that there is not an extra penny to pay for it.

In 1988, the then Secretary of State for Education, Kenneth Baker, announced a doubling of university places. He received all-party support for that initiative. At the time about 15 per cent of UK school-leavers were going into higher education, the lowest in the entire developed world. Today over 30 per cent of all school-leavers do so. As the chattering classes we all knew that this change was necessary so we supported it. But precisely because of that support, nobody bothered to argue for the proposition or to persuade anyone to pay for it. We failed to convince either the taxpayer or the direct beneficiaries to contribute more. Baker recognised this but went ahead anyway, leaving behind what he refers to as his 'ticking time-bomb for the Treasury'.

Post Dearing nothing has changed. There will be no more public money (Mr Brown [the Chancellor] has said so). There will be fees, but no family will have to contribute more (Mr Blunkett [the Education Secretary] has said so). The only change is that the parental contribution will now pay for the means-tested fee instead of the means-tested contribution to maintenance. On the face of it, more money will be coming in because students will be borrowing more. But the Treasury takes the view that all student loans will count as public expenditure just as if they were grants. Thus loans bring in no extra money now. On the face of it, they will do so once loan repayments start to come in, but that process will take at least 20 years, and is, in any case, necessary for future expansion.

The fact remains, however, that the economic prosperity of the nation is increasingly dependent on a highly-educated labour force. Somehow we have to enable more of our population to access that level of education. Dearing suggested ways of doing so, but nothing that we have so far heard of the Government's response achieves it. Indeed, the continuing reliance on parental contributions will make the situation worse.

Research shows that up to 50 per cent of parents fail to pay all (or any) of their 'assessed' contribution. This is a deterrent to access even under the present system, but with some scrimping and a part-time job the 'poor little rich kids' whose folks won't (or can't) pay can usually get by. Parental contributions to pay fees are a much greater deterrent to access: they have to be paid upfront in a lump sum on day one. The only way out of this trap is for colleges to offer generous terms – but that will further erode their fee income, to say nothing of the added administrative costs. It is now widely understood that it is not proposed to make loans available to pay fees. This is because such loans would have to be financed out of the HE budget, making the crisis worse.

For the same reason, the Government has passed by other essential aids to access: an increase of £1,000 per year in the undergraduate mainten-ance package (which everyone agrees is currently too small), and the extension of loans to part-timers and postgraduates.

The proposed fee arrangements – based on means-testing of parents'/ spouses' income and unsupported by a loan – fails to meet core objec-tives. It will deter rather than promote access; and it will provide no extra resources to allow universities to restore the quality of the education they provide.

Much of the problem could be solved if the Government accepted the Dearing recommendation that student loans should be treated differently in the public expenditure accounts. That is probably Sir Ron's most import-ant recommendation. It is entirely possible to do so within International Monetary Fund and EU rules, as, for example, in Australia, New Zealand and Holland. Once this is done, loans can expand to replace enforced dependence on parents (surely an anachronism for people classed as independent adults for all other purposes), to allow students a reasonable standard of living while they study, and to provide for students who are currently unsupported. It would release resources for universities and allow for targeted access initiatives such a support for 16- to 18-year-olds and more FE funding.

There has, as yet, been no formal government response to this recom-mendation but early indications from the [Education Department] are not optimistic. The Department would like to see student loans removed from public expenditure except for a write-off provision as they are in Australia. Such a move would release well over £1 billion per year from the existing education budget and thus solve everybody's problems. The question is whether sufficient political clout can be mustered by the Department and its clients to persuade the Cabinet and, in particular, the Treasury to make these changes in public accounting practice.

A crucial Dearing recommendation which does appear to have been accepted is that student loans should be income-contingent – in other words, repayments are exactly linked to future income. Sir Ron wants the Inland Revenue to make the collections. If students understand that they will have a future commitment to pay x per cent of their income until the loan is paid off, they will feel insured against future low income rather than focusing on the total amount of the debt.

The case for the abolition of the student grant and for the restructuring of university fees needs to be argued but unless the public expenditure issue is sorted out those debates are virtually pointless.

Nicholas Barr and Iain Crawford, 'A Better Class of Students', *Guardian Education*, 9 September 1997, p. iii.

A better class of students

Nicholas Barr and Iain Crawford

Participation in higher education has risen dramatically since Lord Lionel Robbins, Sir Ron Dearing's predecessor, completed his review in 1963. In those days about 5 per cent of UK school-leavers went to university. When Sir Ron published his report in July, that figure had risen above 30 per cent. The increase is a triumph of the welfare state; society would be impoverished, economically and culturally, without that expansion.

That growth has not been painless. Many believe it has come at the expense of quality and done little to change the socio-economic balance of students. Quality has fallen because funding has not been reformed, and because the expansion occurred in two great lurches, rather than by orderly progression of supply and demand. The increase allowed an expanding middle class to send their daughters as well as their sons to college at the taxpayers' expense.

The commitment in 1988, by Kenneth Baker, the former Secretary of State for Education, to move from 15 per cent to 30 per cent participation left a mass system of higher education supported by a funding mechanism designed for an élite system. In defusing his time bomb, we should be clear that the objective is not only to restore quality to pre-1990 levels but also to widen access.

This year the taxpayer will pay about £1.7 billion towards students' living costs, nearly 25 per cent of the higher education budget. About £1 billion of this will be in loans. But this does not bridge the funding gap, since the Treasury treats loans in the public accounts as if they were grants. As loan repayments will filter into the economy slowly, there will be a long wait before the public accounts show any significant extra resources. But the finding time bomb will not wait.

Australia, New Zealand and Holland have realised that by treating loans sensibly in the public accounts – counting as public expenditure only anticipated debt forgiveness (typically 20 to 25 per cent) – and by making loans fair and universally available, they can free resources now to extend access. They do so through loans with income-contingent repayments. Repayments are calculated as a fraction (say 3 per cent) of the graduate's later earnings, usually collected via the tax mechanism.

Income-contingency is the key to improving access. It means that those who can afford to repay do so, and those who cannot are protected from debt. With adequate loans, students go to university, do not pay anything at the time, get their degree and hopefully start earning. When their earnings rise above a certain level, they pay a fraction of their income until they have paid off their loan. What students face is not a debt of perhaps £15,000, but a potential liability to pay a fraction of their future earnings, if those earnings are high enough.

With this approach, we could convert all grants and parental contributions into loans, saving about £1.2 billion immediately and every year. As well as contributing to quality, those resources can improve access. Income-contingent loans are not a deterrent to study, as Australian evidence shows. And the resources can promote access directly – by increasing what students have to live off by 20 per cent, by abolishing parental/spouse contributions, and by extending loans to part-time and postgraduate students.

Most extra lending would not count against the PSBR, so there would be sufficient funds for a real effort to widen access. But the real push must come earlier. University places have largely caught up with qualified school-leavers. Thus widening access means increasing the number of qualified school-leavers. The Dearing Committee report shows that only 16 per cent of 18-year-olds from the lowest socio-economic groups gain two A levels or equivalent; but nearly half enter higher education.

So if poorer students get two A levels, they have a good chance of going to university. One way to help them do so is to use some of the £1.2 billion as targeted grants to encourage them to stay at school.

Nicholas Barr and Iain Crawford, 'Universities in the First Division Should Charge Top Prices', *Guardian Education*, 16 September 1997, pp. ii–iii.

Universities in the first division should charge top prices

Nicholas Barr and Iain Crawford

There is a great fiction in this country. It is that all 150-plus universities and colleges offer degree courses of equal quality, examined to the same standard, with degrees worth the same whichever university confers them.

This fiction will be exposed with the introduction of the proposed flat fee. It was never true and nobody really believed it but that did not matter so much when no one paid explicit fees.

In reality, there have always been élite institutions in terms of academic excellence. Students understand this as soon as they realise the wide range of entrance requirements.

There is a parallel myth – that if something is a basic right, it must be free. But everyone agrees that good nutrition is a basic right, yet people pay for food and, moreover, pay higher prices for higher quality food. It would be regarded as very unfair if everyone had to pay a flat fee for food but some people ate smoked salmon and others baked beans. Yet that is what the Government is proposing for universities.

Flat fees are not only unfair, they also set in train a series of forces which simultaneously reduce the quality of the best universities and make it progressively harder for British students to find places there.

Until now the top institutions have been able to retain parity with the world's best. They used to achieve this through larger block grants from the state. For some time these resources have been inadequate and some top institutions are in danger of relegation from the premier division of the increasingly competitive global higher education league.

Some have sought to maintain their income by charging high fees to (often quite poor) foreign students to subsidise the education of (frequently well-off) British students. That policy, quite apart from being ethically dubious in a country committed to aiding the developing world, will price us out of a lucrative export market.

In higher education, as in most things, quality costs money.

Britain has always had centres of excellence equivalent to the best in the world but the levels of funding received by the top 10 UK universities in comparison with Harvard, Chicago, Berkeley etc., is woefully inadequate. They cannot trade on their past reputations for ever.

These institutions are important to our society and our economy: they carry out vital research for the nation in everything from health to constitutional reform; they teach our finest young minds; their output helps keep us internationally competitive in business and industry, the arts and sciences and they are substantial foreign currency earners.

The introduction of a £1,000 fee does nothing to solve the funding problem. It does not increase total resources for universities (merely shifting parental contributions from maintenance to fees). It also shifts the balance of funding from block grant to money which follows the student, further reducing the Funding Council's ability to divide that total so as to compensate the best institutions.

In principle, a move from centrally determined block grant to money tied to the student (i.e. a form of voucher) is an improvement. Universities are currently told how many students they can accept and what subjects they will study and are heavily penalised for any deviation from these quotas.

They are then told how much they will be paid for doing the job. Such central planning was standard in Eastern Europe 10 years ago but is surprisingly nearly 20 years after the start of the Thatcher revolution.

However, flat fees will do nothing to help the best institutions because they will be left with the same resources per student as the rest.

There is an emerging international consensus that the people who should fix fee levels are the universities themselves, albeit within a strong regulatory framework.

The best institutions face higher costs – not least of staff and research facilities such as laboratories and libraries.

The universities themselves are best-placed to assess their costs and determine appropriate action to maintain quality.

If the Government is not prepared to pay the real cost of the best institutions, students will have to make up the difference.

Given the enhanced earning potential of a graduate from a top university and universal availability of generous income-contingent loans, each student could decide how much to invest in his or her future.

Generous loans make this possible while entirely avoiding the anathema of upfront payments, and income contingency removes the personal risk.

Why does it matter if the Government is not willing to move in this direction? It matters because British students will suffer.

Students going to below-average universities will have to pay the same fee as those going to Oxbridge and the quality of the best institutions will be pulled down towards the average, depriving the brightest British students of the chance of an internationally cutting-edge undergraduate degree.

Alternatively, the best institutions will largely stop teaching British undergraduates (for whom they receive an average of 4,000 a year) and will use the fees from foreign undergraduates (about £8,000 a year) to preserve their excellence and, perhaps, to help a small number of the best British students to study at postgraduate level.

Perhaps that is what politicians want. If that is their vision, they should say so.

It is not ours.

Chapter 11

1998 **An international view**

Nicholas Barr (1998), 'Higher Education in Australia and Britain: What Lessons?', *Australian Economic Review*, Vol. 31, No. 2, June 1998, pp. 179–88.

1 Introduction*

The British and Australian university systems share common roots and common recent problems. The solutions they have adopted, however, show significant divergence.

- By introducing the Higher Education Contribution Scheme (HECS) in 1989, Australia took the right step. In contrast, the British student loan scheme, introduced in 1990, went the wrong way.
- Both countries tightened rather than relaxed central planning of higher education over the 1990s. The Dearing Committee in Britain (UK National Committee of Inquiry into Higher Education 1997a, 1997b) and the government's response (UK Department for Education and Employment 1998b, 1998c) show a clear intention to persist with this strategy. The West Review's discussion paper and final report (Review of Higher Education Financing and Policy 1997, 1998) offer some hope that here, too, Australia might steal a march.

In many ways, the main lesson that Britain can offer Australia on the funding and organisation of higher education is how not to do it.

1.1 Central facts

British higher education expanded from an élite 5 per cent system in 1960 to a mass 30 per cent system by the mid 1990s. Expansion was particularly sharp over the 1990s (as recently as 1990, the participation rate was still only 14 per cent), but with no parallel increase in funding. Australian experience is remarkably similar.

> Increases in access and participation have completed [the] transformation from an élite to a mass higher education system. At the same time, there has been pressure both to restrain expenditure and to address the issues arising from the rapid expansion of the system.
> (Terms of reference of the West review [Review of Higher Education Financing and Policy 1997])

In both countries politicians have been willing to finance higher student numbers but not to maintain real spending per student; and in both countries, despite increasingly parsimonious public funding, the financial freedom of universities has been severely constrained.

Alongside underfunded expansion, both countries also face a second central fact – technological advance and global competition. Returning to a smaller system is therefore not an option.

1.2 Core issues

Both countries therefore face the same two strategic issues.

- *Private funding.* Public funding of a high-quality system is possible – albeit regressive – for a 5 per cent system. It is not possible for a mass system. A mass system therefore requires public funding to be supplemented on a significant scale by private funding. The policy problem, therefore, is to devise a method of bringing in private resources in a way which simultaneously protects both quality and access. As a practical matter this means a system of income-contingent loans; that is, loans where repayment takes the form of x per cent of the graduate's subsequent earnings until the loan has been repaid.
- *Allocating resources.* The second policy question is how most effectively to allocate resources in a large, growing, and increasingly diverse system of higher education – crudely the issue of central planning versus market forces. In the past, universities offered a limited range of fairly standard packages to a limited group of full-time, usually young students. Today, in contrast, the educational package is more complex, is changing, and will continue to change; and there are many more students, their needs are more diverse, and education will increasingly be a repeated exercise. As a practical matter, the task has become too complex for central planning any longer to be possible.

In addition, as argued below, theory supports market allocation as being more effective than central planning for higher education.

The next section briefly sets out the relevant economic theory. The third and fourth parts of the paper tell the UK story, discussing in turn the major recommendations of the Dearing Report and the Government's response. The concluding section offers some thoughts on Australia. Since I would not presume to tell Australia what to do, discussion takes the form of lessons I think the United Kingdom should learn from Australia.

2 Underpinning economic theory

This section takes in turn the two issues just discussed: who should pay for higher education (that is, how costs should be shared between the taxpayer and the student), and how should resources be allocated.

2.1 *Who should pay?*

The conventional argument for subsidising higher education is that it creates external benefits. Though the argument is widely accepted in qual-itative terms, the difficulties of quantification are well known (see Blaug 1976, 1985). I shall take it as read that there is a case for continuing subsidy, but leave open its size, (i) because there is no definitive way of measuring it, and (ii) because-whatever the scientific arguments – the matter is ultimately one to be decided by politicians and the electorate.

Whatever the size of the external benefit, however, there is no contro-versy that higher education creates a private benefit. Thus the theory argues unambiguously that some of the costs should be borne by the student. Since the student typically has little current income, what is relevant is his/her future income – which brings us back to loans. The arguments for income contingency, for both efficiency and equity reasons, are overwhelming. Since they are now common ground between the two countries, I will not belabour the point.[1]

2.2 *Who should decide?*

The issue here is the usefulness of consumer and producer sovereignty. A central question is whether students are sufficiently well informed to make efficient choices. Consumer sovereignty is more useful (i) the better is consumer information, (ii) the more cheaply and effectively it can be improved, (iii) the easier it is for consumers to understand available informa-tion, (iv) the lower are the costs of choosing badly, and (v) the more diverse are consumer tastes.

Higher education does well in terms of these criteria. First, information is available, and more can be made available. There are already 'good universities guides'; and universities increasingly publish detailed information on the Internet. Second, the information, for the most part, is sufficiently simple for the student to understand and evaluate. This process is easier because going to university can be anticipated (contrast finding a doctor to deal with injury after a road accident) so that the student has time to acquire the information he/she needs, and time to seek advice. Third, though it is true that the costs of mistaken choice can be significant, it is not clear that a central planner would make fewer mistakes; moreover, the move towards modular degrees, allowing students to change subjects and, increasingly, institutions, reduces those costs. It should be noted, fourth, that students make choices already. Though the matter is controversial, it can be argued that the assumption of well-informed (or potentially well-informed) consumers holds for higher education.[2]

Finally ((v), above), consumer tastes are diverse, degrees are becoming more diverse, and change is increasingly rapid, and global. For all these reasons, students are more capable than central planners of making choices which conform with their own needs and those of the economy. In contrast, attempts at manpower planning are even more likely than in the past to be wrong.

How useful is producer sovereignty – that is, the economic freedom of universities (I take academic freedom as given)? With an élite system it was possible, as a polite myth, to assume that all universities were equally good and hence could, broadly, be funded equally. With a mass system this myth is no longer sustainable. The characteristics, the quality and the costs of different degrees at different institutions will vary much more widely than hitherto.

Not least to protect the quality of internationally competitive institutions, universities need to be funded differentially, taking account both of the institution's costs and of the demand for places. In principle this could be done by an all-knowing central planner. The problem, however, is too complex for that to be the sole mechanism. A mass system in an increasingly complex world needs a funding mechanism which allows institutions to charge differential prices to reflect their differential costs.

2.3 The resulting system

The theory thus suggests (i) that students should pay for the private benefits they derive from higher education and (ii) that market forces will be useful. It is, however, a huge mistake to imagine that this must mean law-of-the-jungle competition. Outcomes will be influenced by students, by employers, by universities and by government. If students pay a significant fraction of their costs (an inexorable implication of a mass system), they will be empowered to state their preferences. Some students, for example, will demand more time-efficient courses; for example, if the content of a four-year degree is taught over three years without lengthy vacations, students have to finance only three years of living costs. Others will demand more flexible part-time options which can be combined with continuing labour market activity.

Such changes in demand will require universities to respond in ways which are wholly impossible within a centrally planned funding mechanism. Universities need a measure of freedom over the prices they charge, the types of courses they offer and the number of students they accept. Quantity, quality and price would result from the interactions of universities, students and employers within a government-determined regulatory framework. Student demand will be more attuned to continually evolving employer demand than central planning ever could.

Government retains a major influence. It contributes to funding, promotes access, determines the degree of competition and ensures that regulation relating to quality is in place and enforced. At least initially, there is also a strong case for government to establish an upper bound for tuition fees or, perhaps, to establish a norm with permissible variation within a band. That band could be widened over time.

A final, more difficult, question is who should decide on the size of the higher education sector – the government (as in the United Kingdom) or consumer demand (as, for example, in the United States). There is much to be said for the latter so long as arrangements assist quality and access while simultaneously observing macroeconomic realities. Under the approach sketched out above, fees are determined largely by market forces; higher cost universities charge higher fees – but only if students are prepared to pay. Students can borrow to top up any public funding. In such a world (i) consumer demand determines the size of the higher education sector, while (ii) government determines what it is prepared to spend on higher education; that is, how many students it is prepared to fund, and the extent to which it is prepared to fund each. The difference between (i) and (ii) is made up by income-contingent loans.

3 The UK story 1: the Dearing Report

3.1 The backdrop

After more than a decade of increasing government intervention, the 1988 Education Reform Act virtually nationalised higher education. Such central planning was widely criticised.

> In an important sense the main outcome of a cumbersome, complex and yet crude planning process is price control and quantity control. Universities can do little to affect either the number of home students they take or the price they charge. They are underfunded from public sources, and yet their hands are tied as to permissible responses.
>
> [Barnes and Barr 1988, p. 19]

The United Kingdom, in short, had a 'market' in which, so far as home/ European Union students were concerned, price and quantity were determined by the central authorities, a trend which continued inexorably over the 1990s. Though, perhaps, less acute in Australia, these problems will no doubt sound familiar.

On the loans front, too, Britain got it wrong. Until 1990, UK students at a UK university paid no tuition fees and received a tax-funded maintenance grant to cover living costs. The maintenance grant was income-tested on parental or spouse income: students from poorer backgrounds received a full grant; for students receiving less than the full grant, it was assumed that their parents or spouse would make up the difference (so-called parental contributions).

In 1990 a loan scheme was introduced to cover half of living costs, the other half coming from grant and parental/spouse contributions. The loan is disbursed by the Student Loans Company, which also collects repayments. Loans carry a zero real interest rate; that is, the loan incorporates an interest subsidy. People who have borrowed while a student normally repay in 60 equal monthly instalments (that is, repayments are organised like a mortgage or bank overdraft), with repayment deferred in any year in which the graduate's income is below 85 per cent of national average earnings. The source of funds is the Treasury – that is, the taxpayer.

The argument against the scheme is simple – it fails to achieve a single desirable objective. First, and worst, repayments are not income-contingent but organised like a mortgage. Second, it provides no additional resources for universities, and hence does nothing to restore quality. Third, it is hugely and unnecessarily costly in public expenditure terms: students borrow public money; loans carry an interest subsidy; deferments, where a graduate subsequently has low earnings, slow the repayment flow;[3] and administrative costs are high. Finally, the scheme mobilises no private funding at all. These problems were both predictable and predicted (Barr 1989, 1991), and the Education Minister, in Parliamentary debate about the Dearing Report, pointedly remarked that 'Dearing believes that the present loan system is unfair, unworkable and ineffective' (*Hansard* (Commons), 23 July 1997, col. 950). In the late 1980s, faced with similar information, Australia introduced HECS. Though HECS dealt with fee contributions rather than living costs, its critical lesson for the United Kingdom is its income-contingency.

The Dearing Report was published in July 1997.[4] Though its 93 recommendations (listed in the summary report, pp. 42–54, and main report, pp. 370–82) are broad, three elements – quality, access and funding –were central. This paper concentrates on funding, because this is the central debate in both countries (for fuller discussion, including an Australian perspective, see Barr 1998a).

3.2 *Triumphantly right*

Two of Dearing's recommendations – 78 and 80 – are utterly essential and stand out as by far the most important.

Income contingency

'We recommend to the Government that it introduces, by 1998/99, income contingent terms for the payment of any contribution towards living costs or tuition costs sought from graduates in work' (Recommendation 78).

The accounting problem

The UK public accounts are organised on a cash-flow basis (though reform is scheduled for three years time). Thus all student loans count as public expenditure. Because government targets have tended to focus on the current deficit, lending to students crowded out other educational spending, even though much of that lending will subsequently be repaid.[5] As a result, student loans bring in little extra money until the system is mature. The report rightly stresses that it is vital to solve this problem – and does so in remarkably strong language.

> We recommend to the Government that it looks urgently at alternative and internationally accepted approaches to national accounting which do not treat the repayable part of loans in the same way as grants to students.
>
> [Recommendation 80]

The report is right to argue that this problem needs to be fixed fast. It is true that loans will bring in significant additional resources in 20 years time-but (as one Vice-Chancellor put it on the day the Dearing Report was published) you cannot revive a corpse.

The accounting issue (see Barr 1997b) is of limited interest in Australia, since the Australian authorities have already solved the problem (see Australian Bureau of Statistics 1997, Table 12 and pp. 78–9; Barr and Crawford 1997, app. 2) and so, in a different way, have the New Zealand authorities (Barr 1997a).

3.3 *Potentially problematical*

The report's preferred option (Option B in Table 2.2 of the report; see also Table 11.1, below) has three elements:

(i)   50 per cent of student living costs from an income-contingent loan;
(ii) 50 per cent of living costs from a mixture of tax-funded maintenance grant and parental contribution;
(iii) a tuition fee of 25 per cent of average tuition costs.

The first element has already been welcomed. The other two elements are potentially problematical.

Should grants to cover living costs be kept?

The issue is controversial. The argument in favour of grants is that they enhance access. Keeping grants, however, wastes the chance to abolish parental contributions, whose ill effects are well known: they aggravate student poverty, reduce student freedom and have a pernicious gender gradient, particularly for certain ethnic groups (see Barr and Crawford 1997, app. 3). Second, grants are badly targeted: the right income to test is the student's future income, not his/her parents' or husband's current income. That is exactly what income-contingent repayments do – by basing repayment on where people end up rather than on where they start, they get the income test right, and hence increase progressivity in comparison with means-tested grants.

Arguments about flat fees

Recommendation 79 states:

> On a balance of considerations, we recommend to the Government that it introduces arrangements for graduates in work to make a flat-rate contribution of around 25 per cent of the average cost of higher education tuition, through an income contingent mechanism.

In practice, the recommendation is to impose on students a flat fee of about £1,000 per student per year, irrespective of subject studied or university attended – that is, the 1989 version of HECS.

In Britain (as in Australia) the issue of fees is highly controversial.

Table 11.1 The current system, Dearing's preferred option and the Government's response

	Living expenses	*Tuition*
Current system	50% mortgage-type loan 50% grant/parental contribution	Free
Dearing, Option B	50% income-contingent loan 50% grant/parental contribution	£1,000 flat fee from income-contingent contributions
Government		
'Poor' student	100% income-contingent loan	Free
'Rich' student	Parental contribution of 50% of living costs *minus* £1,000 Income-contingent loan, the rest	£1,000 flat fee from parental contributions

View 1: flat fees are bad policy because there should be no fees at all. The counterarguments are, first, that free tuition is unaffordable with mass higher education. Second, graduates, because of their degrees, generally earn more than non-graduates, making a contribution both efficient and fair. Third, charges are levied for most other post-compulsory education and training in the United Kingdom; it is unfair that only full-time under-graduate students – in many ways tomorrow's best off citizens – are completely exempt. Finally, free tuition is unnecessary if universal income-contingent loans are available.

View 2: flat fees are the right way to go, but only as the first step towards variable fees. According to this view, the flat-fee approach worked well in Australia and is a model from which Britain can learn. A move from no fees to variable fees is too big a jump, both for potential students and in political terms, and establishing flat fees therefore an important stepping stone.

View 3: flat fees are bad policy because they hinder the introduction of variable fees, which are both inevitable and desirable.

Why did Dearing take this route on living costs and fees? Dearing was well aware of the arguments about variable fees and the replacement of grant by loan. Why, then, did the Committee retain the grant and go for flat-rate fees? The answer is simple: the accounting problem discussed earlier left them with nowhere else to go. If loans count as public spending, then making them more generous – for example extending loans to replace parental contribu-tions, and extending them to part-time and postgraduate students – adds to public spending. But the Government was committed to existing public spending limits. Thus there was no way to give students more money.

4 The UK story 2: the Government's response

4.1 The response

The Government's initial response to the funding elements of Dearing, on the day the report was published (*Hansard* (Commons), 23 July 1997, cols 949–51), had five key elements, discussed in turn. A later response (UK Department for Education and Employment 1998b, 1998c) added some detail.

(i)   Endorsement of the principle of income contingency. A subsequent announcement, in November 1997, confirmed that collection would be by the tax authorities (see UK Department for Education and Employment 1998b, p. 57).

(ii) A flat-rate, means-tested fee of up to £1,000. The most glaring feature is that the fee will be paid out of the parental contribution; that is, the fee will be upfront and not supported by a loan entitlement (see Table 11.1).

(iii) Replacement of the grant by an income-tested loan entitlement. In conformity with Labour's election manifesto, the grant will be abolished, and replaced by a loan entitlement minus any remaining parental contribution.

The arrangements are complex, so that a simplified numerical example is helpful. Suppose that students are deemed to need £4,000 to cover living costs, made up, under present arrangements (line 1 of Table 11.1) of a loan entitlement of £2,000 and grant/parental contribution of £2,000. Thus the maximum parental contribution (for a student not eligible for any grant) is £2,000. Under Dearing's preferred option, a student receives £2,000 in grant/parental contribution and a £3,000 income-contingent loan to cover the remaining £2,000 of living costs plus the £1,000 tuition fee. Under the Government's proposals, a poor student is eligible for an income-contingent loan of £4,000 to cover living expenses, and does not have to pay a tuition fee. A rich student receives £2,000 in parental contribution, £1,000 to cover the tuition fee and £1,000 towards living costs, and is eligible for an income-contingent loan of £3,000 to cover remaining living costs.

(iv) A lack of enthusiasm for top-up fees. This is problematical. A system of mass higher education is too complex for central price control to be compatible with quality and diversity. At the time of writing Parliament is debating legislation to outlaw additional fees.

(v) A timetable. The Education Minister announced the intention to bring in the fee contribution for all students entering university at the start of the academic year in October 1998.

4.2 Comments

The Government's proposals raise four sets of serious problems: they produce no more resources, put access at risk, create inequities in other ways and cannot be implemented effectively within the proposed time frame. The arguments are summarised very briefly (for fuller discussion, see Barr 1998a; Barr and Crawford 1997).

Problem 1: no more resources. The logic is distressingly compelling.

- Public spending on higher education will not go up (the budget said so).
- Parental contributions (that is, private spending) will not go up (the Education Minister said so).
- Loans to students (the other potential source of private spending) count in their entirety as public spending.

If *public* spending is unchanged and there is no extra *private* spending, there is nothing extra for higher education. Both Dearing and the Government propose a genuine resolution of funding problems in the long run but, as things stand, do not produce any resources in the short run.

Problem 2: potential adverse effects on access. The Government's fee proposals pursue an equity objective through a *price* subsidy (that is, reduced fees for poorer students) rather than an income subsidy through income-contingent loans (for the analytics, see Barr 1998b, ch. 4). The problem with this approach (which is rather Old Labour) is that it can frequently hurt the very people it is intended to help, for example excessive rent subsidies, which have led over the years to waiting lists and labour immobility. It is therefore not surprising that the proposed arrangements, notwithstanding the Government's strong commitment to improve access, are profoundly unhelpful.

Access is harmed in several ways. Student living standards are inadequate because the total of loan and parental contribution is 25 per cent too low to support an adequate standard of living. Second, strengthened reliance on parental contributions, as discussed earlier, makes bad policy worse. Under the Government's proposals, third, the fee contribution is deemed to be paid through the parental contribution, in effect introducing up-front fees. No government committed to access should contemplate such a policy. Finally, all these problems are regressive with respect to gender.

Problem 3: other inequities. Impediments to access are one source of inequity. There are other ways in which the proposals are inherently unfair. First, they focus on starting point rather than outcomes. Lucky the shop-worker's son who becomes a successful barrister, who pays no fees, unlucky the managing director's daughter who becomes a social worker. What matters is not where people start but where they end. Second, price does not vary with quality. It is unfair (and will soon be seen to be unfair and hence politically unpopular) to expect parents to pay the same flat fee at Oxford as at Balls Pond Road Technical College.

Problem 4: the timetable for implementation. Even if the policy were ideal, the timetable is highly ambitious. Such dramatic changes as are being suggested require detailed planning. These are not merely administrative matters, but have major implications for the political acceptability of reform.

In sum, the proposals bring in virtually no new private resources in the short run, are inequitable, and entrench central planning. The move to income contingency will stand the test of time; the flat fees regime will be short lived; and – it is devoutly to be hoped – so will continued reliance on parental and spouse contributions.

5 Thoughts for Australia

Before turning to the Australian debate, a few words on what I am not saying. I am not saying that universities should necessarily or immediately be given unlimited freedom over fees – merely that they should have more freedom than currently. Nor am I opposed to central planning of higher education for ideological reasons, but because market forces plus some regulation will do better than any other method of preserving both quality and access. Some might argue that it is immoral to charge for education on the grounds that education is a basic right. I believe strongly that education is a basic right. But that does not necessarily mean that it should be free. We all agree that adequate nutrition is a basic right, but are happy for food to be supplied by profit-maximising private producers. Where consumers are well informed, equity objectives are better achieved through income transfers than by price subsidies. For precisely that reason we do not send pensioners food parcels, but pay them pensions so that they can buy food at the same shops as the rest of us, at the same prices.

I look at Australia with some envy – and not only because of the crimson rosellas. HECS advanced Australian higher education funding in important ways:

- it introduced a highly effective income-contingent loan scheme;
- it established the principle of tuition fees;
- those fees brought in some extra resources, so that the Australian funding problem is not as acute as the British one.

HECS was undoubtedly the right scheme for 1989, when the Australian system was smaller than it is now. Turning to the West Report, two developments since 1989 are particularly salient.

- Higher education in Australia expanded rapidly, so that participation is now around 40 per cent. In the UK context I have argued that this suggests the need for flexible fees (subject to regulation) within a more market-oriented system of higher education.
- An additional development was the introduction in 1997 of full-fee students, who receive no public subsidy for tuition and are not eligible for HECS. Such an introduction of upfront fees has rightly been heavily criticised (see Chapman 1997b).

Two recommendations of the West Committee's discussion paper are thus particularly relevant.

- *Fees.* 'Institutions should have the freedom to set tuition fees ... Institutions must have the ability to provide a range of courses and delivery options, and to decide the level of resources that are devoted to them. Fee flexibility is also essential to encourage competition ...' (Review of Higher Education Financing and Policy 1997, p. 31).
- *Loans.* 'No student undertaking a first qualification should be required to face the upfront payment of tuition fees ... Students should have access to income contingent loans for the payment of any contribution' (Review of Higher Education Financing and Policy 1997, pp. 29–30).

These views carry through to the final report (Review of Higher Education Financing and Policy 1998, p. 25). From a UK perspective, both recommendations are a target for UK policy to aim at. From an Australian perspective, it is worth noting that a move towards market prices (that is, fees set by universities within a regulatory framework) fully supported by income-contingent loans makes it possible to take the millions of dollars currently spent on general subsidies and use them instead on specific subsidies carefully targeted on groups for whom access is most fragile. Such a move is unambiguously progressive – it benefits tomorrow's less well off at the expense of today's middle class – and, precisely for that reason, is not universally popular. The Australian middle class is vigilant in defence of its perks. In that respect the two countries are identical.

Notes

* Financial support from the Nuffield Foundation is gratefully acknowledged. Many of the ideas in this paper result from collaboration with Iain Crawford. I have also enjoyed many useful discussions about these matters over the years with Mark Blaug and Bruce Chapman.

1   For fuller Australian discussion, see Committee on Higher Education Funding (1988) (Wran Report) and Chapman (1988, 1997a). For UK discussion, see Barr (1989, ch. 5; 1991; 1998b, ch. 13) and UK National Committee of Inquiry into Higher Education (1997a, ch. 20).
2   Note that the answers to these questions differ as between university students on the one hand and school children and their parents on the other. Thus it is not inconsistent to support mechanisms (for example, vouchers and income-contingent loans) empowering consumers in higher education but to oppose them for school education.
3   With income-contingent repayments, precisely *because* repayments are exactly related to income, the threshold for repayment can be fairly low. With mortgage-type repayments, because the graduate pays either zero or a full instalment, the threshold has to be high, slowing the repayment flow.
4   A parallel report on further education (broadly comparable to TAFE) was also published in summer 1997; see UK Further Education Funding Council (1997) and, for the Government's response, UK Department for Education and Employment (1998a).
5   The Labour government elected in May 1997 no longer focuses so tightly on the current deficit; however, its stated educational priorities favour pre-university education, so that the funding problem in higher education remains.

References

Australian Bureau of Statistics 1997, *Government Finance Statistics, Australia,* 1995–96, Cat. no. 5512.0, ABS, Canberra.

Barnes, J. and Barr, N. 1988, *Strategies for Higher Education: The Alternative White Paper,* Aberdeen University Press for David Hume Institute, Edinburgh, and Suntory-Toyota International Centre for Economics and Related Disciplines, London School of Economics.

Barr, N. 1989, *Student Loans: The Next Steps*, Aberdeen University Press for David Hume Institute, Edinburgh, and Suntory-Toyota International Centre for Economics and Related Disciplines, London School of Economics.

Barr, N. 1991, 'Income-contingent student loans: an idea whose time has come', in *Economics, Culture and Education: Essays in Honour of Mark Blaug*, ed. G. K. Shaw, Edward Elgar, Cheltenham [this volume, Ch. 6].

Barr, N. 1997a, 'Student loans in New Zealand', in *Third Report: The Dearing Report: Some Funding Issues*, Volume II, Minutes of Evidence and Appendices, House of Commons Education and Employment Committee, Session 1997–98, HC24 1-II, TSO, London.

Barr, N. 1997b, 'Student loans: towards a new public/private mix', *Public Money and Management*, vol. 17, no. 3, pp. 31–40.

Barr, N. 1998a, 'The Dearing Report and government response: a commentary', Discussion Paper, Centre for Economic Policy Research, Research School of Social Sciences, Australian National University.

Barr, N. 1998b, *The Economics of the Welfare State*, 3rd edn, Oxford University Press, Oxford, and Stanford University Press, Stanford, Calif.

Barr, N. and Crawford, I. 1997, 'The Dearing Report, the government's response and a view ahead', in *Third Report: The Dearing Report: Some Funding Issues*, Volume II, Minutes of Evidence and Appendices, House of Commons Education and Employment Committee, Session 1997–98, HC24 1-II, TSO, London, pp. 88–103.

Blaug, M. 1976, 'The empirical status of human capital theory: a slightly jaundiced survey', *Journal of Economic Literature*, vol. 14, pp. 827–56. [Reprinted in Blaug (1987, pp. 100–28).]

Blaug, M. 1985, 'Where are we now in the economics of education?', *Economics of Education Review*, vol. 4, no. 1. pp. 17–28.

Blaug, M. 1987, *The Economics of Education and the Education of an Economist*, Edward Elgar, Aldershot.

Chapman, B. 1988, 'An economic analysis of the Higher Education Contribution Scheme of the Wran Report', *Economic Analysis and Policy*, vol. 18, no. 2, pp. 171–88.

Chapman, B. 1997a, 'Conceptual issues and the Australian experience with income-contingent charges for higher education', *Economic Journal*, vol. 107, no. 442, pp. 738–51.

Chapman, B. 1997b, 'Some financing issues for Australian higher education teaching', in *Learning for Life: A Policy Discussion Paper* (R. West, Chair), Review of Higher Education Financing and Policy (West Committee), AGPS, Canberra.

Committee on Higher Education Funding (Wran Committee) 1988, *Report of the Committee on Higher Education Funding* (N. Wran, Chair), AGPS, Canberra.

Review of Higher Education Financing and Policy (West Committee) 1997, *Learning for Life: A Policy Discussion Paper* (R. West, Chair), AGPS, Canberra.

Review of Higher Education Financing and Policy (West Committee) 1998, *Learning for Life: Final Report* (R. West, Chair), AGPS, Canberra.

UK Department for Education and Employment 1998a, *Further Education for the Millennium: Response to the Kennedy Report*, TSO, London.

UK Department for Education and Employment 1998b, *Higher Education for the 21st Century: Response to the Dearing Report*, TSO, London.

UK Department for Education and Employment 1998c, *The Learning Age: A Renaissance for a New Britain*, Cm 3790, TSO, London.

UK Further Education Funding Council 1997, *Learning Works: Widening Participation in Further Education* (Kennedy Report), Further Education Funding Council, Coventry.

UK National Committee of Inquiry into Higher Education (Dearing Committee) 1997a, *Higher Education in the Learning Society: Report of the National Committee* (R. Dearing, Chair), HMSO, London; also at http://www.leeds.ac.uk/educol/ncihe.

UK National Committee of Inquiry into Higher Education (Dearing Committee) 1997b, *Higher Education in the Learning Society: Summary Report* (R. Dearing, Chair), HMSO, London; also at http://www.leeds.ac.uk/educol/ncihe.

Part 3

Shifting tectonic plates

The 2004 legislation

Chapter 12

2000 **The benefits of education: what we know and what we don't**

Nicholas Barr (2000), 'The Benefits of Education: What We Know and What We Don't', in *Economic Growth and Government Policy*, Papers presented at a HM Treasury seminar held at 11 Downing Street on 12 October 2000, London: HM Treasury, pp. 33–40.

The essay question I was set has two parts: what are the returns to education; and where do social and private returns diverge? The answer to those questions sheds light on what I take to be the questions the Treasury is *really* asking:

• What is the efficient level of spending on education?
• What is the efficient level of taxpayer subsidy?

This paper argues that these questions – though critically important – can be answered, at best, only indicatively.

The conclusion of a very different literature (Sen, 1999; Barr, 1999; Ravallion, 1996) is that it is not possible to quantify a value-free definition of poverty. Instead, the decision about where to pitch the level of poverty relief depends on social choice constrained by fiscal realities. This does not mean that there should be no poverty studies, but that judgement is needed in interpreting any particular set of results. I shall argue that problems – both of concept and measurement – mean that the benefits to education, similarly, cannot be quantified in any definitive way. A conceptual impasse, it is of course true, cannot be allowed to interfere with operational imperatives. Equally, however, one of the scarcest of all scarce resources is high-grade brain power, which should not be wasted in the search for a Holy Grail.

Section 1 discusses the objectives of education, the key point being that they are multiple and hard to measure. Section 2 discusses the benefits of education and explains the difficulties which arise in trying to quantify them. The implications for assessing the efficient quantity and mix of education spending are assessed in section 3. Section 4 discusses policy making when policy makers are imperfectly informed, looking particularly at tertiary education, the area where policy choices are most diverse and which evokes the greatest controversy.

1 Objectives: what do we mean by a 'good' education?

The objective of education policy is to improve educational outcomes. These outcomes derive from many sources: formal education is one; natural ability is another; good parenting is critical; and there is increasing evidence of the link between childhood poverty and poor educational outcomes.

Improving educational outcomes has both equity and efficiency aspects. Equity is concerned with the distribution of educational outcomes, e.g. whether poorer people end up with fewer qualifications and, as a result, with lower incomes. One of many definitions of equity is that of *equality of opportunity*. This does not mean that everyone (for example) goes to university; it does not even mean that anyone who wishes can go to university. But it does mean that if two people have identical abilities and identical tastes, they receive the same education irrespective of factors which are regarded as irrelevant such as parental income. This definition of equity at least has the advantage that it apportions scarcity in a just way.

Allocative efficiency (sometimes referred to as *external efficiency*) is concerned with producing the types of educational activities which equip individuals – economically, socially, politically and culturally – for the societies in which they live. It embraces the total amount spent on education, and also the division of resources between different types and levels of education. It will depend, *inter alia*, on a country's economic development: in a poor country, efficiency suggests emphasis on basic skills of literacy and numeracy; wealthier countries can afford to spend more on greater diversity of subject matter and on more advanced education. In all these cases, efficiency is concerned with using today's educational resources well (static efficiency), and with using them to promote economic growth (dynamic efficiency).

Efficiency therefore matters. If resources are used inefficiently, they will fail to produce the maximum gain in educational outcomes and, in consequence, will fail to promote growth effectively. If no extra resources are made available, inefficiency means that some people will have less productive (and hence poorer) lives; and if, as a result, growth is lower it means that everyone will be less well-off in the future than they might have been. If extra resources are made available, inefficiency in the education system comes at the expense of better hospitals or roads, or higher personal consumption, deprivations which could be avoided with better use of educational resources.

The efficient level of output, Q^* in Figure 12.1, is that at which the marginal social benefit deriving from any improvement in the education system equals the resulting marginal social cost. To quantify efficiency therefore means that we have to measure (a) the social costs of education and (b) its social benefits. Measuring costs presents no insurmountable problems. The direct costs of the state educational system and its components are set out in the public accounts. Apportioning overheads is not an exact science, but standard methods exist. For people past school leaving age costs should include an estimate of forgone earnings.

Measuring benefits is vastly more difficult. To explain why, it is necessary to look in more detail at what is being measured on the horizontal axis of Figure 12.1, in other words the meaning of 'good educational outcomes'. Discussion frequently portrays the issue as mainly technical, but that view is too narrow. It is insufficiently understood (not least because

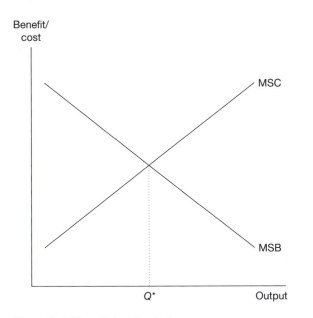

Figure 12.1 The efficient level of output

quantification is very difficult) that the primary purpose of education is to transmit knowledge and skills, *and* attitudes and values. Education is not only technical but also cultural. A central part of its purpose is to produce agreement about values.

To make these arguments more concrete, my teaching actively promotes certain values, for example that what matters is the analytical content of an argument, not the status or gender of the person making it. Contrasting views include: students should never disagree with their teachers; women should listen but not talk; answers get higher marks if they conform with my/LSE's/the government's ideology – all values which have been actively promoted in other times and/or countries, and some – for example the central importance of educating girls as well as boys – still a matter of considerable concern in some countries.

To that extent, the purpose of education is to promote a homogeneity of values. A second set of values, in contrast, promotes diversity, for example the view that disagreement is no bad thing, indeed that active discussion and debate is fundamental to the health of a free society. Related is the value of free expression in elections, with no subsequent retribution by the winners. In the educational context, the underlying value is that disagreement and debate are not only tolerated but are in many ways the purpose of a good education. As another aspect of diversity, families will have different views about subject matter, the role of discipline and the place of religion.

A major issue in any society is the dividing line between the promotion of homogeneity and the boundaries of diversity. Freedom of speech is to be encouraged, but many western democracies make incitement to racial hatred a criminal offence. Diversity and artistic expression are valued, yet many countries have laws against pornography. Inculcating attitudes and values in this way may sound like the educational propaganda of communist education, but with the critical difference that in a free society the values which the educational system seeks to transmit have democratic legitimacy.

Values are important not just because promoting social cohesion is a significant activity in its own right, but also because values are an important ingredient in individual productivity, i.e. the technical and the cultural aspects of education can interact. Education in Communist countries, for example, included values supportive of central planning and totalitarian government, values which hinder productivity in a market economy (for fuller discussion, see Barr, 2001b).

The conclusion to which this leads is that the education package, and hence the meaning of a 'good' education, will depend on the economic, political and social structure of the country concerned. Thus a definitive measure of the benefits of education is not possible. The next section discusses the problem in some detail.

2 Measuring the benefits of education

Attempts to measure the benefits of education face two sets of intractable problems: it is not possible to measure educational outputs, educational inputs or the connection between them (section 2.1); nor (section 2.2) can we take for granted a causal link between education and its outputs. Thus a key problem on which Blaug (1976, 1985) dwells (and which explains the 'slightly jaundiced' view in the title of the first paper) is the difficulty in quantifying the causal link between education and increased individual productivity which lies at the heart of human capital theory. Notwithstanding the strong presumptive arguments in section 3, attempts to quantify the benefits of education rest on shaky foundations, a conclusion which advances in estimation techniques are unlikely to change soon.

2.1 Measuring output and inputs

Output cannot be measured

Since there is no single definition of a 'good' education, there is no unambiguous measure of educational output. It is possible to measure test scores but they are imperfect. First, the connection between test scores and technical skills is by no means simple, so that test results are imperfect even in their own terms. Second, even if tests were a perfect measure of technical skills, educational outputs are much broader. There are consumption benefits for the individual, including the enjoyment of the educational process itself. There are investment benefits, such as greater productivity and, connected, higher pay, greater job satisfaction and increased enjoyment of leisure. Blanchflower and Oswald (2000) show that, holding everything including income constant, education is associated with greater recorded levels of life satisfaction; their results also show that job satisfaction is typically highest among people with advanced levels of education. A third set of deficiencies with test scores as a measure of output is that they take no account of a range of external benefits, including shared values. That most of these externalities are unmeasurable does not make them unreal.

External benefits

Education may create benefits to society over and above those to the individual,[1] of which the following examples are conventionally discussed.

FUTURE TAX PAYMENTS

There is at least one strong external benefit. If education increases a person's future earnings, it increases her future tax payments. Her investment

---

1 For fuller discussion of the theory, see Barr (1998a, Ch. 4 and non-technical appendix).

in education thus confers a 'dividend' on future taxpayers. It is a standard proposition that in the presence of such an external benefit, the resulting flow of investment will be inefficiently small. A standard solution is an appropriately-designed subsidy. For precisely that reason, most countries offer tax advantages for a firm's investment in physical capital.

PRODUCTION BENEFITS

Production benefits arise if education makes someone more productive, and also makes others more productive. The fact that you have become computer literate and hence can use email may make me more productive. Individuals may become more adaptable and better able, to keep up with technological change. The economic spin-offs of an occupationally mobile population are relevant in this context. It is not surprising that much 'high tech' industry occurs in clusters like Silicone Valley, Cambridge (Massachusetts) and Cambridge (England), and education lies at the heart of endogenous growth theory (Romer, 1993). Measuring these benefits is difficult, not least, as discussed below, because it is hard to separate the effects of education from other determinants of a person's productivity, such as natural ability and the quantity and quality of physical capital.

SOCIAL COHESION

Education may create cultural benefits external to the recipient, first, in that a common cultural experience (music, art, literature) may foster communication, both at the time and in the future. There may also be neighbourhood effects: taking children to school, for example, brings people into contact and may foster shared attitudes locally. More broadly, there is evidence (Bynner and Egerton, 2000) of a link between participation in higher education and participation in political activities, community affairs and voluntary work. More broadly still, education is part of the socialisation process: its function in transmitting attitudes and values, discussed earlier, is a critical part of fostering shared attitudes, thus strengthening social cohesion

These externalities, particularly the latter two, raise obvious measurement problems. As discussed below, there are also major conceptual problems. Though the externality argument is strong in presumptive terms, satisfactory empirical verification is lacking. Because of the 'tax dividend' point there is an unarguable external benefit, but it is not possible to show how much.

The conclusion is that it is extraordinarily difficult to measure the output of education, not least because of the problems of measuring non-monetary returns and external benefits.

Connecting inputs and outputs

Even if output could be measured, a further set of problems concerns the connection between output and inputs, shown by the education production function. The first strategic problem is the difficulty of measuring the inputs: it is possible to measure the quantity of some inputs (teachers' and pupils' time, buildings, equipment, etc.), but not the quality of teachers; and inputs like natural ability and the quantity and quality of parenting cannot be measured at all. Second, as discussed already, it is not possible to measure output except in terms of test scores. Hanushek (1986) investigates the research on schooling 'and explores what has been learned and where major gaps remain, focussing on production and efficiency aspects of schools, as opposed to the ultimate uses of education' (p. 1142). In other words, he does not discuss external efficiency (i.e. the contribution of education to cultural and economic goals) but concentrates on internal efficiency, i.e. the effectiveness of the school system in producing educational outcomes such as examination performance. Hanushek (1996) goes into more detail on investment in education, discussing in particular the finding that '[t]hree decades of intensive research leave a clear picture that school resource variations are not closely related to variations in student outcomes . . .' (p. 9). Given the range of missing variables, this result is not surprising.

A third problem in trying to connect inputs and outputs is that the production function itself is hard to estimate. Studies tend to assume (since no other assumption is available) that schools have a single, simple objective – maximising their pupils' test scores. Though that model is analytically tractable and has a surface plausibility, it is fundamentally flawed: it implies, for example, that a school should stop teaching children who are not capable of passing tests.

2.2 Establishing causality: the screening hypothesis

Even if all these measurement problems were solved, a problem remains. Previous discussion implicitly assumed that education leads causally to increased individual productivity. The 'screening hypothesis' questions the causal link, at least for post-primary education, arguing that education is *associated* with increased productivity but does not *cause* it.[2]

The argument has two parts: first, education beyond a basic level does not increase individual productivity; second, firms seek high-ability workers but, prior to employing them, cannot distinguish high-ability workers from low-ability workers, just as insurance companies may not be able to distinguish high and low risks. In that situation, individuals have the incentive to make themselves stand out by some sort of signal. The screening hypothesis argues that post-primary education does exactly that: it gives a signal to prospective employers which it is in the individual's interest to acquire – it signals that he or she is a high-productivity worker. Just as good health may be due more to a naturally strong constitution than to medical care

2 The large literature on this and other aspects of the economics of education is surveyed by Blaug (1976, 1985) and Glennerster (1993).

so, according to this view, is productivity the result of natural ability rather than post-primary education. If we take the hypothesis literally, it means that there is a private benefit to the individual from post-primary education, but no external benefit.

There are various reasons why the strong form of the hypothesis does not hold. It fails, obviously, where education includes professional training, for example medicine. It also fails where there is more than one type of job: since skills and job characteristics are heterogenous, it is necessary to match workers and jobs, so that education has a social benefit as a matching device. Whether the hypothesis has some validity is an empirical matter. The verdict is undecided and will likely remain so, since individual productivity, as discussed above, is partly determined by unmeasurable factors such as natural ability and family background.

3 What is the efficient level of education spending?

In short, it is possible to measure the costs of education, but not the benefits. What, then, can be said about the efficient level of education spending?

3.1 Quantitative analysis

If education (a) increases individual productivity and (b) creates external benefits, the amount of education chosen by an individual in a market system will generally be less than the optimal amount, Q^* in Figure 12.1. One solution is to subsidise education by an amount equal to the external benefits it creates. In contrast, if the screening hypothesis is valid, education has private benefits but no external benefits; thus there is no case for a subsidy for post-primary education. Since it is not possible to measure the output, it is not possible to quantify the external benefits; and since we cannot measure causality, we cannot establish whether and to what extent, education has a screening function. Thus it is not possible to measure the social benefits of education, with two major implications: it is not possible to quantify the efficient level of education spending, Q^* in Figure 12.1; and it is not possible to establish the efficient level of subsidy for post-primary education.

Notwithstanding these difficulties, many studies attempt to measure the returns to education.[3] Glennerster (1998) presents modifications of the DfEE evidence to the Dearing Committee, showing social and private rates of return to a degree. The figures in Table 12.1, like other such estimates, incorporate an 'alpha factor', which is the assumption about the extent to which the higher earnings of people with more education are attributed to that extra education. Thus $\alpha = 0.6$ means that 60 per cent

3 For recent UK evidence, see the Education Department's submission to the Dearing Committee (UK National Committee of Inquiry into Higher Education, 1998), Glennerster (1998, Table 3.8), and Dutta, Sefton and Weale (1999). On the USA, see Card (1999).

Table 12.1 Social and private rates of return to education, 19-year-old men

Social rates of return (%)	Alpha = 0.6	Alpha = 0.8
1985–7	6	7
1989/90 and 1991	7	9
1992–4	7	9
Private rates of return (%)		
1984–7	18	23
1989–91	13	15
1991	11.5	13

Source: Glennerster (1998, Table 3.8).

of extra earnings are caused by extra education; by implication the remaining 40 per cent is due to natural ability. Glennerster makes the point that social class still exerts a non-trivial influence in the UK, so that education might have an important screening function, especially for people from poorer backgrounds (in other words, a person from a poorer background might be considered for a 'good' job only if he or she has a degree). Thus alpha might well be lower in the UK than in the USA, where the influence of social class, it can be argued, is smaller.

Recent papers investigate earnings differentials between identical twins with different educational experience in an attempt to control for ability (hence at least partially addressing the screening issue) and for family background.[4] These results are significant advances on earlier work, but still need to be heavily qualified. They measure the money returns to education, but omit nonpecuniary benefits to the individual, such as the consumption value of education and job satisfaction, and a range of broader social benefits, for example from shared values. As a result, these measures tend to underestimate both private and social benefits to an unknown extent. In addition, to the extent that screening is more of a factor than the estimates pick up, these measures overestimate social benefits (though not private benefits), again by an unknown amount.

For these and other reasons, the causal connection between education and economic growth cannot be quantified. Output growth depends on the increase in the quantity and quality of capital, the increase in quantity and quality of labour, on technological advance and on a range of other factors. Education as a whole affects only one of these variables, the quality of labour (and according to the screening hypothesis not even that), and more advanced forms of education are connected with technological advance. The estimation problem is to separate the quantitative effect of education on the quality of labour and on technological advance, given all the other influences on output, in a situation where measures of output, inputs, and the production function are highly imperfect, and

4 On the USA, see Ashenfelter and Krueger, 1994; Ashenfelter and Rouse, 1998. For recent UK evidence, see Bonjour *et al.*, 2000.

where causality is problematic. It is therefore not surprising that quantitative measures of the link between education spending and economic growth remain problematical.

3.2 Qualitative arguments

This rather gloomy conclusion does not mean that we can say nothing about the connection between education and growth, but that we need to rely on more qualitative analysis. There are three lines of argument which connect education to national economic performance.

Human capital: always important, but arguably more important than ever.

Alfred Marshall, writing over 100 years ago argued that:

> [T]hey [the children of the working class] go to the grave carrying undeveloped abilities and faculties; which if they could have borne full fruit would have added to the material wealth of the country . . . to say nothing of higher considerations . . . many times as much as would have covered the expense of providing adequate opportunities for their development.
>
> But the point we have especially to insist now is that the evil is cumulative. The worse fed are the children of one generation, the less will they earn when they grow up, and the less will be their power of providing adequately for . . . their children; and so on to the following generations.
>
> (Marshall, 1961, Book VI, p. 569)

The essence of Marshall's argument is the high cumulative cost of making the wrong investment decisions. The costs of under-investing in tertiary education in terms of quantity and quality will be much greater than those of expansion which turns out not to have been strictly necessary.

Thus the argument that human capital is important is an old one. A new twist, due to Thurow (1996), argues that it is an even more important determinant of differential national economic performance today than in the past. The simplest way to make the point starts from a conventional production function:

$$Q = f(K, L, M)$$

where output, Q, is related to inputs of capital, K, labour, L, and raw materials, M, through the production function f. Considering each of these in turn:

- In the nineteenth century, access to raw materials was critical. A hundred years ago almost all the largest US firms were involved with raw materials in one way or another. Today, in contrast, value-added comes increasingly from other sources: the material component of computers is a trivial part of their cost; the steel used in a modern car costs less than the electronics.

- Historically, countries with a larger capital stock would typically be richer and so, through higher savings, could invest more than poorer countries, thus further increasing their capital stock, the US being a case in point. With today's global capital markets, domestic investment is less constrained by domestic savings: investment by an entrepreneur in Thailand is not constrained by Thai domestic savings, since he can borrow elsewhere.

- Technology (i.e. the function, f) remains a critical determinant of relative economic performance. Historically, technology tended to be tied to specific countries. Today, not least because information flows are instant, technological advance moves across countries more quickly than hitherto.

Thus f, K and M are less important explanations of differential economic performance today than in the past. The remaining variable, L, thus assumes increasing importance. In short, a combination of technological advance and international competitive pressures makes education a more important source of economic performance than ever.

The nature of technological advance

A connected set of arguments relates to the nature of technological change. First, it takes the form of rising demand for skilled people and declining demand for unskilled workers. Second, change is increasingly rapid. Skills learned when young no longer last a lifetime; thus individuals need skills which are flexible enough to adapt to changing technology and which need updating. These changes explain the movement into the 'information age', meaning a need for education and training which is (a) larger than previously, (b) more diverse and (c) repeated, in the sense that people will require periodic retraining. They also explain the close links between low educational achievement and social exclusion (see Atkinson and Hills, 1998; Sparkes, 1999).

Not least because of the measurement problems already discussed, however, the argument is not a simple one. Technological progress increases the demand for skilled workers, but in specific areas can reduce the need for skills – for example, computers are much more user-friendly than 10 years ago. However, the overall decline in the demand for unskilled labour has been sharp. Thus part of the case for investment in education and training is to ensure that workers have the skills necessary for the application of modern technology. As second part of the case is that investment in human capital – particularly in broad, flexible skills – offers a hedge against technological dynamism. Specific skills may become redundant, but education and training should give people general skills, and therefore saves the resources which would otherwise have to be devoted to retraining labour whose skills had become outdated or, at worst, to supporting workers socially excluded as a result of technological advance. As discussed in Barr (2001b), a problematic legacy of communist education is the narrow, inflexible skills it gave people.

Demographic change

The proportion of older people is rising, presaging high spending on pensions and other age-related activities such as medical and long-term care. The best solution is to increase output sufficiently to meet the combined expectations of workers and pensioners. If the problem is that workers are becoming relatively more scarce, the efficient response is to increase labour productivity. Demographic change is thus an argument for additional spending on investment both in technology and in human capital. Expansion of education and training, it can be argued, is therefore necessary precisely *because* of demographic change.[5]

For all these reasons, notwithstanding the impossibility of quantifying the efficient level and mix of spending on education, training and retraining, the qualitative arguments that education contributes to personal and national goals are strong. The Dearing Committee (UK National Committee of Inquiry into Higher Education, 1997, para. 6.8) endorsed the 'international consensus that higher level skills are crucial to future economic competitiveness', and went on to quote an OECD (1997) study:

> The direction is universal participation: 100 per cent participation with fair and equal opportunities to study; in some form of tertiary education; at some stage in the life cycle and not necessarily end on to secondary education; in a wide variety of structures, forms and types of delivery; undertaken on equal terms either part-time or full-time; publicly-subsidised but with shared client contributions; closely involving partners in the community; serving multiple purposes – educational, social, cultural and economic.

4 Application to tertiary education: making policy when policy makers are imperfectly informed

4.1 Who should pay?

In considering who should pay for tertiary education, the starting point is the assertion that a high-quality mass system cannot be entirely taxpayer

5 For fuller discussion of pensions policy in the face of demographic change, see Barr, 2000.

funded. Thus public funds have to be supplemented by private funds. This conclusion is based not on ideology, but on two deeply practical arguments: large-scale tertiary education is vital; but it is too expensive to rely entirely on public funding. Thus it is necessary to involve private funds. These can come from various sources including the student's family, and student earnings while a student. Both of these have their place. However, the only source of private funds which is both large-scale and equitable is students' future earnings. A well-designed student loan scheme is therefore a core element of a mass system, specifically a wide-ranging system with income-contingent repayments of the sort I have advocated elsewhere.[6]

How should costs be shared between the taxpayer and the individual, i.e. how much subsidy should the various components of tertiary education receive? The theoretical argument is that the student should pay for her private benefit, while the taxpayer contributes a subsidy equal to the external benefit.

This argument commands almost universal acceptance in qualitative terms. As explained in section 2, however, there is no scientifically valid way of measuring the relative sizes of private and external benefits. The following discussion takes it as read that there *is* a case for continuing subsidy, but leaves open its size (a) because there is no definitive way of measuring it, and (b) because – whatever the scientific arguments – the matter is ultimately one to be decided by politicians and the electorate.

Whatever the size of the external benefit, however, there is one strong result – that tertiary education – and especially higher education – creates a private benefit, i.e. the typical student benefits personally from a degree, through higher earnings, greater job satisfaction and/or greater enjoyment of leisure. Thus the theory argues unambiguously that some of the costs should be borne by the individual. Alongside macroeconomic arguments about affordability, microeconomic arguments therefore also point to the centrality of a good student loan scheme.

4.2 Who should make the decisions?

Three questions stand out: are consumers capable of making good decisions; are universities and other institutions capable of making good decisions; and who should decide how large the system should be?

How useful is consumer sovereignty?

I have argued elsewhere (Barr, 1998a, Ch. 13; 1998b) that students are generally able to make efficient choices for two sets of reasons: they are generally well-informed and/or have the time and capacity to make

---

6 See Barr and Crawford (1998a, b) and, for fuller discussion, Barr (2001a, Chs 10–14).

themselves well-informed;[7] separately, tertiary education is becoming increasingly diverse, making the problem too complex for a central planner. Consumer sovereignty is therefore useful. The analysis leads to very different conclusions for school education.

How useful is producer sovereignty?

One aspect – academic freedom – I take as a given. A second aspect – the *economic* freedom of universities – is the subject of heated discussion. With an elite university system of the sort existing in most countries until relatively recently, it was possible, as a polite myth, to assume that all universities were of equal quality, that degrees were worth the same whichever university conferred them, and hence that universities could, broadly, be funded equally. With a mass system this myth is no longer sustainable. The characteristics, the quality and the costs of different degrees at different institutions will vary much more widely than hitherto.

As a result, universities need to be differentially funded to take account both of a particular institution's costs and of the demand for places. In principle this could be done by an all-knowing central planner. The problem, however, is too complex for that to be the sole mechanism. A mass system – and *a fortiori* a mass system in an increasingly complex world – needs a funding regime in which institutions can charge differential prices to reflect their differential costs.

The conclusion this suggests is that producer sovereignty is not just useful; as tertiary education expands and the diversity of its activities increases, it becomes essential. As discussed below, this does not mean unfettered markets.

How large should the system be?

Why is mass tertiary education necessary? Is there an investment argument: would expansion of tertiary education increase the rate of economic growth? Second, should there be expansion for consumption reasons, i.e. would extra resources add sufficiently to the quality of life (for reasons other than output growth) to make expansion efficient? Though these questions are critically important, they cannot be answered as crisply as the questions about consumer and producer sovereignty.

From an investment viewpoint, several arguments for expanding tertiary education were put forward in section 3. First, it can be argued that technological change makes human capital more important than ever as a determinant of national economic performance. The nature of that technological change is leading to rising demand for skilled people and

---

7 As discussed later, while it is true that the generality of students are able to make efficient choices, this is much less true of people from socially-excluded backgrounds, for whom explicit action is needed to increase knowledge and raise aspirations.

declining demand for the unskilled. Its rate of change requires that individuals are retrained periodically – so-called lifelong learning. Those arguments are strengthened by international competitive pressures. To keep up with other countries it is necessary to increase the productivity of capital and labour; if tertiary education contributes cost-effectively to increased productivity there is an efficiency case for expansion. A complementary argument, as the earlier quote from Alfred Marshall brings out, is the downside risk of under-investing rather than over-investing. Finally, demographic prospects strengthen the argument for additional investment in education and training.

These arguments create a strong presumption for increasing the resources devoted to education (for discussion of higher education, see Greenaway and Haynes, 2000).[8] For the reasons set out in section 2, however, the case is strong only in presumptive terms. We cannot state with any precision how much additional investment there should be in total nor, as discussed earlier, how the costs of that investment should be divided between the individual and the state.

Policy when policy makers are imperfectly informed

The preceding discussion suggests the following stylised facts: (a) consumers of tertiary education are generally well-informed; (b) producers are generally well-informed; (c) the optimal size of the sector cannot satisfactorily be quantified.

Let us accept (a) and (b), at least in the weak sense that consumers and producers, if not perfectly-informed, are at least better-informed than central planners, not least because of all the unmeasurable benefits. This suggests that a broad strategy for dealing with (c) is to divide responsibility into two separate decisions:

- Consumers and producers decide on the size of the sector: students apply to institutions; providers decide how many students to accept and what fees to charge; employers decide which graduates they want to employ. These are decisions properly made by the citizenry and by education providers.
- Government decides how much it proposes to spend on tertiary education. This decision is properly the province of government. If public spending falls short of that necessary to meet the choices of citizens

8 In 1995 total spending (public plus private) on higher education in the UK was 0.7 per cent of GDP. The comparable figure in the USA was 2 per cent; the OECD average was 1.5 per cent. In 1996 Argentina spent 0.7 per cent and Chile 1.6 per cent of GDP, respectively (all figures from OECD, 1998, Table B1.1d). At face value, the UK therefore would have to spend an additional, £7 billion per year on higher education to reach the OECD average. Any increase on remotely that scale would have to a significant extent to come from private sources.

and education providers, the difference has to be made up with private spending.

In short, the market decides on total spending, the government on public spending.[9]

4.3 The resulting system

The analysis of this and earlier sections suggests that the providers of tertiary education should set fees, with income-contingent loans covering all tuition charges and living costs which are not covered by taxpayer funding.[10]

Efficiency

The argument for efficiency is that participants are well-informed and all relevant stakeholders – students, universities, employers and government – have an influence on outcomes.

Students pay a part of the cost of their qualification and are therefore better placed to demand greater variation in what universities provide. Students will make choices about which institution they attend; they will make demands about the type of course they go to; they will also make demands about the structure of the qualification – for example whether a degree is part-time or full-time, 3-year or compressed into a shorter time, teaching during the day or in the evening, etc.

Employers can influence outcomes indirectly through their choice of employees. They can also have a direct influence through negotiation about course content. For example, professional bodies such as accountants and social workers already give partial exemption from professional examinations to students graduating from courses whose content takes account of the needs of those professional bodies.

Education providers also have a role, responding to changes in the pattern of demand in ways which are wholly impossible within a centrally-planned funding mechanism. Institutions have to be free to determine price (i.e. the level of tuition fees they charge), quantity (i.e. the number of students they accept) and quality, i.e. the types of courses they offer. Thus they will have economic freedom to parallel their academic freedom.

Finally, government retains a major influence. It no longer controls the system as a central planner, but that does not mean that it is powerless – far from it. Government has a direct role in funding, as discussed earlier.

---

9 This strategy is presented at its simplest; in practice, as discussed shortly, the government would not take an entirely passive role over student numbers or tuition fees.

10 This is the system Iain Crawford and I proposed to the Dearing Committee, subsequently published as Barr and Crawford, 1998a.

It also acts as a facilitator for private funds, for example through its role in implementing a system of student loans. Its second important task is to promote access in the ways described in the discussion of equity, below.

The third role of government is quality assurance. Part of the task is to ensure that regulation is in place and enforced. Incentives, however, are at least as important, for example more generous funding for institutions with better completion rates, subsequent employment rates, and the like. It is also possible to combine regulation and incentives: a minimalist system of quality control would simply require universities to publish timely and accurate performance data on their web sites, for example the destination of its recent graduates, thus giving prospective students the information they needed to vote with their feet (see Cave *et al.*, 1992).

A fourth role of government is to influence the degree of competition between institutions. Tertiary education providers are not the conventional firms of economic theory: they do not make a homogeneous product; they do not maximise profit; and the 'product' is not well-defined (see Winston, 1999). Thus red-in-tooth-and-claw competition is not the best environment for tertiary education. That, however, does not mean that competition has no role. An important task of government is to regulate the extent of competition.[11]

Equity

The system outlined above is also more equitable. First, it improves targeting, since a move from tax funding towards loans particularly in higher education – reduces the subsidy to the best-off. A move towards market prices (i.e. fees set by universities within a regulatory framework) fully supported by income-contingent loans makes it possible to take the large sums currently spent on *general* subsidies and use them instead on *specific* subsidies carefully targeted on groups for whom access is most fragile. Such a move is unambiguously progressive.

The system is more equitable, second, because targeting frees resources to promote access more directly and powerfully than measures which spread subsidies more indiscriminately across the student population. Such policies have several important dimensions. Money is clearly an important ingredient. Scholarships for bright disadvantaged people means that they need a smaller loan or no loan. Access can be improved also by making loans available to all students, full-time and part-time, undergraduate and postgraduate, in further education and higher education.

Information and raising aspirations are also critical. Many people do not progress to further or higher education because they have never thought

11 For fuller discussion of how voucher-type arrangements can encompass anything from completely unconstrained competition, at one extreme, to a mimic of central planning, at the other, see [this volume, Ch. 3]. On equity aspects of vouchers, see Le Grand (1989).

of doing so. Thus mentoring of school children by current university students, preferably from similar backgrounds, is important; so are visits by schoolchildren to universities. Action to improve information is vital for access precisely because students from socially-excluded backgrounds will systematically be badly-informed. Such information activities need to happen early enough to prevent school drop out.[12]

Extra teaching/tutoring is a third ingredient. Finally, since the problems of access to higher education cannot be solved entirely within the tertiary education sector, resources should be used to promote access earlier in the education system.

The approach outlined above is explicitly aimed at a situation where, in the face of complex mass systems of tertiary education, policy makers are imperfectly informed.

- The system is efficient because outcomes are determined not by a single, imperfectly-informed part of government, but by the interacting decisions of students, universities and employers, subject to transparent influence by government.
- Choices, as far as possible, are made in the face of efficient prices, for example, student loans should have an interest rate based on the government's cost of borrowing.
- Flexible tuition fees, flexible student numbers and flexible percentage of taxpayer subsidy allow the system to evolve to accommodate a changing economic and technological environment and changing preferences.

The arrangements are also more equitable than present arrangements because resources are better-targeted and hence can be used to promote access more directly and effectively.

References

Ashenfelter, Orley, and Krueger, Alan (1994), 'Estimating the Returns to Schooling Using a New Sample of Twins', *American Economic Review*, Vol. 84, pp. 1157–73.
Ashenfelter, Orley, and Rouse, Cecilia (1998), 'Income, Schooling and Ability: Evidence from a New Sample of Identical Twins', *Quarterly Journal of Economics*, Vol. 113, No. 1, February, pp. 253–84.

12 The sorts of schemes which are involved include Saturday Schools, which bring schoolchildren from poor areas to university to study on Saturday morning; summer schools, which do something similar during the summer vacation; visit days when schoolchildren can visit a university; visits by academics to schools to make the idea of higher education more tangible; visits by current students, ideally from the same or a similar school, to schools in deprived areas; and mentoring of schoolchildren by university students, preferably from a similar background.

Atkinson, Anthony B., and Hills, John (eds) (1998), *Exclusion, Employment and Opportunity*, London: London School of Economics, Centre for the Analysis of Social Exclusion, CASEpaper 4.

Barr, Nicholas (1998a), *The Economics of the Welfare State*, 3rd edition, Oxford: Oxford University Press and Stanford, California: Stanford University Press.

Barr, Nicholas (1998b), 'Higher Education in Australia and Britain: What Lessons?', *Australian Economic Review*, Vol. 31, No. 2, June, pp. 179–88 [this volume, Ch. 11].

Barr, Nicholas (1999), 'Comments on "Economic Policy and Equity: An Overview" by Amartya Sen', in Tanzi, Vito, Chu, Ke-young, and Gupta, Sanjeev (eds), *Economic Policy and Equity*, Washington DC: International Monetary Fund, pp. 44–8.

Barr, Nicholas (2000), 'Reforming Pensions: Myths, Truths, and Policy Choices', Working Paper WP/00/139, Washington DC: International Monetary Fund, downloadable from http://www.imf.org/EXTERNAL/PUBS/CAT/.

Barr, Nicholas (2001a), *The Welfare State as Piggy Bank*, New York and Oxford: Oxford University Press.

Barr, Nicholas (2001b), 'Reforming welfare states in post-communist countries' in Balcerowicz, Leszek, and Orlowski, Lucjan (eds), *Ten Years After: Transition and Growth in Postcommunist Countries*, Cheltenham: Edward Elgar.

Barr, Nicholas, and Crawford, Iain (1998a), 'Funding Higher Education in an Age of Expansion', *Education Economics*, Vol. 6, No. 1, pp. 45–70 [this volume, Ch. 9].

Barr, Nicholas, and Crawford, Iain (1998b), 'The Dearing Report and the Government Response: A Critique', *Political Quarterly*, Vol. 69, No. 1, January–March, pp. 72–84 [this volume, Ch. 10].

Blanchflower, David, and Oswald, Andrew (2000), 'Wellbeing over Time in Britain and the USA', working paper, presented at the National Bureau of Economic Research Summer Workshop in Cambridge, Mass., July 2000. Downloadable at www.oswald.co.uk.

Blaug, Mark (1976), 'The Empirical Status of Human Capital Theory: A Slightly Jaundiced Survey', *Journal of Economic Literature*, September, pp. 827–56, reprinted in Blaug, Mark (1987), *The Economics of Education and the Education of an Economist*, Aldershot: Edward Elgar, pp. 100–28.

Blaug, Mark (1985), 'Where Are We Now in the Economics of Education?', *Economics of Education Review*, Vol. 4, No. 1, pp. 17–28, reprinted in Blaug, Mark (1987), *The Economics of Education and the Education of an Economist*, Aldershot: Edward Elgar, pp. 129–40.

Bonjour, Dorothe, Cherkas, Lyn, Haskel, Jonathan, Hawkes, Denise, and Spector, Tim (2000), 'Estimating Returns to Education Using a New Sample of Twins', London, Queen Mary Westfield College, mimeo.

Bynner, John, and Egerton, Muriel (2000), 'The Wider Benefits of Higher Education', Wider Benefits of Learning Research Centre, London: Institute of Education, for the Higher Education Funding Council for England in association with the Smith Institute.

Card, David (1999), 'The Causal Effect of Education on Earnings', in Ashenfelter, Orley, and Card, David (eds), *Handbook of Labor Economics*, Elsevier Science B. V.

Cave, Martin, Dodsworth, Ruth, and Thompson, David (1992), 'Regulatory Reform in Higher Education in the UK: Incentives for Efficiency and Product Quality', *Oxford Review of Economic Policy*, Vol. 8, No. 2, pp. 79–102.

Dutta, Jayasri, Sefton, James, and Weale, Martin (1999), 'Education and public policy', *Fiscal Studies*, Vol. 20, No. 4, pp. 351–86.

Glennerster, Howard (1993), 'The Economics of Education: Changing Fortunes', in Barr, Nicholas, and Whynes, David (1993), *Issues in the Economics of the Welfare State*, London: Macmillan, pp. 176–99.

Glennerster, Howard (1998), 'Education', in Glennerster, Howard, and Hills, John (eds), *The State of Welfare: The Economics of Social Spending*, Oxford: Oxford University Press, pp. 27–74.

Greenaway, David, and Haynes, Michelle (2000), *Funding Universities to Meet National and International Challenges*, Nottingham: University of Nottingham, also on www.nottingham.ac.uk/economics/funding.

Hanushek, Eric A. (1986), 'The Economics of Schooling: Production and Efficiency in Public Schools', *Journal of Economic Literature*, Vol. 23, No. 3, pp. 1141–77.

Hanushek, Eric A. (1996), 'Measuring Investment in Education', *Journal of Economic Perspectives*, 10(4), pp. 9–30.

Le Grand, Julian (1989), 'Markets, Welfare and Equality', in Le Grand, Julian, and Estrin, Saul (eds), *Market Socialism*, Oxford: Clarendon Press.

Marshall, Alfred (1961), *Principles of Economics*, 9th edn, London: Macmillan.

OECD (1997), *Thematic Review of Higher Education*, Paris: OECD.

OECD (1998), *Education at a Glance: OECD Indicators*, Paris: OECD.

Ravallion, Martin (1996), 'Issues in Measuring and Modelling Poverty', *Economic Journal*, Vol. 106, September, pp. 1328–44.

Romer, Paul (1993), 'Ideal Gaps and Object Gaps in Economic Development', *Journal of Monetary Economics*, Vol. 32, pp. 338–69.

Sen, Amartya K. (1999), 'Economic Policy and Equity: An Overview', in Tanzi, Vito, Chu, Ke-young, and Gupta, Sanjeev (eds), *Economic Policy and Equity*, Washington DC: International Monetary Fund, pp. 28–43.

Sparkes, Jo (1999), *Schools, Education and Social Exclusion*, London: London School of Economics, Centre for the Analysis of Social Exclusion, CASEpaper 29.

Thurow, Lester (1996), *The Future of Capitalism: How Today's Economic Forces Shape Tomorrow's World*, London: Nicholas Brealey.

UK National Committee of Inquiry into Higher Education (the Dearing Committee) (1997), *Higher Education in the Learning Society: Report 7: Rates of Return to Higher Education*, London: HMSO, also available at http://www.leeds.ac.uk/educol/ncihe.

Winston, Gordon (1999), 'Subsidies, Hierarchies and Peers: The Awkward Economics of Higher Education', *Journal of Economic Perspectives*, Vol. 13, No. 1, Winter, pp. 13–26.

Chapter 13

2002 Evidence to the Education Select Committee 1: funding higher education, policies for access and quality

Nicholas Barr (2002), 'Funding Higher Education: Policies for Access and Quality', House of Commons, Education and Skills Committee, *Post-16 Student Support*, Sixth Report of Session 2001–2, HC445, London: TSO, pp. Ev 19–35.

Executive summary[1,2]

1. This paper puts forward a strategy for achieving two objectives in higher education – improved access and increased quality – about which there is unanimous agreement.

2. Diagnosis. The introduction of income-contingent repayments in 1998 was a genuine and enormous advance. However, two strategic problems remain. First, income-contingency is little understood, causing unnecessary

1 This paper draws on Barr (2001, Chs 10–14), and in part on work while a Visiting Scholar at the Fiscal Affairs Department at the IMF in Spring 2000. It also draws on collaboration on policy design with Iain Crawford for more years than either of us care to contemplate, on advice on factual matters and administrative feasibility from Colin Ward and his team at the Student Loans Company, and on recent work by the three of us on a project advising the Hungarian government. An earlier version was presented at a meeting of the Parliamentary Universities Group.
2 Department of Economics, London School of Economics and Political Science, Houghton Street, London WC2A 2AE, UK.

fear of debt (solutions are discussed in section 4.2). Second, all the funding problems of the current system go back – directly or indirectly – to the subsidised interest rate on student loans. Australia and New Zealand face identical problems for identical reasons.

3. Interest subsidies create three problems. They are badly-targeted, mainly benefiting high-earning graduates in mid career. They are expensive (a recently-developed model estimates conservatively that out of next year's lending to students of £2,500 million about £700 million will never come back because of interest subsidies). Third, because loans are so expensive, the Treasury rations them. Thus interest subsidies, like most subsidies harm the people they are meant to help. There was an experiment with subsidies called Communism. It did not work. The result is that loans are too small, leading to student poverty and extensive use of credit card debt; and loans are means-tested: thus parental contributions and upfront costs continue.

4. Prescription. If graduates pay an interest rate equal to the government's cost of borrowing (not the bank overdraft rate), repayments increase from about 50 per cent of total borrowing to about 85 per cent (the remaining 15 per cent shortfall being mainly due to low lifetime earnings), largely eliminating the fiscal impediment to expanding loans. The move is polit-ically less difficult than it sounds. Interest rates are currently low, so that a move to the government's cost of borrowing involves only a small increase to the rate that graduates pay. Second, a graduate's monthly repayments depend only on her income; thus an increase in interest rates has no effect on monthly repayments, instead affecting the duration of the loan – making it clear that repayments are simply a form of targeted income tax.

5. Policies. Removing interest subsidies is the single essential key to solving current funding problems. The considerable resources thereby released underwrite the strategy for quality and access in section 4. The strategy has three mutually reinforcing elements: flexible fees, a wide-ranging loan system and active measures to promote access.

6. Flexible fees are necessary to reflect diversity, to arrest quality decline and to assist some redistribution of teaching budget towards institutions with more remedial teaching. Specifically, fees should be increased initially to £2,000, but with institutions free to charge less. All fees should be fully covered by a loan entitlement.

7. A wide-ranging loan system.

- Loans should be adequate to cover living costs and tuition fees, making higher education free at the point of use, thus addressing student poverty and freeing students from high-cost borrowing such as over-drafts and credit card debt.

- Loan entitlement should become universal, eliminating the unpopular and complex income test and, at a stroke, getting rid of parental contributions.

The combined effect of these twin elements is equivalent to bringing in universal grants in combination with an income-related graduate contribution (section 4.2). Additional options include extending loans to students in further education and to postgraduates.

8. Active measures to promote access. There are two impediments to access – financial poverty and information poverty. The strategy outlined in section 4.3 aims to address both.

- Grants and scholarships for students from poor backgrounds.
- Extra personal and academic support when students from poor backgrounds reach university.
- Raising the aspirations of schoolchildren.
- More resources earlier in the system, including financial support for 16–19 year olds.

Introduction

1. This paper sets out a strategy for promoting access and strengthening quality. Though explicitly about higher education, the arguments apply equally to the tertiary sector as a whole. Successive sections discuss:

- The many things we all agree about.
- Lessons from economic theory.
- Problems with current arrangements, and key elements of solutions, including an indication of the scale of the prize to be won.
- A policy strategy.

1 What we all agree about

2. Since the finance of higher education is controversial, it is useful to start by setting out some large areas of unanimous agreement.

3. The problem. There is agreement, first, about two core problems:

- Students are poor because the system of support does not give them enough to live on. Two results follow: students have to turn to expensive overdraft and credit-card debt and/or to extensive part-time work; and the parsimony of support is an impediment to access for people contemplating university.
- Universities are poor, creating worries about quality. The UK would have to spend an extra £3.5 billion per year to reach the EU average.

4. Objectives. There is also agreement – strong and universal agreement – about two central objectives.

- Improved access. The socioeconomic mix in higher education has barely changed in 40 years. Everyone supports widening participation in the interests of social justice, and also for reasons of national economic performance.
- Improved quality. Again, there is no disagreement: the quality and diversity of higher education is important for its own sake, and for national competitiveness.

5. Four propositions. Resources are clearly key to achieving these objectives. To that end, the discussion of resources throughout the paper is based on four propositions.

- UK higher education needs substantial additional funding for reasons of national economic performance and because higher education is an important export industry.
- Funding on the necessary scale will not come from the taxpayer, given an ageing population, rising health expenditure, competition from other parts of the education sector and competitive global pressures.
- Reform will therefore be ineffective unless it can deliver an immediate and sustained injection of private funding. The way to achieve this is through a student loan scheme which can draw in private finance on fiscally attractive terms.
- Phasing out the interest subsidy on the current loan scheme is essential to that end. Interest subsidies are costly (about one-third of total lending never comes back because of their cost), distortionary and badly-targeted. Instead of paying an interest rate equal to the rate of inflation (as currently), graduates should pay a rate equal to the government's cost of borrowing (*not* the interest rate on bank overdrafts or credit cards). The considerable savings would be much better used to expand the loan system and for the explicit, targeted measures to promote access set out in section 4.3.

2 Lessons from economic theory

6. Economic theory offers three strong sets of results, summarised here briefly.[3]

7. *The days of central planning have gone*, both for students and for higher education institutions. The system should empower the individual choices of students and potential students. The key theoretical question is whether

3 For fuller discussion, see Barr (2001, Chs 11 and 12).

students are well-informed or can become well-informed. My answer is yes. The role of government is not to plan student choices, but to make sure that students have easy access to timely, accurate and relevant information and – particularly for students from poorer backgrounds – also to advice.

8. The supply side should also be liberalised. Forty years ago, with an elite system, it was possible, as a polite myth, to assume that all universities were equally good and hence could be funded broadly equally. Today we have a mass system, meaning more higher education institutions, more students, and much greater diversity of subject matter – all changes which are warmly to be welcomed. As a result, however, the characteristics and the costs of different degrees at different institutions vary widely. Thus universities need to be funded differentially. In principle this could be done by an all-knowing central planner. In practice, the problem is too complex for that to be the sole mechanism. A mass system in an increasingly complex world needs a funding mechanism which allows institutions to charge differential prices to reflect their differential characteristics.

9. Supply-side liberalisation is not only necessary; it is also desirable. Increased competition between institutions will make them more responsive to student preferences. Some students will wish to study full-time but on an accelerated basis, for example studying for four terms per year rather than three; others, in contrast, will wish to study part-time, for example through evening courses. A system which can offer students and prospective students a wider range of choice is efficient; and the added option of part-time study while continuing to work also assists access.

10. *Graduates should contribute to the costs of their degrees.* A second strong result from economic theory is that higher education should not be free – its costs should be shared between the taxpayer and the graduate. There are two mutually reinforcing arguments.

11. We cannot afford free higher education. The argument is simple. Forty years ago, with a 5 per cent participation rate it was fiscally feasible to rely mainly on public funding to support a high-quality higher education system. The welcome expansion to a 35 per cent participation rate, with aspirations to a 50 per cent rate, however, mean that public funding has to be supplemented on a significant scale by private funding. This is all the more the case because:

12. We should not have free higher education. It is well-known that graduates on average have significantly higher earnings than non-graduates. The Dearing Report (National Committee of Inquiry into Higher Education, 1997, paragraph 18.13) suggests that compared to those without higher

education qualifications who were qualified to enter higher education, those with higher education qualifications:

- have higher employment rates;
- enjoy higher salaries;
- enjoy an average private rate of return of some 11 to 14 per cent.

13. Since higher education creates social benefits it is right that there should always be a taxpayer contribution. But given the robust evidence on private rates of return, excessive reliance on public funding is inefficient. It is also regressive, and hence unjust, since the major beneficiaries of free higher education are the predominantly middle-class participants. A government committed to improving access should not spray scarce taxpayer pounds indiscriminately across the entire student body but should instead target those resources on people for whom access is most fragile.

14. *A well-designed student loan scheme has core features.* The third set of conclusions from economic theory sheds light on the design of student loans. Four features stand out, summarised here only briefly (for fuller discussion, see Barr, 2001, Ch. 12).

- Income-contingent repayments, i.e. loans with repayments calculated as x per cent of the graduate's subsequent earnings until she has repaid her loan, are fundamental. The arguments are now well-understood. Income-contingent repayments instantly and automatically respond to changes in earnings: people with low earnings make low repayments; and people with low lifetime earnings do not repay in full. The effect is to protect borrowers against excessive risk, with gains both in efficiency and in terms of access (see also Barr and Crawford, 1997, evidence to this Committee).
- Large enough to cover all living costs and all tuition fees. This feature makes higher education free at the point of use – the important advance made by the Cubie arrangements in Scotland. Students are no longer pushed towards expensive credit-card debt; and parental contributions can be abolished, a liberation both for students and their parents.
- An unsubsidised interest rate, as explained in section 3.3, is essential for fiscal reasons, for efficiency reasons, and in the interests of access.
- A capacity to bring in private funds. Student loans bring in private funding through students' subsequent repayments. However, there is a net saving to the taxpayer only when the scheme is mature, i.e. when the inflow of repayments from earlier cohorts of students matches or exceeds the outgoings to this year's borrowers. That process takes 15–20 years. If extra resources are needed immediately, it is desirable to have a loan scheme which brings in private money upfront, creating an immediate injection of private finance.

3 Problems with current arrangements[4]

3.1 The good news

15. Income-contingent loans, with repayments collected alongside income tax, were introduced for UK students starting their degrees in or after 1998. This move represents unambiguous progress and deserves loud applause.

3.2 The bad news

16. That, however, exhausts the good news. The problems described below were both predictable and predicted, e.g. Barr and Crawford (1997) in evidence to this Committee.

Student support: impediments to access

17. The system of student support impedes access in several ways.

18. *Deficient loan design.* The current scheme conforms with only one of the four criteria – income-contingent repayments – in paragraph 14. It fails the remaining three badly.

- The loan is too small to cover living costs; it is income tested, so that not all students are entitled to a full loan; and there is no loan to cover tuition fees. Thus the system incorporates upfront charges, students remain poor, and parental contributions continue. All these features impede access.
- The loan incorporates an interest subsidy. The resulting problems are discussed in detail in section 3.3.
- The scheme is capable of bringing in private finance but, because of the interest subsidy, only on fiscally unattractive terms, again, discussed further below.

19. *Continued reliance on parental contributions.* The problems of parental contributions merit additional discussion.

- As a philosophical matter, is it right to force young adults to depend on their parents?

4 For assessment of systems of higher education finance in other countries (the USA, Australia, New Zealand, the Netherlands and Sweden), see Barr (2001, Ch. 13). National Audit Office (2002) reaches very similar conclusions about the problems of the present system, in particular its failure to improve access.

- Student poverty: the scale and volume of unpaid contributions is well known.[5]
- Impediments to access: unpaid contributions cause some students to drop out, and the threat of unpaid contributions deters an unknown number of others from applying in the first place.
- Distorted choices: in other cases, parents pay the contribution, but with conditions attached: 'we will pay, but only if you do a sensible subject.'
- The previous three problems all have troubling gender and ethnic aspects, and the point is, if anything, even stronger in respect of spouse contributions.
- The income test necessary to assess parental contributions is intrusive and has high compliance and administrative costs.

20. It gets worse! Assessment of family income has to take account of whether a student is making maintenance payments (a deduction from his assessable income) or is the recipient of maintenance payments (which may be an addition to his assessable income) (Department for Education and Skills, 2001, Ch 6, paragraphs 54–58). And the relevance of a spouse's income raises the vexed issue of cohabitation: a woman whose husband has a high salary is not entitled to a full loan; nor is one whose partner has a high income – but that requires finding out whether or not a student is cohabiting. Paragraphs B 117–8 of the guidance notes just cited are titled 'Advice on identifying a cohabiting couple'. Such factors – which should lie wholly outside the system of student support – are an inescapable concomitant of an income test.

21. None of this is an attack on family support: where families wish to help, such support should be applauded. The attack is twofold. Policy should not be based on an assumption that parents will support their children. Such an assumption may, at a stretch, have been valid for an elite system of higher education, regarded as a luxury good for middle-class families; it is invalid for mass higher education as an investment good, and totally inapplicable to expanding access. The policy is bad also because

---

5 Barr and Low (1988), using data for 1982–3, found that about half of students entitled to parental contribution received less than they were supposed to, and the shortfall was substantial: students whose parents gave them less than the system supposed received only £33 of every £100 of assessed parental contribution. As a result, one student in thirteen remained below the poverty line even when income from all sources was included. Subsequent work based on 1992–3 data found that 37 per cent of students received less than the assessed parental contribution (Committee of Vice-Chancellors and Principals (1996, p 14), quoting an official survey). Callender and Kemp (2000, p 3) report that: 'by 1998/9, the proportion of students who failed to receive their full assessed parental contribution had doubled to three in ten students. The mean shortfall for these students (average assessed contribution minus average actual parental contribution) was £719.'

it forces students into dependence on parental contributions or spouse contributions, since there is no option to take out a larger loan in place of unpaid contributions.

22. *Complexity.* Annex 1 gives a very simplified explanation of the current system.[6] But student support in practice is so complex that nobody fully understands the system. Someone from a poor background pays no tuition fee and is entitled to a full loan. The assessment of a student's financial position is based on parental income for a younger student, or on his or her spouse's or partner's income. Parental or spouse income has two effects: as income rises, the tuition fee rises; once the fee has reached its maximum (£1,075 in 2001–02), the effect of additional parental income is to reduce the size of the loan to which the student is entitled. All students, however rich their parents or spouse, are entitled to a loan equal to about 75 per cent of the maximum loan except that scholarship and similar income, if high enough, can reduce loan entitlement below that 75 per cent minimum.[7] Such complexity has major ill-effects: students, prospective students, and their parents cannot understand the system; it is a nightmare to administer; and complexity, per se, impedes access.

23. *Inadequate dissemination of information.* Perhaps the greatest impediment to access is the fact that the wider public totally fails to understand income-contingent repayments. The scale of this ignorance cannot be exaggerated. Most people are completely unaware that loan repayments are de facto a form of income tax – but paid only by graduates and switched off once the graduate has repaid what he or she borrowed. In this respect, the Government is deeply culpable over its negligence in vigorously and repeatedly explaining this point. The resulting ignorance unnecessarily aggravates debt aversion and is a further impediment to access. The topic is taken up in detail in paragraphs 63–73.

Universities: impediments to quality

24. The post-Dearing arrangements are also bad news on the supply side.

25. *Continued central planning.* The strong theoretical case against central planning of higher education was alluded to earlier. Though nobody quarrels

---

6 Without wishing to seem frivolous, I challenge Committee members to explain the operation of the income-test by which a student's loan entitlement and tuition fee are assessed, as set out in the guidance notes from the Department for Education and Skills (2001) to the Local Education Authorities, who administer the income test (http://www.dfes.gov.uk/studentsupportissadmin/content/dsp-section-29.shtml, Chapter 6).

7 Originally, a student's loan entitlement was reduced pound for pound with any scholarship income in excess of £1,000 per year. The disregard was subsequently increased; in 2001–02 it is £4,000 (Department for Education and Skills, 2001, Table 5).

with the need for universities to be publicly and transparently accountable, there are few defenders of the particular mechanisms, of which the QAA and RAE are only the tip of the iceberg. In addition, there has been central control of the number of students at each university and of tuition fees – in other words, both price and quantity were determined by the central planner – a situation only partly eased by the proposed lifting of the numbers cap.

26. Such planning impedes quality. Also – and entirely unintended – it impedes access to UK students to the best universities. Again, this was predicted to this Committee:

> A flat fee will continue the erosion of quality at the best universities, which face the biggest shortfalls. If this policy continues, the result will be to deprive British students of the chance of an internationally cutting-edge undergraduate degree in one of two ways. The quality of the best institutions might fall; British students could still get places, but the quality of the degree would be less. Alternatively, the best institutions will largely stop teaching British undergraduates (for whom they receive on average £4,000 per year) and will use the fees from foreign undergraduates (around £8,000 per year) to preserve their excellence. The government is considering trying to prevent British universities from charging additional fees to UK/EU students. Again, this is done for equity reasons; again, it ends up harming the very people it is aimed at helping, in this case by creating a situation where British students will find it harder and harder to get places at the best universities (Barr and Crawford, 1997, paragraph 57).

27. *Inadequate university income.* The immediate post-Dearing arrangements brought universities not an extra penny, for the reasons explained in Barr and Crawford (1997), with worrying effects on quality. The story in 1997, in a nutshell, was as follows:

(a) Public spending on higher education would not go up (the budget said so).
(b) Parental contributions (i.e. private spending) would not go up (the Secretary of State said so).[8]
(c) Loans to students (the other potential source of private spending) counted in their entirety as public spending.

8 'Today the Government announce a new deal for higher education, involving new funding for universities and colleges, free higher education for the less well-off, no parent having to pay more than at present and a fair system of repayment linked to ability to pay' (Hansard (Commons), 23 July 1997, col. 949) (emphasis added). 'Our response to Dearing ensures that fees and maintenance together do not place an increased burden on middle-income families' (ibid., col. 950).

28. There has been some improvement since 1997. Public spending under (a) has increased; debt sales have brought in some private money under (c); and the move from cash-flow to resource accounting has further assisted under (c). These developments are all genuinely welcome; but they do not change the reality that, at its core, the system continues to be publicly funded; and given its greater political salience, student support has crowded out university income. The story in Australia is exactly the same (see Annex 3, paragraph 95), and for exactly the same underlying reason – the interest subsidy on student loans.

3.3 The worst news: interest subsidies

The problem

29. It is important to understand the scale of the problems that interest subsidies cause.

30. *What interest rate?* First, it is important to be clear what I am not saying:

• At present graduates pay an interest rate equal to the rate of inflation. Press discussion of 'market interest rates' evokes worries about high interest rates associated with credit cards and overdrafts. That is not what is meant. The interest rate which graduates should pay on their loans is the *government's cost of borrowing,* i.e. broadly the interest rate the Monetary Policy Committee announces.
• The attack is on blanket interest subsidies. A strong case can be made for targeted interest subsidies – for example someone who is unemployed or caring for young children or other dependants – to make sure that their debt does not spiral upwards. Mechanisms for such targeted assistance are discussed in section 4.2.

31. *Why are interest subsidies such a problem?* Interest subsidies are:

• Regressive. As explained in paragraphs 42 and 43, interest subsidies do not benefit students (who do not make repayments), nor low-earning graduates, but better-off graduates in mid-career.
• Expensive. Interest subsidies are enormously costly. Evidence from debt sales suggests that of all the money lent to students, about one-third never comes back because of the cost of interest subsidies. The scale of the resulting losses is discussed shortly. The high fiscal costs of loans create two further sets of ill-effects.
• Inimical to quality. Expensive student support crowds out university income; thus interest subsidies conflict directly with improved quality.
• Distortionary. Because loans are so expensive, the Treasury rations them. Thus interest subsidies, like most subsidies, create shortages –

like rent control, they end up harming the very people they were meant to help. There was an experiment with price subsidies called Communism. It did not work.

32. In the case of loans, shortages manifest themselves in the following ways:

- The full loan is too small to cover a student's living costs, leading to student poverty.
- Loans are means-tested: as a result parental/spouse/partner contributions continue, and higher education involves upfront costs and charges.
- Loans are restricted, for example are not available to students in further education (impeding access), nor to postgraduates (putting national competitiveness at risk).

Towards a solution: the scale of the prize

33. In short, interest subsidies create a fiscal black hole which aggravates problems both of access and quality.[9] A move to an unsubsidised rate is not just a technicality – it is the single essential key to solving current problems of funding tertiary education. The considerable resources thereby released underwrite the array of major policy advances set out in section 4.

34. *How much extra money?* Suppose graduates pay an interest rate equal to the government's cost of borrowing rather than, as now, the inflation rate.[10] Do the resulting savings make the move worthwhile?

35. Barr and Falkingham (1993, 1996), using LIFEMOD, a microsimulation model, found that for every £100 the government lends, only about £50 is repaid. Of the missing £50, £20 is not repaid because of fraud, early death, and emigration (all of which have a relatively small effect), and

---

9 Other countries are reaching a similar conclusion. New Zealand, having flirted with interest subsidies since 2000, are contemplating reversing that short-lived, ill-advised experiment. A government report published last November, concluded that: 'Participation goals should continue to be supported through a Student Loan Scheme with income-contingent repayments as at present. The Commission believes, however, that the current policy of writing off interest on loans for full-time and low-income students while they are studying is not an effective use of the government's resources. While this policy has decreased the length of time taken to repay loans after graduation, it has also led to an increase in the number of students taking out loans and in the overall level of student debt. To compound matters, the policy has made it possible for learners to borrow money and invest it for private gain (arbitrage). Consequently, the Commission believes that this policy should be discontinued – or that, as a minimum, the incentives for arbitrage should be removed. Any savings accruing to the government as a result of modifying the current loan scheme should be reinvested in the tertiary education system and be used for the benefit of students' (New Zealand Tertiary Education Advisory Committee, 2001, p. 14).

10 Charging a market interest rate on income-contingent loans raises issues under the Consumer Credit Act. Solutions to the problem are outlined in Annex 4.

mainly because some graduates have low lifetime earnings and so never repay their loan in full, and 30 is not repaid because of the interest subsidy. In other words, the interest subsidy converts nearly one-third of the loan into a grant.

36. Previous sales of student debt offer independent evidence. The debt was sold for about 50 pence per pound of its face value. Official estimates suggest that of the missing 50 pence about 15 pence was because of low lifetime income, etc., and 35 pence because of the interest subsidy. The evidence on the interest subsidy is compelling. The government did not use LIFEMOD; thus the official estimates and the simulation results reinforce each other.

37. A recent modelling exercise[11] offers further confirmation. The model is conservative in at least two ways. First, it assumes that the subsidised interest rate is 2.5 per cent, the unsubsidised rate 5 per cent, thus implicitly assuming that the real rate will stay as low as 2½ per cent throughout the lifetime of the loan. Second, the accounting of debt forgiveness is on an accruals basis, even though forgiveness normally occurs only at the end of the loan period.[12] The model takes as its starting point projected loan outgoings for the next academic year of £2,500 million.[13] With debt forgiveness of 15 per cent (i.e. assuming that 15 per cent of student borrowing will never be repaid because of low lifetime earnings, etc.),[14] a move to an interest rate equal to the government's cost of borrowing would release sustainable savings of £700 million per year.[15] That sum could be

11 The model was originally developed by the Chief Executive of the Student Loans Company as part of a joint LSE/SLC project advising the Hungarian Government, and has been adapted to simulate alternatives to the UK system.
12 The calculations assume that a portion of the total debt forgiveness occurs each year, when repayments are due. This gives a higher assessment of the cost of forgiveness than one which reflects the real life position, where the level of forgiveness is known only at the end of the repayment period. The cost is higher because discounting for the loss of purchasing power over time is greater in the earlier years of repayment. The approach was adopted because it represents the most punitive accounting approach that can be taken for costs, depending on the resource accounting policy applied by the Treasury.
13 This is the forecast figure for 2002–3 including income-contingent loans, mortgage loans and hardship loans (the latter two being small). The outturn for 2000–1 was £1,840 million, the forecast for 2001–2, £2,282 million.
14 New Zealand, with longer experience of income-contingent repayments, uses an official estimate of 10 per cent in its public accounts.
15 The gross annual saving from a move to an unsubsidised interest rate is £X million, considerably larger than £700 million. The figure of £700 million is the answer to the following question: the government wants to finance grants by selling bonds which are repaid after n years, where n is commensurate with the maximum duration of the student loan; if repayments, including interest, over n years is £X million, what is the maximum face value of the bonds? The answer is £700 million – the amount that can be spent on grants allowing for the cost of financing those grants. Thus the figure is a very conservative one.

used to finance additional grants and scholarships of up to £700 million. Alternatively, it could be used to underwrite an expanded loan system; with 15 per cent debt forgiveness, it would be possible nearly to triple the total amount of lending. Or the sum could be used for a combination of the two policies.

38. *When will the money be available?* It is necessary at this stage to distinguish the cash-flow costs of loans (i.e. the money which is required now, but which will eventually be repaid), from the fiscal costs (i.e. borrowing which will never be repaid). With the present loan scheme, for each £100 that students borrow (the cash-flow cost), roughly £50 will never be repaid (the fiscal cost). The argument above is that eliminating interest subsidies reduces the fiscal cost of loans from about 50 per cent to about 15 per cent. Though the Treasury will, of course, take cognisance of cash-flow costs, the abolition of interest subsidies makes it possible to have a loan system that is larger, but at the same time has smaller fiscal costs.

39. Seen through the eyes of the Treasury, £700 million is the present value of the annual saving, and is thus a significant and sustainable long-run resource. Seen through the eyes of the Department for Education and Skills, however, the initial savings in cash-flow terms are small.[16] But higher education needs to benefit immediately from the long-run savings. That will require a deal between the Treasury and the Department for Education and Skills for an early injection of additional resources. One way to finance such a deal is by selling a further tranche of student debt, which could yield up to £2 billion. For the reasons explained in the previous paragraph, such a deal makes sense in both educational and fiscal terms.

40. Ensuring low fiscal costs is, of course essential. Once that is done, the Treasury can choose how to deal with the cash flow costs of the loan system. It could do so out of taxation: under resource accounting, the fiscal costs (i.e. lending that is not expected to come back) appears as current education spending, while expected repayments appear in the capital account as a financial asset.[17] With the present loan scheme, about half of lending to students is counted as spending out of the education budget. If there were no interest subsidy, only 15 per cent, or so, of total lending would appear as current education spending, and the 85 per cent expected repayment would appear in the capital account.

16 To oversimplify, if the interest rate students pay rises by 2.5 per cent, the extra interest in year 1 is 2.5 per cent × £2,500 million, ie £62.5 million. In year 2, the saving in cash-flow terms are double that sum, in year 3 triple, etc.
17 Resource accounting has been introduced in the UK only recently. For a description of the way student loans are treated in the public accounts in New Zealand, which has had resource accounting for longer, see Barr (1997), evidence to this Committee.

41. Alternatively, the Treasury could deal with the upfront cash flow costs by bringing in private money to finance the scheme. This can be done in various ways. The debt-sale approach has been extensively discussed (Barr and Falkingham 1993, 1996). There has been less exploration of front-end funding, which has two variants. With retail lending, individual students borrow from private lenders; thus student borrowing is individualized. With wholesale lending, the loans administration borrows private money in tranches of (say) £2 billion, which it then lends to students.[18]

42. *Grasping the nettle.* The scale of the prize is clearly enormous. But political worries about raising interest rates persist. These, however, should not be exaggerated.

- There is already growing support for removing interest subsidies (e.g. Piatt and Robinson, 2001).
- Interest rates are currently low; thus the interest rate would have to rise by no more than 2½ per cent from the rate in the current loan scheme.
- A person's monthly repayments depend only on her income; thus interest rates have no effect on monthly repayments, but only on the duration of repayment. Once such a scheme has been introduced, this feature will become obvious to graduates.
- The wider public should understand who benefits from interest subsidies. Interest subsidies do not help students (it is not students who make loan repayments, but graduates); they do not help low-earning graduates, since unpaid debt is forgiven after 25 years; they do not help higher-earning graduates early in their careers (since monthly repayments are a fraction of earnings, and so are not affected by the interest rate); the only people they help are higher-earning graduates in mid career, whose loan repayments are switched off earlier because of the interest subsidies than would be the case without the subsidies.

43. In sum.

- Interest subsidies are targeted with exquisite accuracy: they benefit successful professionals in mid career. Thus the NUS [National Union of Students] position, defending interest subsidies, is arguing for continued subsidies for those who need it least at a time when they need it least, and the hell with today's struggling inner-city sixth-formers.
- Removing the interest subsidy finances policies to promote access and quality, thus helping students rather than graduates. The proposal is not to eliminate subsidies, but to replace blanket (i.e. untargeted) subsidies by targeted interventions.

18 There has been extensive development work on front-end funding (see Barr, 2001, Ch. 14). The result is not just academic theory, but has been extensively tested with the IMF, Eurostat and financial market actors.

- Income-contingent loans are simply a form of income-tax; and income-tax, together with a write-off after 25 years, bases loan repayments on outcomes, and hence targets subsidies accurately on graduates with low lifetime earnings.

Once students and their parents come to understand these point, their worries and, with them, much of the political hullabaloo, will recede – an issue discussed in detail in paragraphs 63–73.

4 The policy strategy

44. This section sets out a strategy for access and quality with three elements:

- flexible fees, to address the quality issue, and to begin to free universities from unnecessary central planning;
- a wide-ranging loan scheme to empower choice for the generality of students;
- wide-ranging but targeted measures to promote access; these need to start early in the school system.

45. The three elements are a strategy, not just a bunch of ad hoc policies: they are designed to achieve explicit objectives, and the elements are mutually reinforcing. This does not mean that the policies below must be swallowed whole, but does mean that attempts indiscriminately to pick and mix will fail to achieve the policy's objectives.

4.1 Flexible fees

46. *A medium-term aim.* Flexible fees are both necessary and desirable for at least three reasons.

47. To address diversity. Historically, with a small tertiary system and a limited range of subjects, it was possible for central planners to determine funding levels for different institutions, Today, however, the higher education system is large, diverse and complex. As a result, (a) the necessary variation in funding is much greater than formerly and (b) the problem is now too complex for a central planner to have the sole power of decision about how resources should be divided between institutions. Thus institutions should have the freedom to set their own fee levels (that freedom could be constrained).

48. To arrest quality decline. Without higher fees, quality will continue to be eroded and, given flat fees, eroded most at the best institutions.

49. To prevent crowding out. At present, the best institutions tend to receive more funding for teaching in an attempt to protect their quality. This risks crowding out universities with a different mission. With higher fees, the best institutions could paddle their own canoes to a greater extent than currently, freeing resources for institutions which have to do more remedial teaching. Thus – an important and poorly-understood point – flexible fees benefit all tertiary institutions.

50. *Arguments that do not stand up* are of two sorts. It is sometimes argued that students should pay the full costs of tuition. That argument overlooks the significant (albeit hard-to-quantify) external benefits of higher education. There is a strong case for continuing taxpayer subsidy for tuition for all students. Other people argue the opposite – that tertiary education should be entirely funded from taxation. There may be a case for that policy for sub-university education, but, applied to higher education, the argument is flawed. The argument that university education should be free at the point of use (which I support), does not mean that there should be no charges. Free tuition is expensive, and its benefits accrue disproportionately to people from better-off backgrounds, who go on to be among the best-off. Thus free tuition is badly targeted; the money could do much more for access if spent in a way that directed resources specifically at those groups for whom access is most fragile and those who do not benefit financially from their degrees. Lowering tuition charges for higher education in other countries has not improved access. Conversely, introducing the Higher Education Contribution Scheme in Australia in 1989, with tuition charges paid via an income-contingent loan, did not harm access (Chapman 1997).

51. *How high should the fee be?* Taxpayer support plus tuition fees should cover the costs of teaching. At research-intensive universities, fees should be higher to the extent of the value-added in teaching by research-active people, but should not cross-subsidise research.

52. *Pitfalls to avoid.* Though flexible fees are desirable, there should be no 'big bang' liberalisation. As a first step, the flat fee should be increased to £2,000)[19] However, institutions should be free to charge less if they wish, and the ceiling should be raised over time. As indicated below, any increase in the ceiling should be accompanied by an equal increase in the loan entitlement.

4.2 A wide-ranging income-contingent loan scheme

53. The second element in the strategy is a wide-ranging loan scheme. Discussion starts with policy options and then turns to a much-neglected

19 See, similarly, Platt and Robinson (2001) and Council for Industry and Higher Education (2001).

aspect of loans – how to make sure that the public understands the nature of the beast.

Policy options

54. As explained in section 2, a well-designed loan scheme has four characteristics: income-contingent repayments; sufficient to cover all living costs and all tuition fees; with an interest rate equal to the government's cost of borrowing; and capable of bringing in private funds. A loan scheme of this sort opens up the following options.

55. *Universal.* If there is no interest subsidy there is no need to ration loans, which can therefore be made available as a universal entitlement. The administratively complex and politically unpopular means test disappears; so does the relevance of such factors as whether a student is married or cohabiting.

56. *Adequate.* For the same reason, the loan entitlement can be large enough to cover realistic living costs and all tuition fees.[20] A universal, adequate loan has major advantages.

- It eliminates student poverty.
- It makes higher education free at the point of use.
- It makes it possible to abolish parental contributions.
- It frees students from forced reliance on expensive credit card debt and/or the need for extensive part-time work, and thus in substantial measure addresses the worries of middle-class students and their parents, and also the (rightful) complaints by the NUS about the amount of high-cost student debt.
- It is simple for students and their parents to understand.
- It is vastly simpler to administer than current arrangements, since the administratively cumbersome and unpopular means test can be abolished.

There is no need to belabour the helpful political resonances of all these features.

57. *Extending loans to other groups of students.* The scheme could be extended to postgraduate students, starting to address worries about research capacity and national productivity. It could also become a universal entitlement throughout tertiary education, buttressing existing sketchy student support for further education and vocational training, thus contributing to access.

---

20 Extending loans to cover tuition fees raises issues under EU legislation. These are discussed in Annex 4.

58. *Protecting low earners* is a clear priority. Income-contingent repayments do so automatically, since low earners make low repayments, and people with low lifetime earnings do not repay in full. Nevertheless, many people are afraid of rising debt, and interest subsidies were introduced to assuage those fears. As argued earlier, however, interest subsidies are a costly, non-transparent and ineffective way of promoting access, and benefit exactly the wrong people. The policies below are more transparent and better targeted ways of protecting low earners.

59. Scholarships, i.e. grants which do not carry an obligation to make income-contingent repayments.

60. Stopping repayments after 25 years. Scholarships help people at the start of the process. Complete debt forgiveness after (say) 25 years helps them at the end of the process.

61. Targeted interest subsidies based on current income. It is also possible to help people during the process. Under the simplest mechanism, anyone receiving a credit for national insurance contributions – someone who is unemployed or looking after young children – receives an interest subsidy. As an extension (as in New Zealand), anyone whose earnings are so low that his or her income-contingent repayment fails to cover the interest element, similarly receives an interest subsidy.

62. Conditional subsidies. The mechanism in the previous paragraph protects low earners and people with career breaks. However, some of the subsidies benefit people who subsequently have high earnings. Thus there are advantages in terms of fiscal cost and targeting to have a system which pays interest subsidies based on current income, but with a facility to claw back the subsidy element for people who end up with high lifetime income. A workable such scheme has been designed, which the Student Loans Company could administer without difficulty. Such a scheme has major advantages: it gives assistance at the time they need it to people with low income and/or with a career break, facilitating access and preventing people from worrying that their repayment obligation is spiralling upwards; but it is cost free, since the clawback mechanism ensures that only the lifetime poor keep the subsidy. It is also flexible: it would, for example, be possible to give conditional subsidies to some groups (e.g. someone who went travelling after graduation), but unconditional subsidies to others (e.g. someone looking after young children or elderly dependants – analogous to current proposals to assist teachers with their loan repayments).

Understanding income contingency: some equivalence propositions

63. Past failures adequately to explain income-contingent loans has created unnecessary disquiet. Medical practitioners sometimes talk about 'the

worried well' – people who are in good health, but whose life is made less happy by misplaced worries that they are not well. Analogously, it can be argued, 'worried debtors' are concerned that student loans will be a millstone. Students perceive a large debt, but miss two important points of context. First, repayments are merely an addition to their future income tax. Thus the risk they take is no different from the risk we all face that at some time in the future the basic rate of income tax might increase (I am old enough to remember a 33 per cent basic rate). Second, they do not see how much they will pay over the years in income tax or national insurance contributions, nor what they will spend on food (or drink) over a 25-year period. None of these items cause people to worry, despite the fact that someone who starts on average earnings and remains on average earnings all his working life, will pay nearly £300,000[21] in income tax and national insurance contributions over a 35-year career, a topic discussed more fully in Annex 2.

64. Alongside the policy design in the previous paragraphs, it is thus imperative to explain what is going on. I am not at this stage digressing into political presentation, but want instead to point out some analytical equivalences which should inform explanation.

65. The following schemes are all analytically identical.

66. Scheme 1: An income-contingent loan. Earlier discussion described an income-contingent loan, for which graduates make repayments of x per cent of their earnings until they have repaid the loan at an interest rate equal to the government's cost of borrowing. What has been missing thus far in government action is a clear explanation that a person's loan repayments are, in effect, a form of income tax: a person's repayments track changes in his or her earnings instantly and automatically, and thus nobody repays more than he or she can afford.

67. The point is fundamental. Suppose we start from the argument (NUS, etc.) that higher education should be paid out of taxation. But that means that the costs of higher education are paid by the generality of income recipients, including low earners, non-graduates, pensioners and the like. It is widely acknowledged that this is unfair. To deal with that unfairness, some people have argued that higher education should be financed through a graduate tax, which can be thought of as additional income tax, but paid only by the beneficiaries of higher education. But a graduate tax has its own unfairness, since people with high lifetime earnings repay considerably more than they have borrowed (this is true of any successful professional, without having to refer to extreme cases like Mick Jagger or

21 In today's prices, assuming annual real earnings growth of $2\frac{1}{2}$ per cent.

Stelios Haji-Ioannou).[22] To address the latter problem, it is suggested that a graduate tax should not have an indefinite duration, but should be capped, i.e. 'switched off' once a person has repaid an agreed contribution towards the costs of his/her degree. *An income-contingent loan is exactly that* – it is a graduate tax which is capped at 100 per cent of the initial sum borrowed. Put another way, the only difference between a graduate tax and an income-contingent loan is the duration of repayment: with a graduate tax, repayment lasts (say) 25 years, regardless of how much a person has borrowed or repaid; with an income-contingent loan the duration of repayment bears an exact relation to the initial amount borrowed.

68. Thus income-contingent repayments can be described as repayment of debt. But with equal accuracy they can be described as a form of targeted income tax – targeted by being imposed only on graduates and by being 'switched off' once the loan has been repaid. This is a form of taxation that is more efficient and fairer than funding via the entire body of taxpayers.

69. Scheme 2: Free higher education. If loans are universal and adequate to cover all living costs and all tuition fees, higher education is free at the point of use. Thus the system can be described as free higher education, paid for by a targeted income tax or a graduate contribution. To repeat, the only difference from tax funding is that (a) the tax is paid only by those who have been to university and (b) the additional tax is capped.

70. Scheme 3: Universal grants plus a graduate contribution. Suppose that all students receive a grant large enough to cover their living costs and tuition fees; and suppose that the system is financed by an extra x pence in the pound added to a person's income tax rate. The contribution does not go on for ever: it is 'switched off' once a person has contributed an amount equal to the grant he/she received; and nobody pays for more than (say) 25 years. Thus the scheme is simple: there is a universal grant, financed by a graduate contribution payable for a maximum of 25 years, but for some people a shorter time.

71. Two additional points specify the scheme precisely:

* The duration of the graduate contribution bears an exact relation to the amount of grant a student has received. Though administratively complex, this is precisely the task that the Student Loans Company

22 As explained in Annex 3, a graduate tax has problems in addition to being unfair: it leads inescapably to continued reliance on public funding; it is a hypothecated tax; and it raises difficult boundary problems.

currently performs: higher earners repay their grant more quickly; lower earners take longer and are further protected in the ways outlined in paragraphs 58–62; and nobody makes contributions for more than 25 years.

- Students for whom access is fragile are helped in the ways set out immediately below. The scholarships and other forms of financial help they receive do not make them liable for a graduate contribution.

72. Since the three schemes are equivalent, any is an accurate description of the system of student support. If this were better understood – particularly the very close relation of income-contingent repayments to tax funding – the problem of the 'worried well' would be greatly diminished.

73. A point in conclusion: the equivalence arguments in the previous paragraphs are analytical and should be judged on the quality of their logic. They are not presentational arguments based on logical thin ice.

4.3 Active measures to promote access

74. Income-contingent loans measure ability to pay on the basis of where a person ends up, i.e. his or her subsequent income. This is the best approach for students from better-off backgrounds, who are generally well-informed about the benefits of tertiary education. However, students from socially-excluded backgrounds are typically badly informed. Precisely for that reason, a wide range of additional measures to promote access – the third leg of the strategy – is necessary.

75. Put another way, it is not only financial poverty which impedes access, but also information poverty. Any strategy for access therefore needs two elements:

- those which involve money, and
- those which involve information and raising aspirations.

The following are no more than indications of the scale of necessary actions.

76. *Grants and scholarships in higher education.* Money measures include scholarships for students from poor backgrounds. They could be based on parental income, but should also include money for schools and universities to award to students from poor backgrounds. There should be financial incentives to universities to widen participation; and universities would, in any case, wish to gather resources for scholarships to enable them to recruit the brightest students, regardless of their financial background.

77. For some students the biggest hurdle is to realise that they are good enough to do well in higher education: for them, scholarships which make their first year entirely free give them a risk-free opportunity to test their abilities and to become well-informed about higher education. Once such a student does well in the first year, he or she will be much more prepared to take out at least a partial loan for the rest of the degree.

78. *Extra personal and intellectual support in higher education.* A second ingredient in promoting access is extra personal and intellectual support, at least in the early days, for access students to make sure that, once a student starts at university, he or she gets the necessary support to make the transition. It is no good persuading someone to go to university if he or she is then allowed to sink without trace.

79. *Raising aspirations of school children.* Action is also needed much earlier. Information and raising aspirations are critical. The saddest impediment to access is someone who has never even thought of applying to university. The sorts of schemes involved include Saturday Schools, which bring schoolchildren from poor areas to university to study on Saturday mornings; summer schools, which do something similar during the summer vacation; visit days, when schoolchildren can visit a university; visits by academics to schools to make the idea of higher education more tangible; visits by current students, ideally from the same or a similar school, to schools in deprived areas; and mentoring of schoolchildren by current university students, preferably from a similar background. Such activities needs to start early, e.g. at age 12.

80. *More resources earlier in the system.* Problems of access to higher education cannot be solved entirely within the higher education sector. Thus more resources are needed earlier in the education system, which is where the real barriers to access occur.[23] This includes more resources for teaching. It also includes financial support for 16–18 year olds.

5 Conclusion

81. At risk of sounding repetitive, the root of all the funding problems of the present system go back – directly or indirectly – to the interest subsidy on student loans.

- Interest subsidies aggravate the shortage of resources in the sector, compete with university funding, cause loans to be inadequate, crowd out expenditure to promote access, and are deeply regressive.

23 Educational exclusion has a clear connection with broader social exclusion – for example, less than 25 per cent of children in care in the UK end up with any formal educational qualification.

- Setting the interest rate that graduates pay equal to the government's cost of borrowing is the key to addressing all these problems and, on a conservative estimate, yields some £700 million per year. That sum is important for its own sake; it is even more important because a fiscally cost-effective loan scheme can leverage a much greater volume of private finance. Specifically, with no increase in long-run fiscal costs, it would be possible nearly to triple total lending, or to combine a smaller expansion of loans with additional grant expenditure.
- Grasping the nettle makes possible the policies for access and quality set out in section 4.
- The move is less difficult than it sounds – perhaps the political equivalent of the 'worried well'. In Sweden and the Netherlands graduates pay an interest rate broadly equal to the government's cost of borrowing, and the matter is not regarded as in any way noteworthy; and Australia and New Zealand are currently facing the same reality as the UK.
- In contrast, if the interest subsidy is not eliminated, we might as well all pack our bags and go home.

Annex 1 The student support system before and after 1998

82. Table 13.1 summarises in simplified form (and with rounded numbers) the system of student support for students who started their degree between 1990 and 1997, and that for students who started their degree in 1998 or later.

83. The old system was introduced gradually. When fully phased in, it operated through:

(a) 50 per cent of student living costs from a mortgage-type loan;
(b) 50 per cent of living costs from a mixture of grant and parental contribution;
(c) no tuition fees paid by the student.

84. The arrangements since 1998 have three components:

(a) an income-contingent loan;
(b) replacement of the grant by a loan entitlement which is partially income tested;[24]
(c) an income-tested tuition fee.

---

24 Poor students are eligible for 'a maintenance loan of the same value as the current grant and loan package' (*Hansard*, (Commons), 23 July 1997, col. 950).

Table 13.1 Student support: the system until 1998 and the current system

	Living expenses	*Tuition*
The system until 1998	50 per cent mortgage-type loan; 50 per cent grant/ parental contribution	Free
The current system 'Poor' student	100 per cent income-contingent loan	Free
'Rich' student	Parental contribution of 25 per cent of living costs; income-contingent loan the rest	£1,000 flat fee from parental contributions

85. To amplify the current system:

* 'Poor' students (i.e. where parent/spouse net income is below about £18,000 per year) pay no tuition fee and are eligible for an income-contingent loan intended to cover 100 per cent of living costs.
* 'Rich' students (whose parents' or spouse's net income is above about £34,000 per year) pay the full £1,000 fee. They are entitled to an income-contingent loan equal to 75 per cent of the maximum loan. It is assumed that the parental contribution pays the tuition fee and 25 per cent of living costs.
* In between, loan entitlement and fees are calculated on a sliding scale.[25]

86. To illustrate these arrangements with a simplified numerical example, suppose that it is estimated that students need £4,000 to cover living costs, made up, under the old system (line 1 of Table 13.1) of a loan entitlement of £2,000 and grant/parental contribution of £2,000. Thus the maximum parental contribution (for a student not eligible for any grant) is £2,000.

87. Under current arrangements, a poor student is eligible for an income-contingent loan of £4,000 to cover living expenses, and does not have to pay a tuition fee. A rich student receives £2,000 in parental contribution, £1,000 to cover the tuition fee and £1,000 towards living costs, and is eligible for an income-contingent loan of 3,000 to cover remaining living costs.

Annex 2 An unsubsidised interest rate: how much extra for graduates?

88. What is the effect on repayments if graduates pay an interest rate equal to the government's cost of borrowing rather than (as currently) the rate of inflation?

---

25 Herein lies much of the complexity – for details, see Department for Education and Skills (2001) (http://www.dfes.gov.uk/studentsupportl/ss-admin/content/dsp-section-29.shtml, Chapter 6).

89. Answer 1: Monthly repayments. The change has no effect on a graduate's monthly repayments. Since loans are income-contingent, repayments depend only a person's monthly income. Thus the higher interest rate affects the duration of repayments but not the amount of the monthly repayment.

90. Answer 2: Total repayments. On average, it is estimated that students will take 15–20 years to repay their loans (since the system of income-contingent repayments is new, estimates are all that we have). The model referred to in paragraph 37, estimates that at today's prices if a graduate takes 15 years to repay his loan, the extra interest payments on a loan of £12,000 from removing the interest subsidy is about £3,700. The comparable figure if he takes 20 years to repay is £4,700. Thus a plausible estimate of the additional interest repayments of an average student taking 17½ years to repay is £4,250.

91. Some comparators. These numbers need to be seen in context.

- With even a modest graduate premium (15 per cent) and real wage growth (including career progression) of 5 per cent, a graduate will earn £270,000 more than a non-graduate over a 35-year career. The extra interest payments are a minuscule price for those benefits.
- Over 35 years, a non-graduate on average earnings pays about £520,000 in income tax and national insurance contributions; with a graduate premium of 15 per cent, the equivalent figure for a graduate is about £600,000. Thus the additional interest payment is equivalent to a tax increase of about 0.7 per cent.
- Over the lifetime of the average loan, a graduate will spend on average £25,000 on alcohol. To spend £25,000 out of after-tax income a person paying basic rate income tax, etc., has to earn £37,000. Thus it would be possible to finance the additional interest payments by having one booze-free day per week till the loan has been paid off.

92. The figures in the previous two paragraphs are in cash terms. The equivalent figures in present value terms, at a 5 per cent discount rate, are as follows. On a loan of £12,000, the present value of the extra interest payments is £2,880 over 15 years, or £3,350 over 20 years; thus the average student will pay around £3,115 in additional interest payments. Over a 35-year career, the extra earnings of a graduate are £105,000. The present value of the income tax and NICs paid over 35 years by a non-graduate on average earnings is £195,000; for a graduate the comparable figure is £228,000. The present value of expenditure on alcohol over 17 years by an average graduate is £14,000, requiring pre-tax earnings of nearly £21,000.

Annex 3 An open-ended graduate tax: problems but no solutions

93. An open-ended graduate tax (i.e. one which is paid for, say, 25 years irrespective of a person's earnings) creates major problems.

94. *Continued reliance on public funding.* Since a graduate tax is irredeemably a tax, it cannot be privatised. It merely continues public funding through a different route. Thus the flow of private finance via graduates' repayments is slow in coming, and hence does nothing to improve access or quality in the short term.

95. Even in the medium term, a graduate tax does not necessarily produce extra resources for higher education, since increasing flows of private finance in (say) 10 years time can be offset by reduced public funding. This is exactly what has happened in Australia, whose Higher Education Contribution Scheme (HECS) was introduced in 1989 with the express aim of increasing resources for higher education. That aim remains unfulfilled.

> A year-long investigation into Australian higher education by a senate committee has found the nation's university system in crisis and in need of substantial public investment over the next 10 years.
>
> The committee found that universities were seriously underfunded and were worryingly reliant on non-government sources of revenue, notably on fee income from foreign and local students (*Times Higher Education Supplement*, 19 October 2001, p. 10).

96. In sharpest contrast, a well-designed loan scheme could bring in private funds from day one, in ways which avoid these problems.

97. *Closes options which a loan scheme leaves open.* As discussed in section 4, above, a scheme which avoids interest subsidies makes possible a wide variety of highly desirable options, such as making higher education free at the point of use – options which the fiscal cost of a graduate tax entirely rules out.

98. *Unfair.* A graduate tax is unfair (and hence politically unpopular) for several reasons:

- People are compelled to make continuing contributions, with no option to pay upfront if they wish.
- Those contributions are unrelated to the cost of their higher education.
- The contributions will be considerable for a successful professional, and can be enormous, e.g. for the Mick Jaggers or Stelios Haji-Ioannous of this world.

99. *Hypothecation.* What happens to the revenue from a graduate tax?

- If it is simply another source of income for the Consolidated Fund, it is a tax, pure and simple, and higher education continues to be publicly funded.
- If it is explicitly dedicated to higher education, it is a hypothecated tax – a mechanism which (with the exception of the national insurance fund) the Treasury has always regarded as an anathema. Any such move would be a major policy shift. Such a shift might be worth discussing if the potential gains are great, but that is not the case here.

100. *Boundary problems.* A graduate tax is (a) compulsory (contrast loans, where students can choose whether or not to borrow), and (b) binary (contrast loans, where students can choose how much to borrow), and thus creates major boundary problems as between:

- Different occupations. Do all UK students pay the graduate tax? Doctors? Nurses? Intending teachers? Once a group is granted an exemption, there will be pressure to extend it, and considerable difficulty in removing an exemption from any group.
- Different modes of study. Does the graduate tax apply equally to full-time and part-time students? What about Open University students?
- Different parts of the UK. A major problem arises because taxation operates on a UK basis but the responsibility for higher education is devolved. A graduate tax thus opens up a Pandora's box – for example, the Scottish Executive could ask for a different form of graduate tax, or could opt out altogether. If the graduate tax is not the same throughout the UK, would an English person who studied in Scotland pay the English rate or the Scottish rate? Would the answer be the same for a Scot who studied in England? Ditto Northern Ireland (over half of whose students attend universities in the Republic of Ireland or the mainland)?
- Different parts of the EU. Does the graduate tax apply to UK graduates who studied in other EU countries (or elsewhere); and how are EU students at UK universities treated?

101. All these boundary problems raise major practical problems for the tax authorities as well as creating a potential political minefield.

Annex 4: Legal issues

Income-contingent loans and the Consumer Credit Act

102. Though income-contingent student loans are not made under the Consumer Credit Act (CCA), it is desirable that they stay as close as possible to the Act and to other relevant financial legislation.

103. The problem is as follows. Under the CCA, loan agreements have to specify interest charges across the life of the contract. That is possible only if the repayment flow is known. This is not a problem for a conventional (mortgage-type) loan, but is not possible with income-contingent loans, where repayments depend on a person's (unknown) future income stream and hence have an unknown duration. The issue was sidestepped in 1997–98 by arguing that the current student loan, which is indexed to the retail price index, is below the low interest threshold for the CCA.[26] Since that threshold is low, an unsubsidised loan would almost certainly exceed it, if not now, then at some time in the future.

104. There are two potential avenues to resolving the problem:

(a) revise the CCA to accommodate income-contingent loans; or
(b) ensure that the legislation bringing in new student support arrangements explicitly excludes those arrangements from the CCA via Statutory Instrument.

Approach (b) presents no obvious problems: a loan which charges the government's cost of borrowing is within the spirit of the CCA; the process in (b) is simpler and quicker than (a); and it leaves it open subsequently to amend the CCA if the government so wished.

Loans for fees and compliance with EU legislation

105. At present, UK students are eligible for a loan which covers (part of) their maintenance, but not their tuition fees. If loans covered fees, it would be illegal to deny loans to students from other EU countries studying in the UK.[27] A court case is currently testing whether it is legal to deny such students access to maintenance loans. In considering the coverage of loans, the following points are relevant.

106. Loans to cover fees are highly desirable because they make higher education free at the point of use. Thus the issue of EU-compliance should

26 The England, Wales and Northern Ireland Teaching and Higher Education Act 1998 (THEA 1998), s22(4) and s22(9) provide that Secretary of State may only charge compound interest rates required to maintain the value in real terms of the outstanding amounts of the loan, which shall at no time exceed the 'specified rate for low interest loans'. This 'specified rate for low interest' is defined in s22(9) as the rate specified for exemption purposes under s16(5)(b) of the Consumer Credit Act 1974 (CCA 1974). The Scotland Teaching and Higher Education Act 1998, s29 inserts amendments to the Education (Scotland) Act 1980, (ESA 1980). The ESA 1980 s.73B(6) includes the same provision as s.22(9) of the THEA 1998, and therefore defines the low interest rate as a rate that will ensure exemption under the CCA 1974.

27 The post-Cubie arrangements in Scotland, by ensuring that students face no upfront charges, in effect extends loans to cover fees, thus raising serious problems of compliance with EU law.

be addressed in the medium term; and it might have to be addressed in the short term even for maintenance loans, depending on the outcome of court case mentioned above. The problem should not be exaggerated. The loan contract that students currently sign entitles them to income-contingent repayments while within the UK tax net, but requires them to make mortgage (or similar) repayments if they work abroad. This process is already embedded in the procedures of the Student Loans Company and works well. In the short run it could be extended to EU students.

107. A better starting point is to note that foreign students are a good thing, not a bad thing. Higher education is – and should continue to be – a major UK export industry whose benefits are both direct (income from overseas students) and indirect (future UK exports). A properly designed loan scheme is self-funding apart from non-repayments from the lifetime poor, which introduce a social policy element into the scheme. Extending the scheme to EU students is thus feasible on the basis that each government agrees to cover the social policy element of loans for its own citizens.

References

Barr, Nicholas (1997), 'Student Loans in New Zealand', in *Third Report: The Dearing Report: Some Funding Issues, Volume II, Minutes of Evidence and Appendices*, House of Commons Education and Employment Committee, Session 1997–98, HC241-II, (TSO, 1997), pp. 119–21.

Barr, Nicholas (2001), *The Welfare State as Piggy Bank: Information, Risk, Uncertainty, and the Role of the State*, Oxford: Oxford University Press.

Barr, Nicholas and Crawford, Iain (1997), 'The Dearing Report, the Government's Response and a View Ahead', in *Third Report: The Dearing Report: Some Funding Issues, Volume II, Minutes of Evidence and Appendices*, House of Commons Education and Employment Committee, Session 1997–98, HC241-II (TSO), pp. 88–103.

Barr, Nicholas and Falkingham, Jane (1993), *Paying for Learning*, Welfare State Programme, Discussion Paper WSP/94, London: London School of Economics.

Barr, Nicholas and Falkingham, Jane (1996), *Repayment Rates for Student Loans. Some Sensitivity Tests*, Welfare State Programme, Discussion Paper WSP/127, London: London School of Economics.

Barr, Nicholas and Low, William (1988), *Student Grants and Student Poverty*, Welfare State Programme, Discussion Paper WSP/28, London: London School of Economics.

Callender, Claire and Kemp, Martin (2000), 'Changing Student Finances: Income, Expenditure and Take-up of Student Loans among Full- and Part-time Higher Education Students in 1998–9', London: Department of Education and Employment Research Report RR213.

Chapman, Bruce (1997), 'Conceptual Issues and the Australian Experience with Income Contingent Charges for Higher Education', *Economic Journal*, 107/442 (May), 738–51.

Committee of Vice-Chancellors and Principals (1996), *Our Universities, Our Future, Special Report 4: The Case for a New Higher Education Funding System*, London: Committee of Vice-Chancellors and Principals.

Council for Industry and Higher Education (2001), *The Funding of UK Higher Education: The CIHE Submission to the Comprehensive Spending Review*, London: Council for Industry and Higher Education,

Department for Education and Skills (2001), *Higher Education Student Support in England and Wales 2001–02: Chapter 6: Assessing Financial Entitlement* (http://www.dfes.gov.uk/studentsupport/ss-admin/content/dsp-section-29.shtml, Chapter 6).

National Audit Office (2002), *Widening Participation in Higher Education in England*, Report by the Comptroller and Auditor General, HC 485, Session 2001–02, London: TSO.

National Committee of Inquiry into Higher Education (the Dearing Committee) (1997), *Higher Education in the Learning Society: Main Report*, London: HMSO.

New Zealand Tertiary Education Advisory Committee (2001*), Shaping the Funding Framework: Fourth Report of the Tertiary Education Advisory Committee: Summary Report*, Tertiary Education Advisory Committee, Wellington, New Zealand, November (http://www.teac.govt.nz/fframework.htm).

Piatt, Wendy and Robinson, Peter (2001), *Opportunity for Whom? Options for Funding and Structure of Post-16 Education*, London: Institute for Public Policy Research.

Chapter 14

2002 **Evidence to the Education Select Committee 2**

Iain Crawford (2002), 'Funding Higher Education: Policies for Access and Quality: Supplementary Memorandum', House of Commons, Education and Skills Committee, *Post-16 Student Support*, Sixth Report of Session 2001–2, HC445, London: TSO, pp. Ev 44–5.

Factors exacerbating student poverty: real and perceived

1. It is unanimously agreed that the current student support package is too small and needs to be enlarged. In addition, policy should address two factors – one real and one perceived – that additionally and unnecessarily exacerbate student poverty, and create misinformation.

- *Student inexperience in financial management.* The lack of experience, knowledge and self discipline, in handling personal finance of a significant number of new undergraduates is a contributory factor to student poverty. While accepting that the state student support package is inadequate, the lack of ability to manage personal finance makes the problem worse for a large proportion of students.
- *Inadequate information.* Lack of authoritative information on available state and commercial financial support mechanisms means that ignorance and scaremongering are real deterrents to access and create an unjustified sense of discontent amongst participants.

Suggested measures: student loan payments

2. State Student Loans should be paid monthly rather than three times per year. Students would give their bank account details when applying for their loan; loans would be paid by electronic transfer. It is unreasonable to expect students, many of whom are without experience of the world beyond school, to manage their money in the way that it is paid to them at present, when most adults rely on regular monthly or even weekly payments.

3. It should be administratively possible to move to such a system. In the new Hungarian system, loans are paid in monthly instalments, with a double-payment in the first month to cover such things as rent deposits, new textbooks, etc.

4. Such a change would help to remove some of the "end of term" student poverty. It would also marginally improve the Student Loans Company's cash flow.

Suggested measures: information

5. It is clear, from research by commercial banks and others, that there is a lack of knowledge and understanding of Student Loans Company (SLC) loans among prospective students. This is partly because of changes since the system was introduced, partly because of disinformation promoted by opponents of the system, and partly because of a general paucity of personal finance knowledge amongst secondary school and sixth form students.

6. There is an urgent need for a campaign to educate prospective students, their parents and advisors about all aspects of student financial support, as well as advice on budgeting and personal finance management. As discussed in paragraphs 75–79 of Nicholas Barr's submission, there are two impediments to exclusion – shortage of money and shortage of information. That evidence (paragraph 79) stresses the importance of making sure that prospective students are well-informed about the educational side of universities; a co-equal element is to make sure that they are well-informed about the financial side. The activities outlined below are therefore not a minor PR element, but a fundamental part of any well-conceived strategy to promote access.

7. Commercial banks spend a great deal of time and resources trying to address the information gap with their student customers. The retail banks' motivation is entirely commercial: they regard the student market as very important, and spend hundreds of pounds per account on marketing, free overdrafts and other inducements.

8. It is not in the commercial interest of banks for students to keep getting into budgeting problems. It adds to banks' administrative costs and, if they get too strict, risks losing customers who in the long run would be very profitable.

9. There is, therefore, scope for such a campaign to be sponsored jointly by the Government/SLC and the retail banks. Since banks are prepared to expend substantial resources on the student market, it is likely that they would be prepared to co-operate with Government in a campaign to educate secondary school students about state support and personal banking. Indeed which retail bank could afford to be seen not participating in such an exercise? In a joint campaign, the Government and the banks could mutually reinforce their messages.

10. Some commercial banks are already working on projects in schools. They all have a lot of information on student spending and borrowing patterns. Through their campus branches and specialist student centres they talk to thousands of students and they spend a lot of money finding out what students want and need.

11. While it should be assumed that banks will behave in their own commercial self-interest, it should be recognised that their interests can coincide with those of students and government, in that they can promote access by explaining that finance should not be a worry.

12. Substantial financial resources and research data are available for such a joint information campaign. This would enable government to bury the disinformation and to promote the reality of the loan scheme – in particular the low interest rate and the income-contingent repayment system which removes all the normal risks attached to commercial debt. It would enable the banks to educate their prospective customers to their mutual benefit. Both banks and government could explain the difference between commercial rates and the government rate of borrowing!

Nicholas Barr and Iain Crawford, 'Access for All', *Guardian Education*, 16 July 2002, p. 13.

Access for all

Nicholas Barr and Iain Crawford

Britain's universities are underfunded and the proportion of students from the lowest two socio-economic backgrounds has not changed significantly in 40 years. Thus higher education funding damages national economic performance and [harms access].

The report into post-16 student support by the education select committee – perhaps for the first time since the 1963 Robbins report – puts forward the start of a coherent strategy for addressing these problems. As long-time critics of the funding policies of all governments for the past 15 years we do not say that lightly.

Getting to grips with access and quality requires money – lots of it. Where from? Relying on large increases in taxpayer support in the comprehensive spending review is unrealistic given global economic turbulence and the demands of the NHS and schools.

The select committee's proposals make a strong start by substantially reducing the interest subsidy in the loan scheme, recommending that students should pay an interest rate equal to the government's cost of borrowing, currently about 4% (not commercial credit-card or overdraft rates). This change releases £800m a year to spend on access.

Since 1998 student loans are no longer organised like a mortgage or overdraft, with fixed repayments. Instead, repayments are calculated as a percentage of a graduate's income. Thus repayments vary month by month with earnings, just like a tax but with two important differences: it is not paid for ever, but only until the loan is paid off; and it is paid only by those who have benefited financially from a degree. Thus the truck driver does not pay for the degree of an old Etonian.

But the interest rate on student loans is equal to the inflation rate, i.e. is subsidised. So who benefits? The subsidies do not help students (only graduates make repayments). They do not help low-earning graduates, since unpaid debt is eventually forgiven. They do not help high-earning graduates early in their careers – repayments depend only on earnings; interest rates only affect the duration of the loan. The only people the subsidies help are higher-earning graduates in mid-career, whose loan repayments are switched off earlier because of the subsidy.

The question is whether we want to continue to pay subsidies whose main effect is to help wealthy people become wealthier. The NUS argues that the subsidy should continue because some benefits spill over to less well-off graduates. It is supporting subsidies for those who need it least at a time when they need it least, and the hell with struggling inner-city sixth-formers.

Much better to take the £800m and use it to finance a range of benefits aimed explicitly at improving access. Grants for students from poor backgrounds mean that they have no loan, or a smaller loan.

Our attack on blanket interest subsidies is not an attack on targeted subsidies. It is both possible and desirable to pay an interest subsidy to people who are unemployed or looking after young children or with low earnings.

Outreach to children in school is also essential. The saddest barrier to access is a child who never even thinks of going to university.

There are also benefits for the rest of the student body. If loans are no longer leaky they can (and should) be large enough to cover all living costs and all tuition fees; and a full loan can (and should) be made available to all students. This eliminates student poverty.

The select committee's recommendations redirect a substantial proportion of the £800m into grants and targeted subsidies. A student from a particularly needy background might get a full grant. And all students are eligible for a full loan. The select committee's proposals have the potential to transform the funding landscape. A government so publicly and rightly committed to promoting access should grab the opportunity.

The committee kindly recommended that the DfES should talk to us about our research in this area before concluding its review. We'd be delighted to do so, if invited.

Nicholas Barr, 'A Way to Make Universities Universal', *Financial Times*, 22 November 2002, p. 21.

A way to make universities universal

Nicholas Barr

The turbulent debate about financing higher education is entirely unnecessary. There is a solution that is simple, workable and with important advantages for all concerned.

Everyone agrees on the core problems. Britain's universities are underfunded, students are poor and the proportion of students from the lowest socioeconomic backgrounds has not changed significantly in 40 years. Inadequate funding of higher education puts national economic performance at risk and sells the poor down the river.

There is also unanimous agreement about two crucial objectives: strengthening quality and improving access. I believe the way to achieve those objectives is to make three changes.

First, increase the tuition fee to £3,000. That would give universities additional resources to improve quality, benefiting UK students and restoring the sector's considerable export potential. Institutions should be allowed to charge lower fees if they wish and students should be helped to pay the charges.

Thinking on fees is often muddled. Many would agree that higher education is a right – but it does not follow that it must always be free. Food, equally, is a right, yet nobody demonstrates outside shops or restaurants.

Another confusion is between social elitism, which is abhorrent, and intellectual elitism, which is both necessary and desirable. There is nothing inequitable about intellectually elite institutions. The fairest system is one in which the brightest students are able to study at the most intellectually demanding institutions irrespective of their socioeconomic background.

The second element is larger loans. The good news is that, since 1998, student loans are no longer organised like a mortgage or bank overdraft but have income-contingent repayments – calculated as a percentage of a graduate's income and collected alongside income tax. The bad news is that the loan package is too small. After using her loan to pay her hall fees, my niece has £100 left for the rest of the year. Therefore the loan should be large enough to cover all tuition fees and living costs and should be universally available.

Implementation of these two changes would eliminate upfront fees (the Student Loans Company would send the fee payment directly to the university), making higher education free at the point of use, as in Scotland. It would end student poverty. It would do away with parental contributions. It would free students from expensive credit card debt and long hours in part-time work. The system would be easy to understand and much simpler to administer than current arrangements.

These two changes are equivalent to introducing universal full grants paid from taxes. All students would be entitled to the full loan, so no one would be forced to pay anything when going to university. Income-contingent repayments differ from a tax in only two ways: they do not go on forever; and they are paid only by people who have been to university and benefited financially from their degree. The taxes of the truck driver would not be used to finance the degree of an Old Etonian.

This proposal is also economically literate. More generous student support implies higher spending. But if the repayment mechanism is well designed (for example, with targeted interest subsidies rather than the blanket interest subsidy in the current scheme), graduates' repayments will cover the cost of that support, except for people with low long-term earnings. Additionally, with a well designed system the Treasury could, as in the past, meet some of the cash-flow costs by selling off student debt.

The third essential element is active measures to promote access. There are two causes of exclusion: financial poverty and information poverty. Any strategy for improving access needs to provide resources and raise aspirations. Scholarships – such as higher education maintenance allowances – are vital. So are financial incentives for universities to widen participation. Action to inform schoolchildren and raise their aspirations is equally important. The saddest impediment to access is never even thinking about going to university. Intervention needs to start early, perhaps at the age of 12.

A package of higher fees, bigger loans and better information would enhance quality and promote access. It is educationally, fiscally and administratively sound. It should form the core of the government's white paper on higher education.

Chapter 15

2003 The Higher Education White Paper: a critique

Nicholas Barr (2003), 'Financing Higher Education: Lessons from the UK Debate', *Political Quarterly*, Vol. 74, No. 3, June 2003, pp. 371–81.

Though directly an assessment of the 2003 White Paper on higher education in England and Wales,[1] this paper offers analysis and strategic conclusions that apply to all advanced countries. After introductory discussion, successive sections weigh up current arrangements (generally unfavourably), assess the White Paper strategy (generally favourably) and discuss the follow-up actions necessary to ensure that the strategy works. A concluding section stresses political leadership, portrays two contrasting futures and summarises broader lessons for policy design.

Introductory matters

Higher education in the UK faces three widely agreed problems: universities are underfunded, students are poor, and the proportion of students from poorer backgrounds has not changed significantly in forty years. Thus higher education funding puts national economic performance at risk and sells the poor down the river.

There is also agreement about core objectives: strengthening quality and diversity, and promoting access, both for their own sakes and for reasons of national economic performance. Thus the argument is not about what we are trying to do but about how best to do it.

Economic theory offers strong messages for financing higher education.[2]

First, the days of central planning have gone. The case against central planning is not ideological, but rooted in the economics of information. The essence of the argument is that students (in sharp contrast with school-children or people with complex medical problems) are well-informed, or potentially well-informed, consumers, and hence better able than planners to make choices which conform with their interests and those of the economy. Though that proposition is robust for many students, there is an important exception: people from poorer backgrounds might not be fully informed, with major implications for access, discussed below.

On the supply side, central planning, whether it was ever desirable, is no longer feasible. In response to technological change, advanced countries increasingly have mass higher education, meaning more universities, more students and greater diversity of subject matter. Thus the myth of parity of esteem and relative parity of funding is no longer sustainable. In principle, differential funding could be implemented by an omniscient central plan-ner, but the problem is too complex for that to be the sole mechanism: mass higher education requires a funding regime in which institutions can charge differential prices to reflect their different costs and missions.

A second lesson from economic theory is that students should contribute to the cost of their degree. It is true that higher education creates benefits beyond those to the individual – benefits in terms of growth, the trans-mission of values and the development of knowledge for its own sake. Thus taxpayer subsidies should remain a permanent part of the landscape. However, students also receive significant private benefits, making it efficient and equitable that they bear some of the costs. This leads to the third set of lessons from economic theory.

Well-designed student loans have core characteristics.

- Income-contingent repayments, i.e. repayments calculated as x per cent of the borrower's subsequent earnings, collected alongside income tax, are essential. They protect access because the loan has built-in insurance against inability to repay; and because repayments are collected alongside income tax, they also protect the borrower from the risk of making an unsecured loan. Income-contingent repayments have a profound effect that is insufficiently understood by politicians and the public.
- Loans should be large enough to cover all fees and living costs, resolving student poverty and promoting access by making higher education free at the point of use.
- Loans should attract an interest rate broadly equal to the govern-ment's cost of borrowing. The huge problems caused by interest subsidies are discussed below.

Before the White Paper: a wedding and four funerals

This section assesses current arrangements. The lesson other countries could usefully follow is the introduction in 1998 of loans with income-contingent repayments.[3] Having campaigned with Iain Crawford for many years for that result, I warmly welcome the move.

The bad news is that that is all the good news. The current system has four strategic flaws, offering lessons to other countries of policies to avoid or to phase out: central planning continues; the system is complex; loans are too small; and loans attract an interest subsidy.

Problem 1: central planning continues in three guises. Tuition fees (£1,125 in 2003/4 in England and Wales) are centrally determined for UK and EU students. There is also control of student numbers. Not the least of the resulting anomalies is that universities which recruit too many students may be penalised. In good communist tradition, the central planner determines both price and quantity. In the same tradition, control is heavily bureaucratic. Assuring teaching quality is a worthwhile activity, but the procedures during the latter part of the 1990s involved vast amounts of paperwork. They also bore another hallmark of central planning: a counter-productive one-size-fit-all process.

Problem 2: the system of student support is vastly complicated, with major ill-effects: nobody can understand the system; it is a nightmare to administer; and complexity, per se, impedes access.

Problem 3: loans are too small. The full loan (£4,000 outside London in 2003/4) does not cover all living costs; not all students get the full loan; and there is no loan to cover fees. Thus students are poor, forcing them to rely on their parents, to use expensive credit card debt, and/or to spend long hours earning money. These factors all impede access.

Problem 4: loans attract an interest subsidy. Under the present system, the interest rate on student loans is equal to the inflation rate, i.e. a zero real rate of interest. This is policy design of such cleverness that it achieves not a single desirable objective.

- The subsidy is enormously expensive, currently around £800 million per year.
- It impedes quality. Student support, being politically salient, crowds out the funding of universities.
- It impedes access. Loans are expensive, therefore rationed and therefore too small.
- It is deeply regressive, the main beneficiaries being successful professionals in mid-career.

The last point bears explanation. Interest subsidies do not help students (graduates make repayments, not students). They help low-earning graduates only slightly, since unpaid debt is eventually forgiven. They do not help high-earning graduates early in their careers – with income-contingent loans, monthly repayments depend only on earnings; thus interest rates *have no effect on monthly repayments,* but only on the duration of the loan. Thus the major beneficiaries are successful professionals in mid-career, whose loan repayments are switched off earlier because of the subsidy than would otherwise be the case.

What should the government do? Iain Crawford and I have long advocated a strategy with three legs.[4]

Leg 1:   Variable fees bring in additional resources to improve quality. Students should be helped to pay the charges, as described below. It is of central importance that charges should be deferred: thus graduates make repayments, not students.

Thinking on fees is often muddled. Many people agree that higher education is a right, but it does not follow that it must always be free; food, equally, is a right, yet nobody demonstrates outside shops or restaurants. Another confusion is between social elitism, which is abhorrent, and intellectual elitism, which is both necessary and desirable. There is nothing inequitable about intellectually elite institutions. The access imperative is a system in which the brightest students are able to study at the most intellectually demanding institutions irrespective of their socioeconomic background.

Leg 2:   Adequate and universal income-contingent loans. The loan should be large enough to cover fees and realistic living costs, and should be available to all students. This package eliminates upfront fees (the Student Loans Company would send fee payments directly to the university), making higher education free at the point of use, as in Scotland. It ends student poverty. It eliminates parental contributions. It is easy to understand. It is vastly simpler to administer than current arrangements. And, as discussed below, the package is equivalent to restoring grants.

Leg 3:   Active measures to promote access. There are two causes of exclusion: financial poverty and information poverty. Any strategy to promote access must address both. Grants are vital; so are financial incentives to universities to widen participation; and so are extra resources to provide intellectual support at university for students whose road to university has been hard, to make sure that, once they arrive, they get the support necessary to make the transition. Action to inform schoolchildren and raise their aspirations is equally critical. The saddest impediment to access is someone who has never even thought of going to university. Action needs to start young.[5] A final set of measures to promote access, discussed below, helps low earners after they leave university.

The White Paper strategy

The content of the White Paper is wide-ranging. Discussion here is limited to the funding proposals.

The term 'top-up fees' conflates three separate questions: should fees be the same at all universities or different; should students pay fees upfront or deferred; and should universities receive fees upfront or deferred? The White Paper answers all three questions correctly. From 2006 fees will no longer be fixed, but variable between 0 and £3,000 a year. There will no longer be an upfront charge, since fees will be fully covered by a loan. Universities, however, will receive the fee income upfront.

The White Paper seeks to promote access directly in at least three ways. It brings back a grant of at least £1,000 per year. Fee remission continues, as at present: people from poor backgrounds will not pay the first £1,125 of any tuition charge, and some students might be exempt from the entire £3,000 charge. Finally, a new Office for Fair Access (OFFA) will ensure that universities charging fees above £1,125 have well-designed plans to widen access and carry those plans out.[6]

Student support continues essentially as at present. The maximum maintenance loan remains broadly unchanged, and entitlement continues to be income tested, i.e. parental contributions continue. Loans attract a zero real rate of interest, i.e. interest subsidies continue. The income threshold at which loan repayments start will be raised from its current level of £10,000 to £15,000 in 2005.

Research funding will be more focused, not least to protect the UK research base, to which the White Paper has an explicit commitment.

Public spending is set to increase significantly over the next three years.

Seen through the eyes of lurid press coverage, the proposals look horrible – high fees, large debts. That view is thoroughly misleading. The White Paper strategy has two elements: (a) it redistributes from better-off to worse-off, and (b) it ends communism, i.e. brings in genuine competition.

Strategy element 1: redistribution from better-off to worse-off

The underlying principle is that those who can afford to pay more do so, releasing resources to improve quality and promote access. Economic theory is particularly useful to explain what is going on. The White Paper proposes two sets of actions (see Figure 15.1):

- a price increase, raising the average tuition fee from p_0 to p_1. This leads to a movement *along* the demand curve from a to b. Taken alone, this action obviously reduces demand and harms access. However, (i) the fees are deferred for everyone, and (ii), there are also:
- targeted transfers to groups for whom access is fragile. This moves their demand curve *outward*, increasing their demand to c.

Thus the strategy is deeply progressive. It shifts resources from today's best-off (who lose some of their fee subsidies) to today's worst-off (who receive a grant) and tomorrow's worst-off (who, with income-contingent repayments, do not repay their loan in full).

Three sets of supporting arguments are important. First, the main disparity in participation occurs when people leave school at 16. Of those with A-level results good enough to go to university, 90 per cent do so, with little socioeconomic variation. Thus spending to improve GCSE scores does more for access than subsidising fees for people who would have gone to university anyway.

Second, other ways of paying for higher education are unfair. A graduate tax (i.e. an additional x pence on income tax until retirement, or for a fixed period such as twenty-five years), is unfair because repayments are unrelated to the cost of a person's degree.

Flat fees, i.e. the same fee at all universities, are unfair for two reasons. It is unfair if a student at Banbury University pays the same fee as one at Oxford. Secondly, as Iain Crawford and I predicted – not least in our earlier article in *Political Quarterly* – flat fees discriminate against British students.[7]

As for tax funding, there are at least three problems. First, it does not work – access has barely improved in forty years. Second, it will not happen: higher education will always lose out to the NHS, nursery education and school education. Third, it should not happen. Higher education confers a benefit on society as a whole, and to that extent should continue to receive tax funding. Beyond that, however, tax funding is deeply regressive. If the money comes from general taxation, the taxes of the hospital porter pay for the degree of the old Etonian. If it is unfair for graduates to pay more of the cost, as the proponents of tax funding argue, it is even more unfair to ask non-graduate taxpayers to do so. The counter-argument is to make taxation more progressive. Suppose the government raised

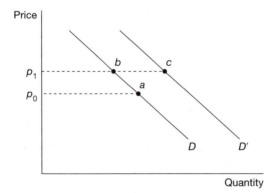

Figure 15.1   The White Paper's twofold strategy to promote access

£5 billion that way. The question that proponents of tax funding must then answer is: why should that money be spent on the best and the brightest who will disproportionately go on to become the richest, rather than on nursery education, vocational education, action to improve the staying-on rate after age 16, and more generous grants?

A third set of supporting arguments notes that the proposals can be viewed from perspectives very different from those portrayed in the press. The White Paper can be regarded as restoring universal grants. Higher education is largely free at the point of use: the Student Loans Company squirts money into the student's bank account to cover her living costs and into the university's bank account to cover her tuition fees. The graduate subsequently makes income-contingent repayments, which differ from income tax in only two ways: they do not go on forever, and they are paid only by people who have been to university and benefited financially from their degree. In short, income-contingent loans are logically equivalent to a grant financed by an income-related graduate contribution.

Another perspective is to think of student loans as extending social insurance. We pay national insurance contributions now so as to get our pension later, i.e. we redistribute to ourselves over our life cycle. Student loans are exactly the same – students receive a 'pension' now for their university education, repaid through their own subsequent contributions.

Core argument 1: in conclusion, deferred variable fees are equitable.

- They resolve the serious inequities of tax funding, a graduate tax or flat fees.
- Those who can afford to pay a larger contribution do so, where 'can afford' refers to their income after graduation, i.e. to outcomes.
- The system protects access in two ways: students face no upfront charges; and graduates repay only if their earnings warrant.
- As illustrated in Figure 15.1, the system actively promotes access because it frees resources to increase the staying-on rate after age 16 and to restore grants, thereby focusing resources on those who need help most, rather than spending wastefully and regressively on blanket subsidies.

Strategy element 2: the end of communism

Completely separately, variable fees shift the balance of power from the central planner and producers to students and employers by (a) giving universities an independent source of income and (b) strengthening competition.

Core argument 2: variable fees make funding open-ended. If fees are set by government, rising fee income can be offset by falling taxpayer contributions. Thus government controls the total volume of resources going into higher education – funding is closed-ended. Australia is a graphic example: government introduced centrally set fees in 1989 to address a funding crisis; the system is now back in crisis. Equally, and as predicted in our earlier article,[8] the introduction of fees in the UK has not netted any extra money. A graduate tax has the same problem: government controls the volume of resources going into higher education, and universities compete in a zero-sum game. With variable fees, universities have an independent income source. The central planner no longer determines the funding envelope.

Core argument 3: variable fees introduce competition. My support for competition is not ideological. Competition does not always improve outcomes. Most particularly, it is beneficial only where consumers and producers are well-informed. This, it was argued earlier, is the case for universities, but not for school education. Thus competition in higher education matters greatly, empowering the choices of students, and indirectly also employers. The change in the balance of power is fundamental to creating a diversified system fit for its purpose in a technological age. This is not an argument for law-of-the-jungle competition. Government has an important continuing role, but as regulator and setter of incentives, not as central planner.

The resulting changes will be significant. The days are gone when higher education was based on a unitary model of three or four years of full-time academic study in institutions devoted to teaching and fundamental research. Diversity today has many dimensions:

- Period of study: it should be possible to study part-time, staying in one's current job. Equally, accelerated study should be possible, e.g. studying over the summer to complete a degree in two years, reducing living costs and facilitating earlier return to work.
- Level of degree: there should be a seamless line of progression from sub-degree study to undergraduate and postgraduate degrees.
- Coverage: degrees can and should cover increasingly diverse areas.
- Type of training: degrees can offer academic training, vocational training, or both. This is nothing new – medical degrees are high-quality vocational training.
- Type of research: research can be fundamental, or applied, or assisting local economic development. All are important; all are properly part of higher education.

The potential benefits from competition are large, but so are the resulting changes, creating political opposition. The supply-side response is predictable. The White Paper strategy has profound implications for the management of universities. The elite universities – like Poland and Hungary in 1990 – welcome the new freedoms, but some institutions are unenthusiastic, seeing the new arrangements as more a threat than an opportunity. The demand-side response is also understandable. Students, like the Poles in 1990, see prices rising, but not yet the resulting benefits. Once the changes are in place, students should greatly prefer the new system, which transforms their power by giving universities strong incentives to offer them such things as accelerated courses and part-time options.

Making the strategy work

I argued in the previous section that the White Paper strategy promotes access by transferring resources from better-off to worse-off people; and that it promotes competition, and hence diversity. This section considers what needs to be done to ensure that the strategy is translated into action, discussing in turn actions to promote access, policy to ensure that central planning stays dead, and matters for future consideration.

Promoting access

If the White Paper is to succeed in widening access, action is needed (1) to publicise what income-contingent loans mean, and (2) to improve further the student support package.

It is vital to increase public understanding of income-contingent loans. One of the roots of current problems is that David Blunkett responded to the Dearing Report in July 1997, at a time when the Inland Revenue had not yet agreed to collect repayments (which was not decided until November 1997), forgoing a golden opportunity to explain why the new loan scheme was dramatically better than the old one.[9] Partly because of that timing problem, the government has been woefully inadequate in publicising income contingency; and the absence of such publicity has created a vacuum filled by a misplaced obsession with headline debt figures, fanned by lurid newspaper articles.[10]

Income-contingency changes everything.

- Repayments are like income tax: people with low earnings make low repayments or no repayments; and repayments instantly and automatically track changes in a person's pay packet.
- A larger loan has no effect on monthly repayments, only on duration; thus
- higher fees do not affect monthly repayments, and
- larger maintenance loans do not affect monthly repayments; equally,
- a higher interest rate does not affect monthly repayments.

Ministers should stop talking about debt, and instead concentrate on key messages:

- It is a payroll deduction, not debt.
- Students get their higher education free – it is graduates who make repayments, and then only to meet part of the costs and only if their earnings warrant.

- If it is unfair to ask graduates to pay more of the cost (as the proponents of tax funding argue), it is even more unfair to ask non-graduate taxpayers to do so.

Nor should the size of the debt be exaggerated. A £20,000 loan seems large because people (and newspapers) focus on the stock of debt, rather than the flow of repayments. Yet we mostly think about expenditure in flow terms, so that cumulative totals seem shocking. On plausible assumptions, over a forty-year career a current graduate will pay (in cash terms) about £850,000 in income tax and national insurance contributions, and will spend about half a million pounds on food. As an alternative comparator, it is possible to repay £10,000 of student debt in ten years by giving up a smoking habit of a packet of cigarettes a day. Quite rightly, no student or parent loses sleep over a career tax debt of approaching £1 million, because he/she looks at such figures through the other end of the telescope – i.e. in terms of monthly, income-related repayments rather than as cumulative totals. Student debt – given income-contingent repayments – is the same. It is not like a bank overdraft or credit card bill, but a payroll deduction alongside income tax and national insurance contributions.

A second set of actions to promote access is to improve the student support package, to ensure the outward shift of the demand curve in Figure 15.1. The full grant should be higher. As discussed earlier, students from poor backgrounds may be less well-informed and hence more debt-averse. Thus grants are an essential element in promoting access.

The maintenance loan should also be higher. Because the current loan does not cover realistic living costs, many students face a combination of poverty, heavy and expensive credit card/overdraft debt, and excessive hours in part-time work. Debt aversion arises in part because student loans and credit card debt become conflated in people's minds.

The continuing interest subsidy, however, makes larger maintenance loans costly. One way out is as follows. Suppose realistic living costs outside London are £6,000. The government should offer *all* students a second maintenance loan of £X, where £X is the amount that brings a student's total maintenance package to £6,000, at a stroke eliminating student poverty and abolishing compulsory parental contributions. Similar loans should be offered to postgraduates. The interest rate on the second loan should equal the government's cost of borrowing.

The political difficulties of such a move should not be exaggerated. Students would welcome both the improvement in their standard of living and the fact that they could borrow the extra money at the government's borrowing rate rather than the credit card rate.

Ensuring communism stays dead

The second leg of the White Paper strategy is a more competitive environment for higher education. Ensuring that the policy intent is realised requires (1) consideration of the fees cap and (2) a sustained real funding increase over the medium erm.

The fees cap 'will apply throughout the life of the next Parliament, and it will rise annually in line with inflation so that it keeps its real value' (White Paper, para 7.31).

The cap needs to be high enough (a) to pay the best universities the rate for the job and (b) to bring in competition, and low enough (c) to ensure that the White Paper proposals are politically sustainable and (d) to give universities time to put in place management suitable for a competitive environment.

Given these criteria, the initial cap of £3,000 is probably right. However, its duration – the life of the next parliament – is too long. If the cap is too low for too long, a critical bulk of universities will charge the maximum, approximating a system of flat fees. The result will be to reintroduce closed-ended funding and thus to restore central planning by the back door.

It is equally necessary to ensure a sustained increase in university income. In the medium term, more resources will come through variable fees. However, clawback by the Treasury over the next ten years (as in Australia) would put quality at risk. From 2006, students will face higher fees. If the quality of their university experience fails to match those higher fees, the new arrangements could come under political threat. Adequate tax funding during the initial phase is therefore essential.

Matters for future consideration: reducing the interest subsidy

As with the fees cap, it is important to introduce reforms that are politically sustainable. Even so, it is worth another look at the interest subsidy, since its cost considerably dilutes the redistributive power of the proposals, putting at risk the pro-access leg of the White Paper strategy.

As discussed earlier, the blanket interest subsidy achieves not a single desirable objective. The White Paper proposals aggravate matters by increasing the cost of the subsidy. First, loans will be larger, to cover tuition fees, increasing the cost of the interest subsidy proportionately to increased loan outgoings. In addition, the repayment threshold will be increased from £10,000 to £15,000, the effect of which is to increase the cost of the subsidy *disproportionately*. The combined effect of the two changes could easily increase the cost of the subsidy to £1.2 billion *per year*.[11]

As explained earlier, that expenditure is targeted with exquisite accuracy on exactly the wrong people at exactly the wrong time. The resources could and should be used instead to finance a series of pro-poor policies.

- There should be more assistance for poor students at university, including (a) a larger grant, (b) raising the income threshold below which people qualify for a grant and (c) offering 'super grants', covering all costs, to some students in their first year.

- There should also be better support for the generality of students, including (d) increasing the full maintenance loan and (e) abolishing the income test, so that all students are eligible for a full loan.
- More generous assistance for people with low incomes after graduation should include (f) freezing the real value of debt for people with low income (i.e. a targeted subsidy), covering low-income workers and people who are unemployed, (g) giving a similar subsidy to people taking career breaks to care for young children or elderly dependants (even better, government could signal its support for such activities by writing off 5 per cent of outstanding debt for each year of caring activities), (h) writing off (say) 10 per cent of the debt of nurses in the NHS and teachers in the state education system for each year of service, and (i) restoring debt forgiveness after twenty-five years, thus offering protection to people with low lifetime earnings. In present-value terms the cost of giving up repayments in later years is small.

The Department for Education and Skills argues that such mechanisms are complex and expensive to administer. Neither argument stands up.[12] The correct argument is the opposite: eliminating the blanket interest subsidy makes it possible to eliminate the income test for loans, thus significantly reducing administrative costs.

Again, the political difficulty of such moves should not be overstated. The Netherlands and Sweden charge a positive real rate of interest, a matter that is taken for granted in those countries. A higher interest rate does not add a penny to a student's monthly repayments, not does it affect the headline debt figure. And a commitment by government to spend the resulting extra resources on the targeted interventions just described would make it difficult for the National Union of Students to argue against the move without laying themselves open to charges of fighting to protect middle-class perks using access as a fig leaf.

Conclusion: two futures

The White Paper aims to do two fundamentally important things.

- *To shift resources from today's well-off to today's and tomorrow's worse-off.* Those who can afford to pay more do so, releasing resources for targeted transfers.
- *To end communism.* Variable fees create competition, shifting the balance of power from the central planner and producers to consumers.

Will the strategy succeed? The answer depends on the political will to follow through, in particular:

- To improve information about the deal for students. *The single most important and immediate task for government is to create understanding that repayments are not debt, but a payroll deduction.*
- To reduce the interest subsidy to release resources for the access strategy.
- To relax the fees cap over time to ensure that the end of communism is irreversible.

Outcome 1 Failure to take off: a political downward spiral

The story is of:

- failure to convince students and their parents that this is not a case of heavy debt; political ructions continue. Hence there is:
  - inability to reduce the interest subsidy, hence insufficient resources to promote access and continuing rationing of loans by the Treasury, further aggravating the politics of higher education finance, and hence
  - inability to raise the fees cap, restoring communism and its companion, underfunding.

As a result, in five years' time we will be back in crisis, as in the incomplete reforms of 1997. But this time would be a final farewell to world-class universities.

Outcome 2 Take-off a virtuous political spiral

With political leadership, the beneficial outcomes are self-reinforcing:

- Publicity and education get student debt from the overdraft bit of people's brains to the payroll deduction bit.
- In a calmer political environment, it is possible to reduce the interest subsidy, freeing a large volume of perversely targeted resources for the many pro-poor, pro-access policies outlined earlier, further improving the politics of reform; hence
- the fees cap can be raised in stages, bringing in the benefits of competition and increasing resources for universities.

The result is a vibrant, diverse and responsive system of higher education, at its best world-class, with strongly progressive funding matching the brightest students with the best universities irrespective of their socioeconomic background.

The strategic lessons for other countries are clear. With mass tertiary education:

- variable fees are essential for quality and diversity;
- in the interests of access, however, fee charges should be deferred through a loan entitlement;
- loans should have income-contingent repayments, and should attract an interest rate broadly equal to the government's cost of borrowing.

Acknowledgements

This paper draws on my fifteen-year collaboration with Iain Crawford, on assistance from Colin Ward and his team at the Student Loans Company on factual matters and administrative feasibility, and on work by the three of us advising the Hungarian government. A fuller version of this paper is published as Nicholas Barr, 'Financing Higher Education in the UK: The 2003 White Paper', House of Commons Education and Skills Committee, *The Future of Higher Education, Fifth Report of Session 2002–03, volume II, Oral and written evidence*, HC 425-II, TSO 2003, pp. Ev 292–309 (hereafter Barr 2003), downloadable from http://econ.lse.ac.uk/staff/nb.

Notes

1 Department for Education and Skills, *The Future of Higher Education*, Cm 5735, London, The Stationery Office, 2003. Available at http://www.dfes.gov.uk/highereducation/hestrategy.
2 On the underlying economic theory, see Nicholas Barr, *The Welfare State as Piggy Bank: Information, Risk, Uncertainty, and the Role of the State*, Oxford, Oxford University Press, 2001, chs 10–12. For a broader defence of the welfare state in terms of the same body of theory, see Nicholas Barr, *The Economics of the Welfare State*, 3rd edn, Oxford, Oxford University Press, 1998.
3 Australia and New Zealand already have such a system; for discussion of higher education finance in other countries, see Barr, *The Welfare State as Piggy Bank*, ch. 13.
4 See Nicholas Barr, 'Making Universities Universal', *Financial Times*, 22 November 2002, p. 21 [this volume, p. 267], and, for fuller discussion, Nicholas Barr, 'Funding Higher Education: Policies for Access and Quality', House of Commons, Education and Skills Committee, *Post-16 Student Support*, Sixth Report of Session 2001–02, HC445, London, Stationery Office, 2002, pp. Ev 19–35, and supplementary memoranda, ibid., pp. Ev 45–7, Ev 130–3 and Ev 133–4.
5 See Polly Toynbee, 'Help Toddlers, and then Let Students Pay their Own Way', *Guardian*, 22 January 2003.
6 See *Widening Participation in Higher Education*, London, Department for Education and Skills, 2003.
7 Nicholas Barr and Iain Crawford, 'The Dearing Report and the Government's Response: A Critique', *Political Quarterly*, Vol. 69, No. 1, January 1998, pp. 72–84 [this volume, Ch. 10]; on the specific prediction, see p. 80.
8 Ibid., p. 78.
9 For assessment of the Dearing Report and the government's response, see ibid.
10 Students and parents have legitimate worries, but mostly exaggerated or misplaced – see Barr 2003, paras 121–30.
11 For fuller discussion see ibid., paras 104–20.
12 Ibid., paras 107–19.

Nicholas Barr and Iain Crawford, 'Myth or Magic?', *Guardian Education*, 2 December 2003, pp. 20–1.

Myth or magic?

Nicholas Barr and Iain Crawford

Nicholas Barr and Iain Crawford, architects of the top-up fees policy, argue that their critics in and outside the Commons are harming the very causes they mean to support. The government's approach is the most progressive way to provide higher education free at the point of use and redistribute resources to the worst off.

We all want to strengthen the quality of higher education and improve access. But there are widespread misunderstandings about the government's proposals to do so.

Misunderstandings about tax funding

The proposals rightly incorporate a large and continuing taxpayer contribution to higher education because of its social benefits. But that process can go too far.

'Free' higher education fails on quality. There is universal agreement that universities are underfunded. As the last 40 years show, higher education always loses out to the national health service and schools.

Free higher education also fails on access. Last year only 15% of children whose parents are manual workers went to university, compared with 81% of the children of professionals.

Free higher education redistributes to the best-off. Some 82% of British working-age adults have not been to university. Getting them to pay the lion's share of higher education is like subsidising champagne. Many people would welcome a more progressive tax system. But the way to spend the extra money is not on the best and the brightest who mostly go on to become the richest, but on strengthening pre-school education and nutrition, raising the staying-on rate post-16, improving vocational education, and restoring generous grants.

So, the zero fees option – advocated by the National Union of Students, the Liberal Democrats and, recently, the Conservatives – fails to achieve a single desirable objective.

Misunderstandings about flat fees

Some people argue that fees should be the same at all universities. This approach makes sense if all degrees are the same, but overlooks the need for today's higher education to be much more diverse than it has been historically in terms of subject, approach (academic or vocational), part-time or full-time. Thus degrees – rightly – are different.

Separately, it is self-deluding to pretend that all degrees are equally good – students with the best A-levels apply to Oxbridge and similar universities, not to their local college. Policy based on this pretence is bad policy. What really matters is not the instrument – fees – but the outcome: that bright people from poor backgrounds should be able to go to the best universities.

Given the faulty initial assumption, it is not surprising that flat fees fail both on quality and fairness. They perpetuate Treasury control, denying universities an independent source of finance and exerting downward pressure on quality. The risk is that the world's great universities will end up concentrated in America.

Flat fees are also inequitable.

Unfair 1: They give the largest subsidy to the best universities, which have the highest proportion of middle-class students.

Unfair 2: They impose the same charge at Balls Pond Road College as at Oxford – Labour backbenchers should find this outrageous – and lead to the absurd situation where Balls Pond Road is legally prevented from reducing its charge.

Unfair 3: Flat fees discriminate against UK students by giving the best universities an incentive to recruit overseas.

Unfair 4: They prevent redistribution within higher education: if some universities can be more self-financing, resources can be redirected to institutions with more remedial teaching, for example through the Higher Education Funding Council's widening access premium.

Unfair 5: The Office for Fair Access loses its only powerful weapon – the right to withhold permission to raise fees.

Misunderstandings about the type of debt

If the government's proposals left students with large credit card-type debt – high interest rate, short repayment period and enforced repayment, even if earnings are low – we would join Labour backbenchers on the barricades.

But that is not the proposal. Income-contingent loans, introduced in 1998, transform the landscape in ways that the government has not done a good job in explaining. A graduate repays 9% of earnings above £15,000, so that someone earning £18,000 repays £270 per year, or £5.20 per week.

Thus loans have inbuilt insurance against inability to repay. Low earners make low or no repayments, and people who never earn much do not repay their loan.

This is not credit card debt, but a payroll deduction. A picture of a graduate's payslip would make this clear.

By abolishing upfront fees, the proposals make higher education free for students. When someone goes to university, the Student Loans Company squirts money into their university's bank account for their fees and into their bank account for living costs. When they leave university, the graduate is faced with a payroll deduction.

We pay national insurance now to finance our pension later; income-contingent higher education contributions are exactly analogous.

Misunderstandings about the size of the debt

Many students and parents are scared by talk of up to £20,000 debt. But that figure should be seen in context. It seems large because we think of expenditure on a weekly basis, so that cumulative totals seem shocking. But over a full career a typical graduate will pay about £850,000 in income tax and national insurance contributions and will spend half a million pounds on food. Quite rightly, nobody loses sleep over a career tax debt approaching £1 million because he/she looks at the figure through the other end of the telescope, in monthly terms. Student debt – given income-contingent repayments – is no different.

Misunderstandings about variable fees and access

If the proposals were simply to allow variable fees we would, once more, be on the barricades. But the proposals have two mutually supporting elements. First, they bring in variable fees, but those fees are deferred and paid only by those who can afford to pay.

Second, part of the resources released by those fees is targeted on people for whom access is fragile, precisely so that bright students from poor backgrounds can go to the best universities.

As a result the strategy promotes access. Flat fees (let alone no fees) try to promote access by subsidising higher education for everyone; this spreads subsidies thinly, and largely on people who do not need help. Variable fees are fair, first, because they release resources to promote access for those who need help most. Second, they facilitate redistribution within higher education. And third, they allow expansion of UK student numbers.

The strategy also assists quality. Funding becomes open-ended: if tax funding falls, each university has a policy response under its own control. In addition, the approach creates incentives for institutions to respond to the demands of students and employers, thus contributing to diversity, choice and quality, and also to access because institutions will face incentives to provide more part-time degree options.

The combination of income-contingent loans, deferred variable fees, and measures to promote access, makes the government's proposals deeply progressive. Higher education is largely free at the point of use. The strategy shifts resources from today's best-off (who lose some of their tuition subsidies) to today's worst-off (who receive a grant) and tomorrow's worst-off (who, with income-contingent repayments, do not repay their loan in full).

That does not mean that the proposals are perfect. They should be made even more progressive through larger grants and higher maintenance loans. A well-designed package to promote access would also raise the staying-on rate post-16, which is where the real barrier to access occurs.

Nicholas Barr, 'A Good Deal for All the Family', *The Times Educational Supplement*, 23 January 2004, p. 21.

A good deal for all the family

Nicholas Barr

Lurid coverage of top-up fees gives the impression that parents will have to find £3,000 in fees for each year each child goes to university, and that each child will end up with £15,000 of credit-card debt.

If that were true, I would join the rebels on the barricades. It is not true. The Higher Education Bill helps universities, who get more money to improve quality, and helps families because of its emphasis on improving access.

Promoting access has two ingredients. The first is to make sure that people get A-levels. Irrespective of background, 90 per cent of young people who get respectable A-levels go to university. Thus what matters is to increase the staying-on rate post-16. Programmes like AimHigher and education maintenance allowances are designed to do exactly that.

The second ingredient is that university should be free, or largely free, for students. That is not true at present. Many students or their parents have to pay tuition fees of £1,125 per year, there are virtually no grants, and the loan to cover living costs is too small, forcing students to rely on a mix of parental contributions, credit-card debt, overdrafts or long hours.

If the Bill goes through in broadly its present form, what will things look like for someone starting university in 2006 or later?

University will be largely free for students. The present upfront fee disappears. Fees will vary from zero to a maximum of £3,000, but students and parents will not pay; instead, the Student Loans Company pays on the student's behalf. It also pays money into the student's bank account for living costs.

Thus students benefit because upfront fees disappear, and because the Bill increases the loan for living costs to a much more realistic level.

Students from poor backgrounds benefit even more because the Bill brings in grants of £1,500 per year. They will also be let off the first £1,200 of any tuition fee, though there is talk of converting that fee remission into an additional grant, in which case the grant will be £2,700 per year.

Parents also benefit because the abolition of upfront fees sharply reduces the parental contribution, leaving them, at most, to contribute towards living costs.

These benefits are financed, first, by taxpayers, who will continue to pay some five-sixths of the higher education budget. The rest will come from graduates through their loan repayments.

Loan repayments are a payroll deduction, not credit-card debt. At present, loan repayments are 9 per cent of each graduate's earnings above £10,000 per year. Under the Bill, repayments will be 9 per cent of earnings above £15,000. Thus someone earning £18,000 will repay £270 per year, or £5.19 per week, a deduction on his or her payslip alongside income tax. This point is clear to anyone who graduated in 2001 or later.

A credit-card debt of £15,000 is seriously scary. A student loan debt of £15,000 is not. Over a working life a typical graduate will hand over about £850,000 in income tax and national insurance contributions. His or her food bill will be about £500,000 (and we do not even mention drink). Parents do not lose sleep over their children's future tax bills. Nor should they over their student loan repayments.

Compared with present arrangements, all graduates gain because the increase in the repayment threshold from £10,000 to £15,000 reduces their monthly repayments. Low-earning graduates gain because nobody earning below £15,000 has to pay anything, and also as any loan not repaid after 25 years will be forgiven.

The only people who will, over time, pay more than now are higher-earning graduates, whose loan repayments will cover higher fees than at present. This is right. They are among the better-off; their repayments are related to their earnings; and nobody repays more than he or she has borrowed. Furthermore, improving access means helping people in school and pre-school to maximise their chances of staying on till A-level,

The bottom line is that university is largely free for students; it is graduates who make repayments. Those who campaign for university to be 'free', that is, entirely paid out of taxation, are campaigning to benefit tomorrow's better-off graduates. This is puzzling.

These arrangements apply to all students, including people doing degrees en route to becoming teachers. There are additional benefits for potential teachers. Most people doing a postgraduate certificate in education get a training bursary of £6,000. On completing their induction year, teachers in some subjects (maths, science, modern languages, technology and English) receive a 'golden hello'. Under a further useful innovation, a pilot scheme allows the student loans of new teachers in shortage subjects to be written off over time (10 per cent for each year in the state system, so that after 10 years' teaching the loan has been forgiven).

Unsustainable claims by politicians are not unusual. But when the Government claims that the Higher Education Bill is a good deal for universities and for families, it is right.

Part 4

Onwards and outwards

Chapter 16

Financing higher education: a universal model

In July 2004, the Higher Education Act became law. As earlier chapters make clear, this is a cause for celebration. The new legislation, however, is only a way station, not an end point. This chapter draws together the threads running through the book and considers the future. The first section reflects on what has been learned from economic theory and the experience of other countries. The second section summarises our solutions in terms of policy and – equally important – implementation. The third section considers the unfinished agenda, both technical issues and, acutely relevant in many countries of the wider Europe, political aspects. The final section argues that our strategy applies to a wide range of countries.

1 What have we learned?

1.1 Lessons from economic theory

Three lessons from economic theory, set out in the chapters in Part 1, permeate the book: the days of central planning have gone; graduates should share in the cost of their degrees; and well-designed student loans have core characteristics.

The days of central planning have gone

As discussed in Chapter 3, the argument against central planning is not ideological, but rooted in the economics of information. The literature on the communist economic system (see Kornai 1992, Ch. 9) makes the important distinction between extensive and intensive growth. During the period of extensive growth, surplus inputs, notably agricultural labour, could be brought into the industrial sector, characterised by rapid growth in the Soviet Union in the 1930s. Intensive growth, when surplus inputs had been used up, depends on technological advance and more efficient use of inputs. Central planning became progressively less able to cope with the combination of scarce inputs and more advanced technology, manifested by declining, and in some of the communist countries negative, growth rates in the 1980s and 1990s.

The analogy with higher education is appropriate. Fifty years ago, university systems were small and covered a limited range of subjects. Today, because of technological advance and for other reasons, there are more universities, more students and many more subjects. The problem has become too complex for central planning to bring about efficiency. Central planning is no longer feasible.

Nor is it desirable. One of the major arguments running through the book is that students are generally well informed, making consumer choice useful. The combination of (*a*) well informed consumers and (*b*) large numbers of highly diverse qualifications, including philosophy and aircraft engine maintenance, suggests that competition is likely to be more effective than central planning at improving outcomes.

Though that proposition is robust, there are two significant caveats, to both of which discussion returns shortly.

- Students from poorer backgrounds might not be well-informed, with implications for access generally and debt aversion in particular.
- Though the approach gives a greater role to students, employers and universities in making choices about subject, content and mix, it does not imply unrestricted markets. Rather, the analysis points to regulated markets.

Graduates should share in the cost of their degrees

A graduate contribution is efficient in microeconomic terms because most graduates derive a private benefit from their degree and because the efficiency of competition is strengthened by price signals. It is necessary for fiscal reasons, given the high cost of mass higher education and competing fiscal pressures such as population ageing. It improves equity by reducing the regressivity of a system in which the degrees of mainly better-off people are paid for by people who on average are less well-off. If graduate contributions are central, it follows that so are student loans.

Well-designed student loans have core characteristics

As we have argued noisily over 16 years to all governments, and permeating all the chapters of this book, well-designed student loans have income-contingent repayments, are large enough to cover tuition fees and realistic living costs, and charge an interest rate related to the government's cost of borrowing.

The balance between market and state

The argument that consumer choice and competition are beneficial does not deny an important and continuing role for government, which remains an important stakeholder alongside students, universities and employers.

One part of the government's role is to empower demand:

- As partial funder of higher education, not least because of external benefits arising from teaching and (perhaps even more strongly) research.
- As organiser of student loans, to provide a mechanism for individual consumption smoothing in the face of capital market imperfections.[1]
- As promoter of access. Consumption smoothing may be sufficient for people who are well informed, but further action is needed for those who are not.

On the supply side, government has a role:

- As regulator, to ensure that satisfactory quality assurance is in place. Consumers may be well informed, but that does not mean that they are perfectly informed, justifying quality-assurance for reasons of consumer protection. As discussed in Chapter 13, such quality control does not have to be intrusive or bureaucratic.
- As setter of incentives. In addition to aiming transfers at particular individuals to promote access, government properly sets incentives in other ways. It can target resources towards particular subjects. Even if students and employers are well informed, that does not deny government the right to views about subject mix. For example, governments might wish to offer additional resources to subjects like classics, music or drama or (a permanent worry of governments) to engineering.
- As actor to influence the degree of competition. The fewer the constraints imposed by government the stronger is competition, and vice versa. Thus without introducing central planning, government can influence the extent of competition, with different answers possible for different subjects. Degrees in economics, law and business management, for example, with high demand and relatively low fixed costs might well be highly competitive. On the other hand, a case can be made for more muted competition in subjects like classics or music (for which demand is low), or chemistry or engineering, where demand is low and fixed costs (laboratories and equipment) high.

1 For a proposal for private income-contingent loans, see Palacios Lleras (2004).

1.2 Lessons from country experience

The lessons from economic theory are reinforced by the experience of different countries with fees and loans.

Financing universities: lessons about fees

Three lessons are worth pondering: fees relax the supply-side constraint; big-bang liberalisation of fees can be politically destabilising; but failure to liberalise is also a mistake.

FEES RELAX THE SUPPLY-SIDE CONSTRAINT

Policy makers face a nasty dilemma. Large taxpayer subsidies create supply-side constraints by exerting downward pressure on student numbers or on quality. In countries with less public funding per student, these problems are not so acute, but in that case, high charges (necessitated by limited public funding) put access at risk. Thus high subsidies can harm access on the supply side, but their absence can harm it on the demand side. This is the dilemma which the strategy in the next section is designed to resolve.

It is not only the total volume of private spending that matters, but also the way it is determined. With flat fees, government controls total funding. If rising fees are offset by declining public expenditure the only change is in the balance between public and private funding. In 1989, Australia introduced centrally-set tuition fees to address a funding crisis. Over the years, fee income increased but tax funding fell back. By 2000 the system was back in crisis. Reforms in 2003 partially liberalised fees.

BIG-BANG LIBERALISATION CAN BE POLITICALLY DESTABILISING

In 1992, New Zealand introduced fees, which were set by universities and on which no constraints were imposed by government, and income-contingent loans which charged a positive real interest rate and were large enough to cover fees and realistic living costs. Though close to the policy design advocated in earlier chapters, mistakes were made in political implementation. First, the liberalisation of fees was to some extent big-bang, giving students and parents little time to prepare or to adjust expectations. Second, inadequate attention was paid to politics: having implemented the reforms, the government stopped campaigning for them; nor did the government do enough to explain to students and parents the considerable advantages of income-contingent repayments. As a result, when nominal student debt rose over the years, worried middle-class parents created political pressures. The scheme was diluted in 2000.

FAILURE TO LIBERALISE IS ALSO A MISTAKE

There are two problems if higher education is 'free' or has low fixed fees. Quality suffers because the higher education budget has to compete with other budgetary imperatives; as a result, real funding per student declines. Access also suffers. If places are scarce, it will tend to be middle-class students who get them; and if places are not scarce, the need to finance a mass system typically crowds out resources to promote access.

Financing students: lessons about loans

Country experience offers four potential lessons: income-contingent loans do not harm access; interest subsidies are expensive; positive real interest rates are politically feasible; and the design of the student loan contract is important.

INCOME-CONTINGENT LOANS DO NOT HARM ACCESS

As discussed in Chapters 1 and 11, Australia introduced loans with income-contingent repayments in 1989 to cover a newly introduced tuition charge. Chapman's (1997) assessment (see also Chapman and Ryan 2003) finds that: (1) overall participation increased after 1989 and, superimposed on that trend, (2) women's participation grew more strongly, and (3) the system did not discourage participation by people in the lowest socio-economic groups.

There are two sets of reasons why this result should not be surprising: the income-contingent mechanism is designed explicitly to reduce the risks borrowers face; and fees supported by loans free resources to promote access.

A recent study from Statistics Canada offers empirical support particularly for the latter argument. Canada liberalised fees in the early 1990s but without a parallel increase in loan entitlement and with no additional expenditure on scholarships. Predictably, access suffered. In the mid-1990s, the maximum amount that students could borrow was increased, with knock-on increases in other forms of student support. Again predictably, access improved, notwithstanding that the Canadian loan scheme is not income-contingent. The report (Corak *et al.* 2003, p. 14) concluded that:

> There is a clear positive correlation between parental income and university attendance, and this correlation . . . became stronger during the mid-1990s when tuition fees began increasing significantly. This change reflected declines in participation rates of youth from middle income families. . . . The correlation, however, declined during the latter half of the decade reflecting rises in participation of those from the lowest income groups. This pattern is consistent with the fact that

the changes in the Canada Student Loans Program raising the maximum amount of loan occurred only after tuition fees had already begun to rise (p. 14).

INTEREST SUBSIDIES ARE EXPENSIVE

The simulations by Barr and Falkingham (1993, 1996) reported in Chapter 8 found that of every £100 lent out to students, about £30 is never repaid because of the cost of the interest subsidy. Official estimates connected with the sale of student debt by the UK government in the late 1990s put the figure at about one-third. The two sets of evidence reinforce each other since they were independent and based on different methodologies, the latter with a market test.

New Zealand offers confirmation. Under reforms introduced in 2000, students were charged a zero *nominal* interest rate while still at university (previously a real interest rate related to the government's cost of borrowing was charged from the time the student took out the loan); in addition, the interest rate after graduation was frozen at somewhat below its previous rate. The impact was striking. Before the changes, official estimates suggested that £90 out of every £100 lent would be repaid. After the changes, it was estimated that only £77 would be repaid (New Zealand Ministry of Education 2002, p. 7). The change is so expensive precisely because the subsidy applies to *all* students. A key message is that seemingly small adjustments can be very expensive.

POSITIVE REAL INTEREST RATES ARE FEASIBLE

In the Netherlands and Sweden, as in New Zealand until the changes in 2000, a real interest rate broadly equal to the government's cost of borrowing is charged from the moment the student takes out the loan. Both elements are taken for granted. As discussed, inter alia, in Chapter 13, with income-contingent loans a higher interest rate does not increase a graduate's monthly repayments, only the duration of the loan.

CONTRACT DESIGN IS IMPORTANT

International labour mobility is high and, with enlargement of the EU, likely to increase, raising questions about default if a person emigrates. In Australia, loan repayments are part of a person's tax liability, so that someone who is outside the Australian tax net has no liability to make repayments. With interest subsidies this is a costly error. In the UK, in contrast, the loan contract includes collection of repayments through the tax system, but does not exempt a person outside the UK, who has to make mortgage-type repayments. Though default and administrative costs are somewhat higher for people working abroad, the effect is not large.

2 The strategy

This section sets out solutions based on economic theory and drawing on country experience, giving equal stress to strategic policy design and to implementation.

2.1 The policy strategy

The later chapters in the book put forward a strategy with three elements.

> *Leg 1: Variable fees* promote quality in two ways: they bring in more resources; and, by strengthening competition, they improve the efficiency with which those resources are used. A mistake to avoid is big-bang liberalisation.
>
> *Leg 2: A good loan scheme* has income-contingent repayments, is large enough to cover fees and realistic living costs, and charges an interest rate related to the government's cost of borrowing. A fundamental mistake is blanket interest subsidies, which are hugely expensive, and which distort policy by crowding out policies with greater power to improve access.
>
> *Leg 3: Active measures to promote access.* Income-contingent loans measure ability to pay on the basis of where a person ends up (that is, his or her subsequent income). This is the right approach for students from better-off backgrounds, who are generally well informed about the benefits of going to university. A wide range of proactive measures to promote access is necessary precisely because not everyone is well informed.

Money is clearly central. Measures include grants and scholarships for university students from poorer backgrounds, thus measuring ability to pay in terms of where a person starts. A second ingredient is extra personal and intellectual support for students for whom access is most fragile, to make sure that, once a student starts at university, he or she gets the support necessary to make the transition. It is also important, third, to offer financial assistance young people to encourage them to complete their school education.

Action is also needed much earlier. Information and raising aspirations are critical. The importance of good information both to promote efficiency and to empower individuals has been a central theme of this book. Poor information – defined broadly to include culturally ingrained attitudes – harms access deeply: many people from poorer backgrounds do not apply to university because they have never thought of doing so; others rule it out for the wrong reasons; and poor information is one of the roots of debt aversion. Thus it is essential to raise aspirations, to demystify higher education, and to improve the extent to which people are aware of the benefits of a degree and of the options available to them. Measures include mentoring of schoolchildren by current university students, preferably from similar backgrounds, and visits by schoolchildren to universities for weekend lectures, visit days, summer schools and the like. Such activities need to happen soon enough to prevent high school drop out. The main mistake is to underestimate the information challenge.

Finally, problems of access cannot be solved entirely within the higher education sector. Extra resources are needed to strengthen earlier education, which is where the real barriers to access occur. Given the increasing evidence (Feinstein 2003) that the roots of deprivation go back to pre-school years, such activity needs to start early.

This package – deferred variable fees, income-contingent loans, and active measures to promote access – is designed as a strategy in which the three elements reinforce each other. Taken together, they are more efficient and more equitable than other arrangements, including 'free' higher education. Each element can be crafted in different ways (e.g. the range over which fees can vary, the way in which the interest rate on loans is determined, the system of scholarships, etc.), and with differing weights, to reflect differences in national objectives and different constraints. The strategy is applicable to any country that can do an effective job in collecting income tax – and hence collecting loan repayments. In contrast, any policy that does not have all three elements will be less efficient and/or equitable. In that sense – a claim not made lightly – this is a dominant policy strategy.

Chapter 1 summarised our predictions over the past 16 years. The prediction now is that, provided the 2004 Act is implemented as planned:

- variable fees notwithstanding, student numbers will continue to rise;
- the socio-economic mix in higher education will widen, but, given the deep roots of deprivation, improvement will take time.

As discussed below, the UK arrangements, though promising, remain work in progress.

2.2 *The reform process*

Strategic policy design of the sort just described is only part of the story. Successful reform depends on a tripod of skills:

- policy design;
- political implementation;
- administrative/technical implementation.

A tripod, by its construction is stable, but loses stability if any of the legs is weak or missing.

Implementation – defined as the plans and actions which translate policy (words on paper or in speeches) into action on the ground – requires discussion. When President Kennedy promised that the US would put a man on the moon by the end of the 1960s he was pronouncing policy. Implementation was the province of scientists, aeronautics engineers, materials scientists, etc., pulled together by the National Aeronautics and Space Administration (NASA). It was also the province of politicians, who needed to ensure public support sufficient to justify the large NASA budgets approved by Congress.

The UK Beveridge Report established a policy for contributory social insurance, together with family allowance and a national system of social assistance. Implementation involved persuading the public, including employers, of the rightness of the policy (a task to which Beveridge devoted considerable energy), and establishing institutions able to collect contributions, maintain contributions records, verify entitlements, and calculate and disburse benefits in a timely and accurate way.

The importance of implementation is underestimated. Typically a person with one of the skills in the tripod will fail fully to grasp the importance of the other two. There is much lip service, but little real understanding. Academics, whose expertise is policy design, ignore implementation or underestimate it; politicians may not give enough weight to the coherence of policy or to meeting its administrative requirements (e.g. by allowing enough time and by including an adequate administrative budget). Administrators and other technical experts may take a blinkered approach, or be reluctant to reform for other reasons.

Effective implementation requires both the right skills mix and the right sequencing. On the first, a Ministry of Finance will contain macroeconomists, microeconomists and statisticians, all skills essential to policy design. In addition, implementation requires skills that are just as demanding, *and are different skills*. The idea that if one understands the policy one can establish a programme for implementing it (an error to which academics are perhaps particularly prone) is generally false. A family doctor might diagnose a pain as appendicitis and recommend an operation, but the operation takes place only after confirmation by the surgeon who will actually wield the knife. The surgeon, moreover, would not dream of operating until the anaesthetist had confirmed that the patient could take the strain, nor go ahead without the anaesthetist in attendance.

The sequencing point is simple but even less well understood: implementation skills are an integral part of reform, not an add-on. They must be involved at the stage of policy design, not bolted on after policy is set. There is a deeply flawed view that policy involves 'higher' skills: higher-level people design policy, which is then handed over to the peons to implement. This is, quite simply, wrong: the three sets of skills are hierarchical neither in level nor chronologically.[2]

2 Barr, Crawford and Colin Ward (of the UK Student Loans Company) would sit round the table with our Hungarian counterparts (see the discussion in section 3.2). Any of us, while speaking about his patch, would constantly be looking for nods from the other two to confirm that what he said fitted with their parts of the puzzle.

In the context of student loans, it is unwise to embark on reform without analytical design skills, strong and sustained political support, and technical expertise.

- Policy matters: the package in the previous section is designed as a robust, strategic whole.
- Politics matters: reforming higher education requires strong political leadership. In its absence, reform takes a long time; and political mishandling can muddy the waters, making reform harder than it needs to be. The UK in the 1990s exemplifies both problems. Without strong political leadership reform may be impossible (at the time of writing most countries in Western Europe had yet to grasp the nettle of tuition fees). In sharp contrast, strong leadership can lead to rapid reform, Australia in the late 1980s, New Zealand in the early 1990s and Hungary in the early 2000s being cases in point.
- Administration matters: many countries have student loans; but default rates are often high even in advanced countries, and are a major and continuing problem in developing countries.

Our experience suggests five sets of lessons for reformers:

Get a network

Reform inevitably has many links and interactions. In the case of higher education, these include politicians, Parliamentarians, the Education Department, the Treasury, the tax authorities, the National Statistical Office, the Vice-Chancellors, the student loans administration and student organisations. Thus a reliable network is essential.

Get broad support

This requires a lot of work. Political sustainability has a range of ingredients. It is necessary, first, that there is sufficient strength and breadth of political support, ideally cross-party support. A second ingredient is the duration of support. Reform of higher education finance is not an event but a process. Reform does not end when the legislation is passed, but needs continuing commitment, both to ensure necessary adjustments as events unfold, and to sustain continuing political support. Reform which is regarded as a single, once-and-for-all event runs the risk of neglect, discredit and eventual reversal. A third element is the depth of political support. It is not enough for the top echelons of government to understand the proposals, which need to be understood and supported throughout government *and* administration. Without that depth of shared understanding, the original plan risks being implemented badly or, at worst, actively subverted by lower levels of government or administration.

A separate, but important, source of support is the media. In the UK, parents and students see 'high fees, high debt'. The press (and not just the heavyweight press) is integral to explaining the argument to the wider public.

Get a tripod

In our case, Barr and Crawford covered strategic policy design and practical politics, respectively and, latterly, Colin Ward and Hugh Macadie of the Student Loans Company provided administrative and financial-market expertise.

Get a lot of patience

Reform is rarely fast. In the British context, hostility to reform has been widespread, some of it for entirely honourable reasons, some of it for motives which do not bear close scrutiny.

Loans passed into law in 1989 and variable fees in 2004 because the Education Ministers (Kenneth Baker and Charles Clarke, respectively) championed them, in the latter case with strong public support from the Prime Minister. But their successes were hard won.

- Many politicians opposed loans in the late 1980s; having got used to that idea, they opposed the introduction of fees in 1997; and the opposition to the 2004 legislation to introduce variable fees was strident.
- The Treasury opposed expansion in the early 1990s on the grounds that its cost-effectiveness was unproven; and we were told to our faces by Treasury officials in early 1990 that improving access was not an objective of government policy.
- The Education Department argued against income-contingent loans in 1989 and 1990 on the mistaken grounds that they could not be implemented,[3] and opposed the abolition of blanket interest subsidies in 2003 on the mistaken grounds that the policy would harm the poor and/or that targeted interest subsidies would be expensive to administer.[4]
- Vice-Chancellors (with a few honourable exceptions) continued to argue for the status quo. Their underlying policy was public funding, supported by personal contacts between Vice-Chancellors and their connections in government and administration. In clinging to this elite-to-elite approach, the Vice-Chancellors as a body failed even to do the one thing on which the entire sector could agree – to promote the importance of higher education to the country as a whole – and thus failed to create the groundswell of political support necessary to sustain public funding.

3 See Barr (1990) for counter-arguments to departmental opposition to income-contingency.
4 For a critique of the Education Department's position, see Barr (2003, paras. 104–120); see also Education and Skills Committee (2003, volume I, paras 182–4 and 207–9).

Get a life

There are times when a topic is at the top of the political agenda, when activity should be intense, and times when it is off the agenda. During the latter times it is generally counter-productive to raise the issue too frequently. And there are times of intense frustration, when reforms are lost because of misplaced opposition, for example the failure to put into place income-contingent loans in 1990 or variable fees in 1997. At such times it is good to have other professional and personal activities to which to turn.

Most of the policy strategy in section 2.1 is set out in Chapter 5, published in mid-1989. If the strategy is so right, why, it might be asked, did it take so long? It took so long for lack of cross-party support, for lack of support from the civil service, notably the Education Department, and for lack of support from the university sector and, in consequence, for the lack of any sustained campaign to increase public understanding. In countries with strong political leadership and a history which had muddied the waters less, reform can be considerably faster.

3 The unfinished agenda

The previous section offers solutions to avoidable problems, including (1) unsustainable public spending, (2) benefits that are hijacked by the middle class, (3) loans that are absent or badly designed, so that they bring in few extra resources, (4) economic constraints on universities, reducing incentives to efficiency, and (5) design features which are expensive (interest subsidies), administratively demanding (income testing), or both. These problems are widespread, though (2) and (4) are less of a problem in systems with variable fees.

The package in section 2.1 is designed explicitly to address these problems. The three elements offer a benchmark against which countries can assess policy directions. The US, it can be argued, does well on Leg 1 (variable fees) but less well on Leg 2 (loans are not income-contingent, nor collected as a payroll deduction, and generally attract an interest subsidy) and Leg 3 (where scholarship arrangements can be criticised as parsimonious and complex). In 2003, Australia partially liberalised fees under Leg 1, but its loan scheme, though with income-contingent repayments, includes a blanket interest subsidy and (perhaps for that reason) does not cover living costs for most students. New Zealand came close to achieving all three elements of the policy in the 1990s but was burnt because the politics came unstitched. Most countries in mainland Western Europe and the Nordic countries have yet to address fees under Leg 1, and with few exceptions, have work to do on loans.